# new success

# Pre-Intermediate
# Students' Book

## with Active Book

Stuart McKinlay
Bob Hastings

**4**

CD 1.1   Texts recorded on Class CD

**5**

# It's me!

**Read, listen and talk about** identity.
**Practise** the Present Simple and Present Continuous; state/action verbs; personality adjectives
**Focus on** expressing interest; reading for the main ideas.
**Write** a personal introduction.

## GRAMMAR AND LISTENING

1 Look at the photos. What can you say about Jade, the girl with the phone, just by looking at the photos?

- How old is she?
- Where does she come from?
- Anything else about her?

2 Read what people who know Jade say about her. Match the texts with the speakers.

a father   _2_
b mother   ___
c brother   ___
d teacher   ___
e boyfriend   ___
f friend   ___

**1** Jade's very quiet and she rarely takes part in class discussions. But she always writes excellent essays.

**2** I come from Scotland but my wife's English. I think my kids are quite proud to have some Scottish blood in them!

**3** Jade's three years younger than me. We get on OK, I suppose. Luckily, she usually spends her free time with her boyfriend so I don't see her very often.

**4** Jade is doing really well at school at the moment – I'm so proud of her. She still spends all evening on the phone to Marc. I think she's talking to him now.

**5** I know Jade from Kendo classes. She's getting pretty good at it! People think Jade's very serious but she's got a fantastic sense of humour.

**6** She's such a caring person – I really love her. We're working hard for our mock exams this term so we don't see each other so often in the evenings.

6

**3** CD1.2 Listen and answer the questions.

1 What is Jade's surname?
2 What is her home town?
3 What's her nationality?
4 How old is she?
5 Which are her best subjects at school?
6 What does she want to study at university?
7 What sort of school does she go to?
8 Why doesn't she see her boyfriend after school very often?

**4** CD1.3 What kind of person is Jade? Which words describe her? Listen again and check.

big-headed quiet clever funny
modest outgoing caring serious
romantic selfish talkative hard-working

**5** Look at your answers to Exercise 1. Were any of your predictions correct?

## Work it out

**6** Match sentences 1–5 with definitions a–e.

1 She usually spends her free time with her boyfriend. ☐
2 We're working hard for our exams this term. ☐
3 She's talking to Marc. ☐
4 I come from Scotland. ☐
5 She's getting pretty good at Kendo. ☐

a a fact that doesn't change
b a routine or a habit
c something that's temporary
d something that's changing
e something that's happening now

## Check it out

**Present Simple and Present Continuous**

We use the Present Simple for routines/habits and facts that don't change.

She usually spends her free time with her boyfriend.
I come from Scotland.

**Time expressions:** *never, rarely, often, sometimes, usually, regularly, always*

We use the Present Continuous for things happening now, temporary situations and change and development.

She's talking to Marc.
We're working hard for our exams this term.
She's getting really good at Kendo.

**Time expressions:** *at the moment, these days, now, nowadays, this term/year*

**7** Choose the correct forms.

1 He *isn't watching / doesn't watch* a match now. He's in the library.
2 Tim *often watches / is often watching* football matches with his friends.
3 *Do you work / Are you working* or can I come in?
4 My English *is getting / gets* a lot better.
5 He usually *stays / is staying* in his flat in London but he *stays / is staying* with his parents at the moment.
6 I *spend / am spending* more time with my girlfriend these days.

**8** CD1.4 Listen and answer the questions.

1 What kind of music does Jade usually listen to?
2 What music is she listening to at the moment?
3 What kind of books does Jade enjoy?
4 What is she reading at the moment?

**9** Answer the questions with the prompts below or your ideas. Then interview your partner and tell the class what you find out.

jazz classical soul techno hip-hop
metal rock pop indie reggae folk

crime fantasy science fiction horror
short stories classic novels

| | You | Your partner |
|---|---|---|
| 1 What sort of music do you usually listen to? | I usually listen to … | Robert likes … |
| 2 What bands are you listening to these days? | | |
| 3 What sort of books do you enjoy? | | |
| 4 What are you reading at the moment? | | |

**10** CD1.5 Listen to what is happening in Jade's life these days. Complete the sentences with the correct verbs.

1 Jade _____ a bit tired at the moment.
2 Her mock exams _____ quite well.
3 She _____ Marc just at the weekends nowadays.
4 She _____ on better with her brother these days.

**11** What is happening in your life at the moment? Tell your partner.

I'm … at the moment. I'm also … these days.

## READING AND SPEAKING

**1** In groups, discuss the questions.

1 Are you proud of where you come from? Why?
2 Which of these adjectives do you associate with the people from your city/region/country?

funny  generous  hard-working  punctual
laid-back  loud  polite  sophisticated
passionate  reserved  romantic  serious

**2** [CD1.6] Read the article quickly and decide what the main idea is. Don't worry about new words.

1 It's good to be proud of your country.  ☐
2 The Olympic Games are changing.  ☐
3 National differences are still important but less than before.  ☐

**3** Read the article again and <u>underline</u> the words or phrases that show the main idea of each paragraph. Again, don't worry about new words.

**4** Use your <u>underlined</u> words to help you match headings 1–6 with paragraphs A–E. There is one extra heading.

1 Cosmopolitan society ☐
2 Communication brings us closer ☐
3 Friendly competitors ☐
4 National conflicts ☐
5 A sporting example ☐
6 Something new is coming ☐

## CELEBRITY COMMENT

This week's guest writer in Celebrity Comment is Britain's new star athlete **Tiago Larsson**.

# Waving the Flag

**A** Most of us are proud of where we come from. We sing our national anthems and wave our flags; we cheer when our country wins a gold medal; we feel different from other nationalities. But the world is changing and it's changing fast and a global community is on its way.

**B** New technologies are breaking down the borders between people. The Internet is helping us to get to know each other. You don't need a passport or a visa to talk on Messenger or Skype. I chat with friends from lots of different countries and I don't mind where they come from. All I know is we enjoy the same things. It's not where you're from that matters the most; it's who you are that really counts.

**C** Foreign travel too is bringing us together. My mother comes from Brazil, my father's from Sweden, but I live in London and I compete for Great Britain. I speak Swedish, Portuguese and English and in today's world I'm not so unusual. In my neighbourhood you can hear more than a dozen languages, you can eat food from all around the world and there's a wonderful mixture of music and art.

**D** Nationality is still important to us: we follow our flags with pride and compete against other nations. But just because someone comes from another place, doesn't mean they're our enemy. I know lots of athletes from other countries. We're rivals but we get on well and respect each other.

**E** I enjoy national differences, but I'm delighted the divisions between people are disappearing. I love the closing ceremony of the Olympic Games: the athletes from all the different countries are wearing their country's colours, but they're all holding hands, singing the same song and waving the same flag.

**5** Look back at Exercises 2–4 and choose the correct words in Train Your Brain.

> **TRAIN YOUR BRAIN** | Reading skills
>
> **Understanding the main ideas**
>
> When you want to understand the main ideas in a text:
> 1 *Don't worry about / Check* any words you don't know.
> 2 As you read, decide what the main ideas of each *sentence / paragraph* are.
> 3 *Memorise / Underline* a few words or phrases to help you remember the main ideas.

**6** In pairs, say what Tiago thinks about these things. Do you agree with him?

• The importance of nationality in today's world
• The effect of new technologies
• Mixed nationalities
• Competition with other countries
• The closing ceremony of the Olympic Games

**7** Match verbs 1–7 with their collocations a–g. Use a dictionary to help you.

1 wave ☐     a the border
2 travel ☐     b the national anthem
3 sing ☐     c flags
4 emigrate to ☐     d abroad
5 cross ☐     e your nationality
6 change ☐     f a passport/a visa
7 apply for ☐     g a foreign country

**8** Complete sentences 1–6 with collocations from Exercise 7.

1 I don't have enough money to _____ for my holidays.
2 To visit the USA, you have to go to the Embassy and _____ .
3 If you can't find a job here, you can _____ .
4 Because of the security check, it takes hours to _____ .
5 If you marry someone from this country, you can _____ .
6 Before an international match the players _____ while the fans _____ .

**9** Read the sentences and tick the three you agree with the most. Then compare your answers with a partner's.

1 I'm proud of my nationality. ☐
2 I don't mind where my friends come from. ☐
3 I'd like to live in a multilingual society. ☐
4 It's important to respect foreign traditions. ☐
5 I get on well with people from other places. ☐
6 I enjoy music and food from other countries. ☐

**9**

## VOCABULARY | Personality

**1** Think Back! **Choose the personality adjectives that describe Jade.**

| + | caring, cheerful, clever, funny, generous, hard-working, laid-back, lively, modest, outgoing, polite, quiet |
|---|---|
| − | big-headed, boring, bossy, lazy, loud, mean, pessimistic, rude, selfish, serious, shy, stupid |

**2** CD1.7 **Match the positive and negative adjectives in Exercise 1. Use a dictionary if you need to. Then listen and repeat.**

caring → selfish, cheerful → ...

**3** Choose the correct answer.

**1** Lara loves meeting people. She's very

_____ .
  **a** friendly     **b** generous     **c** selfish

**2** The British are quite _____ . They feel uncomfortable with strangers.
  **a** confident     **b** punctual     **c** shy

**3** Tom's _____ . He thinks he's number one.
  **a** big-headed     **b** helpful     **c** tolerant

**4** My brother is _____ about the future.
  **a** jealous     **b** optimistic     **c** serious

**5** Dan's very _____ . He always has a smile on his face!
  **a** cheerful     **b** polite     **c** rude

**6** Jo's _____ . She always tells us what to do.
  **a** modest     **b** bossy     **c** talkative

**4** In pairs, follow the instructions.

- Choose five adjectives that describe your personality and two that don't.
- Tell your partner what your adjectives are. He/She guesses which two do NOT describe you.

**5** Tick four sentences that match your personality. Then tell a partner.

1 I'm someone filled with self-belief. ☐
2 Sometimes I'm not sure who I am. ☐
3 Sometimes I make no sense. ☐
4 Sometimes I'm miserable. ☐
5 I've got all the answers. ☐
6 Sometimes I'm perfect. ☐
7 I like to be by myself. ☐
8 I hate to be alone. ☐
9 I am special. ☐

**6** CD1.8 Song. Go to page 120 and follow the instructions.

## GRAMMAR AND WRITING

# TeenLife Quiz

## How outgoing are you? Take our personality quiz to find out!

### Tick the statements which are true for you.

**1** I prefer to go dancing than to watch a film on my own. ☐

**2** I never forget my friends' birthdays. ☐

**3** I always ask for an explanation if I don't understand. ☐

**4** I belong to at least one club or association. ☐

**5** I want to be famous one day. ☐

**6** I hate spending a lot of time indoors by myself. ☐

**7** Everyone agrees that I'm easy to get to know. ☐

**8** I love going to parties and clubs. ☐

**9** I always answer my mobile phone – even when I don't know who is calling. ☐

**10** I believe it's always better to say what you think. ☐

**1** In pairs, look at the cartoon and discuss the questions.

1 What is the girl doing?
2 Why is she doing it?
3 How often do you watch films?

## Work it out

**2** Look at these examples and answer the questions.

I **watch** a lot of films.
I **love** films.

1 Which verb describes …
   a an action?
   b a state (thoughts, feelings, beliefs)?
2 Which of these verbs can you use in the Present Continuous?

## Check it out

### State and action verbs

We use simple and continuous tenses with action verbs. The meaning of the verb doesn't change.

I watch a lot of films.  →  I'm watching a film now.
I leave school at 3 p.m.  →  I'm leaving school now.

We can only use simple tenses with state verbs (*hate, like, love, need, remember, taste, think*, etc.).

I love films.  NOT  I'm loving films.
I don't like sport.  NOT  I'm not liking sport.

### Mind the trap!

The verb *think* can describe both states and actions but the meaning changes.

I'm thinking about (considering) getting that new phone.

I think (believe) it's too expensive.
NOT  I'm thinking it's too expensive.

**3** Do the quiz. Then look at page 120 to find out what kind of person you are.

**4** Read the quiz again and underline all the state verbs.

**5** Tick the correct sentences and correct the wrong ones.

1 What are you thinking about? ☐
2 Jack isn't liking the book. ☐
3 I'm listening to a great piece of music. ☐
4 George doesn't know the answer. ☐
5 I'm sorry but I'm not agreeing with you. ☐
6 I'm thinking my answer is wrong. ☐
7 You aren't understanding the joke. ☐

**6** Complete Michel's message to the website with the correct forms of the verbs in brackets.

● ● ●

SEARCH  www.englishcontacts.con  ✕

# ENGLISHCONTACTS

Posted by Michel at 14.37

My name's Michel and I'm 22. I ¹_____ (come) from Belgium but this year I ²_____ (study) English in London. I ³_____ (love) cooking and I ⁴_____ (want) to become a professional chef. I'm cheerful and friendly and I ⁵_____ (like) reading crime novels – at the moment I ⁶_____ (read) a book by P.D. James. I also enjoy sports and I ⁷_____ (belong) to a football club. Thanks to my course, I ⁸_____ (think) my English ⁹_____ (get) better and now I ¹⁰_____ (understand) more when people speak to me.

If you share my interests, please write to: mich@wbml.be

**7** Read Michel's message again. Tick the things he writes about.

age ☐
nationality ☐
personality ☐
family ☐
where he lives ☐
how well he knows English ☐
hobbies, interests, sports ☐

**8** Now write a short introduction about yourself for the *EnglishContacts* website. Write about the things in Exercise 7.

I hate spending a lot of time indoors by myself.

**1 Richard**

**3 Carmella**

**2 Sandra**

## LISTENING AND SPEAKING

**1** Look at photos 1–3 and decide what jobs the people have. Do you think they are good at their jobs?

**2** CD1.9 Listen and check your ideas for Exercise 1. For each person, choose three adjectives that describe them best.

1 **Richard:** confident, bossy, outgoing, popular, reserved
2 **Sandra:** caring, lazy, rude, talkative, cheerful
3 **Carmella:** selfish, helpful, friendly, serious, tolerant

**3** CD1.10 Think Back! Listen and decide how the people seem to be different in private. Write two adjectives for each person and compare them with a partner.

1 Richard    _____   _____
2 Sandra    _____   _____
3 Carmella   _____   _____

**4** CD1.10 Listen again. Are the statements true (T) or false (F)?

1 Cheryl is a journalist. ☐
2 The interview is happening before the concert. ☐
3 Richard says he is feeling ill. ☐
4 Sandra is late for her evening class. ☐
5 She isn't sleeping enough these days. ☐
6 Sandra wants to become a nurse. ☐
7 Ben is working on his English project at the moment. ☐
8 Carmella's children don't cook for her very often. ☐

**5** In pairs, complete the conversation between Sandra and her boss. Practise saying your dialogue and perform it to the class.

**Student A**
You are Mrs Barr, Sandra's boss at the department store. You are unhappy with Sandra because you think she is rude to customers and spends too much time talking to her friend Lucy. You want her to look for another job.

**Student B**
You are Sandra. You know you aren't doing your job very well these days but you're very tired – you're working long hours at the store and you are doing a course (Health Studies) at college in the evenings. Your dream is to become a nurse in the future. Perhaps you could work shorter hours?

Sandra   I hope it's not bad news, Mrs Barr.
Mrs B   I'm sorry to say that there are some problems. The first thing is you're often ¹_____ . Secondly, you're ²_____ at the moment.
Sandra   I'm sorry, Mrs Barr. I know I'm not ³_____ these days. The problem is I'm really ⁴_____ . I ⁵_____ ten hours a day at the moment and I ⁶_____ as well.
Mrs B   Oh, what ⁷_____ ?
Sandra   Health. You see I want ⁸_____ in the future. That's why I really need the money.
Mrs B   A nurse? I see. Well, I want to give you another chance. But I think you ⁹_____ too hard at the moment. Perhaps you should work shorter hours?
Sandra   ¹⁰_____ .

**6** Are you a different person in private to how you are in public? Tell your partner using personality adjectives.

*I am different/the same in private and in public. I am ...*

# SPEAKING

**1** [CD1.11] Listen to the two dialogues. What's the difference between them?

**2** [CD1.11] Study Speak Out. Listen to the second dialogue again and complete it with expressions from Speak Out. Then, in pairs, practise saying the dialogue.

**Sam** What do you do at weekends, Rob?
**Rob** I read a lot and I write poetry too.
**Sam** Oh ¹_____ ? ²_____ !
**Rob** Yes, I love it. What about you? What do you do in your free time?
**Sam** Well, I play the guitar.
**Rob** ³_____ ? ⁴_____ !
**Sam** I'm playing a concert tonight, actually.
**Rob** ⁵_____ ? ⁶_____ ! Where?
**Sam** It's at the arts centre.
**Rob** ⁷_____ ? ⁸_____ ! What time?

---

**SPEAK OUT** | Expressing interest

| Echo questions | | Other expressions |
|---|---|---|
| Have you? | Has he? | Really? |
| Do you? | Does he? | Brilliant!/Great!/Wow!/Cool! |
| Can you? | Can she? | How interesting! |
| Are you? | Is she? | What an interesting thing to do! |
| Is it? | Are there? | That sounds brilliant/great/ cool/good/interesting! |
| | | That's brilliant/great/cool/ good/interesting! |

---

**3** [CD1.12] Listen and repeat some of the phrases from Speak Out.

**4** [CD1.13] Reply to sentences 1–6 with echo questions from Speak Out. Listen and check. In pairs, practise saying the echo questions.

1 There are some cool shops there. _____
2 I'm bilingual. _____
3 My sister can speak Italian. _____
4 I come from Lisbon. _____
5 My home town is very beautiful. _____
6 I've got three sisters. _____

**5** [CD1.14] Listen to the sentences and answer with the correct echo question.

**6** Write down three things you do in your free time. Use the prompts in the box. Then compare with a partner.

read    play board/computer/role games
chat online    dance    keep fit
play/listen to music    paint/draw
play sports    make clothes
do puzzles    go to the gym

**7** Complete sentences 1–8 with information about your life. Then work in groups of three and make dialogues. Take turns.

**Student A**
1 I've got _____ .
2 I like _____ .
3 I'm interested in _____ .
4 My parents come from _____ .
5 I'm getting much better at _____ these days.
6 I can _____ .
7 In my free time I _____ .
8 There's a fantastic new _____ in town.

**Student B**
Have you?
Do they?
Are you?
Can you?
Do you?
Is there?

**Student C**
How interesting!
That's excellent/cool!
Really?
That sounds brilliant/great!
What an interesting thing to do!
Wow!

A I've got some new CDs.
B Have you?
C Really?

**8** Look at the cartoon and complete the caption with the correct echo question.

He goes to ballet classes at weekends, you know.

_____ ?

# On our way

**Read, listen and talk about** future plans; travel and leisure.
**Practise** structures for future intentions and arrangements; indirect questions.
**Focus on** making and responding to suggestions.
**Write** formal emails (asking for information).

# GRAMMAR AND SPEAKING

**1**  Ask and answer the questions in pairs.

  1 Do you enjoy travelling?
  2 Which countries interest you the most? Why?

**2**  In pairs, complete the cartoon with captions a–d.

  a Excuse me. Could you tell me which country we are in?
  b I'm *really* tired. We need another holiday.
  c What about Europe? It's small but people say it's quite interesting.
  d English breakfast included.

## Work it out

**3**  Look at the text for frames 3, 5, 6 and 8 in the cartoon and answer the questions.

  Which sentences talk about:
  a a definite plan/arrangement for the near future?
  b an unfinalised plan, future intention or ambition?

## Check it out

### Future intentions and arrangements

To talk about future intentions, ambitions or unfinalised plans we use *going to*.

We're going to visit Europe this summer.
I'm going to ask that policeman for help.

To talk about definite plans/arrangements in the near future we use the Present Continuous. We usually mention the time and/or place as well.

We're flying to London in four hours.
We're coming home on Friday.

**4**  Choose the best answers in situations 1–6.

  1 You see a friend on the platform at the station. He says: I'm *catching / going to catch* the 4:14 train to London.
  2 Your ferry is delayed for six hours! You're very angry. You say: I'm *writing / going to write* a letter of complaint.
  3 Your friend asks you to babysit this evening. You can't help. You say: I'm *meeting / going to meet* my friends at eight.
  4 A friend has a holiday brochure from the travel agent's. She says: I think I'm *visiting / going to visit* Scandinavia this year.
  5 Your five-year-old brother is watching a science fiction film. He says: I'm *exploring / going to explore* space when I grow up.
  6 Your friends are packing a tent into their car. They say: We're *going / going to go* camping.

## Mind the trap!

With leisure activities (*hike, swim, sail, camp, fish, sightsee*, etc.) we use the correct form of *go* + the *-ing* form of the leisure activity.

I go skiing at weekends. NOT I ski at weekends.

I'm going skiing tomorrow. NOT I'm skiing tomorrow.

I'm going to go skiing this winter. NOT I'm going to ski this winter.

**5**  In pairs, ask about your future plans. Use the Present Continuous or *going to* and the times below.

  tonight    this weekend
  next summer/winter holidays

  A What are you doing this weekend?
  B On Saturday evening I'm meeting a friend. I think I'm going to play squash on Sunday morning.

**6**  **CD1.15** Complete the dialogue with the Present Continuous or *going to* and the verbs in brackets. Then listen and check.

  **Pam**  Hi Tom! How are things?
  **Tom**  Hi Pam, we're really busy. We're just packing our suitcases. We ¹_____ (leave) for the airport in a few minutes.
  **Pam**  Where ²_____ (you/go)?
  **Tom**  We ³_____ (go) to Poland for a week. We ⁴_____ (fly) to Krakow at midday.
  **Pam**  Are you staying in Krakow all week?
  **Tom**  No, we ⁵_____ (stay) there for three nights. We've got a reservation in a guest house in the city centre.
  **Pam**  What ⁶_____ (you/do) there?
  **Tom**  Well, we ⁷_____ (sightsee) and I ⁸_____ (take) lots of photos. Then if the weather's good, we ⁹_____ (hike) in the Tatra mountains for a few days.
  **Pam**  Lucky you! I'm not sure where to go on holiday this year. I ¹⁰_____ (pop) in to the travel agent's on my way home.

**7**  In pairs, change the dialogue in Exercise 6 with the prompts below.

  • train station/half past ten
  • France/fortnight/catch a train/Paris/ eleven o'clock
  • stay/Paris/for the whole fortnight?
  • no/the first week/reservation/hotel/near/ Eiffel Tower
  • visit museums/practise my French/then/ cycling/Normandy

**8**  In pairs, read your dialogue from Exercise 7. Then do it again from memory.

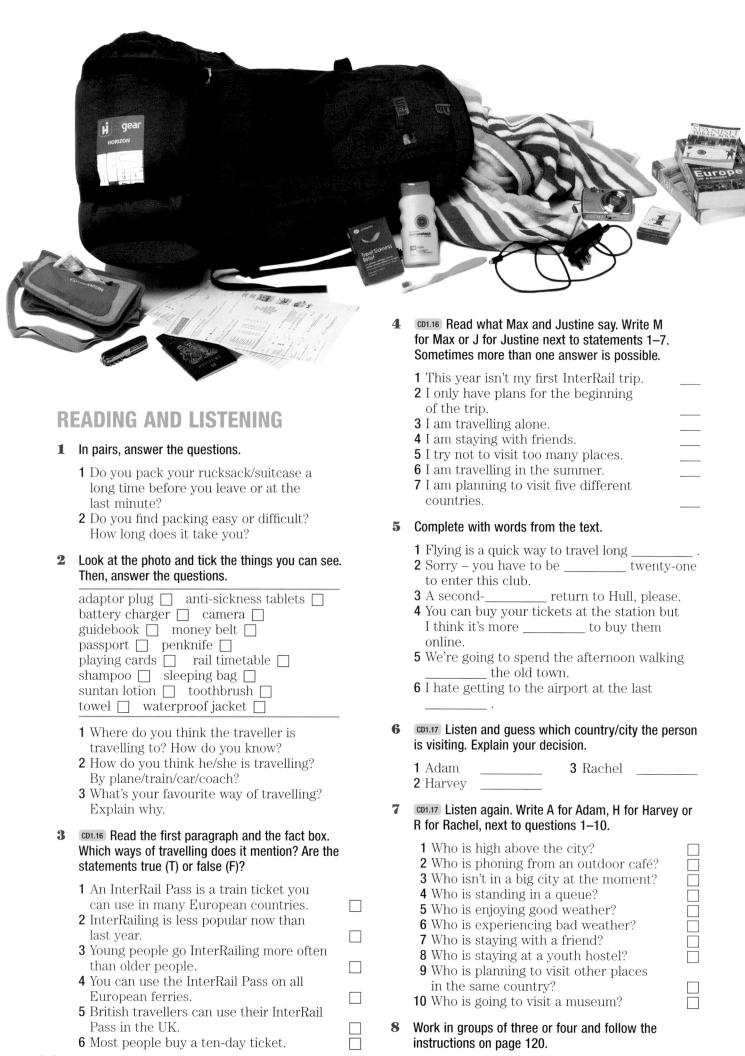

## READING AND LISTENING

**1**  In pairs, answer the questions.

   1 Do you pack your rucksack/suitcase a long time before you leave or at the last minute?
   2 Do you find packing easy or difficult? How long does it take you?

**2**  Look at the photo and tick the things you can see. Then, answer the questions.

adaptor plug ☐  anti-sickness tablets ☐
battery charger ☐  camera ☐
guidebook ☐  money belt ☐
passport ☐  penknife ☐
playing cards ☐  rail timetable ☐
shampoo ☐  sleeping bag ☐
suntan lotion ☐  toothbrush ☐
towel ☐  waterproof jacket ☐

   1 Where do you think the traveller is travelling to? How do you know?
   2 How do you think he/she is travelling? By plane/train/car/coach?
   3 What's your favourite way of travelling? Explain why.

**3**  CD1.16 Read the first paragraph and the fact box. Which ways of travelling does it mention? Are the statements true (T) or false (F)?

   1 An InterRail Pass is a train ticket you can use in many European countries. ☐
   2 InterRailing is less popular now than last year. ☐
   3 Young people go InterRailing more often than older people. ☐
   4 You can use the InterRail Pass on all European ferries. ☐
   5 British travellers can use their InterRail Pass in the UK. ☐
   6 Most people buy a ten-day ticket. ☐

**4**  CD1.16 Read what Max and Justine say. Write M for Max or J for Justine next to statements 1–7. Sometimes more than one answer is possible.

   1 This year isn't my first InterRail trip. ___
   2 I only have plans for the beginning of the trip. ___
   3 I am travelling alone. ___
   4 I am staying with friends. ___
   5 I try not to visit too many places. ___
   6 I am travelling in the summer. ___
   7 I am planning to visit five different countries. ___

**5**  Complete with words from the text.

   1 Flying is a quick way to travel long _____ .
   2 Sorry – you have to be _____ twenty-one to enter this club.
   3 A second-_____ return to Hull, please.
   4 You can buy your tickets at the station but I think it's more _____ to buy them online.
   5 We're going to spend the afternoon walking _____ the old town.
   6 I hate getting to the airport at the last _____ .

**6**  CD1.17 Listen and guess which country/city the person is visiting. Explain your decision.

   1 Adam _____  3 Rachel _____
   2 Harvey _____

**7**  CD1.17 Listen again. Write A for Adam, H for Harvey or R for Rachel, next to questions 1–10.

   1 Who is high above the city? ☐
   2 Who is phoning from an outdoor café? ☐
   3 Who isn't in a big city at the moment? ☐
   4 Who is standing in a queue? ☐
   5 Who is enjoying good weather? ☐
   6 Who is experiencing bad weather? ☐
   7 Who is staying with a friend? ☐
   8 Who is staying at a youth hostel? ☐
   9 Who is planning to visit other places in the same country? ☐
   10 Who is going to visit a museum? ☐

**8**  Work in groups of three or four and follow the instructions on page 120.

**16**

# Travelling Light

Driving a car for long distances is stressful. Flying is quick but frustrating – flights are often at inconvenient times, there are hours of waiting, watching the clouds below quickly becomes boring. That's why for many people, going by train is the best way to travel. It's quiet and relaxing, you can get up and walk around and it's also a great way to meet people. One problem is that train tickets can be expensive. But the new InterRail Global Pass is a cheap and convenient way of travelling around Europe. InterRailing is becoming more popular again and every year a quarter of a million people choose this way to travel. Seventy percent of them are under the age of 25.

**We talk to two experienced InterRailers …**

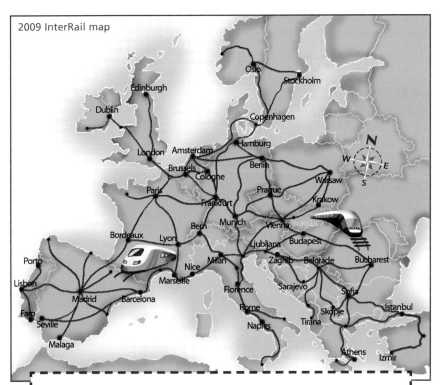

2009 InterRail map

## Max, 22, a student from Newport

This is my third time InterRailing. This year I'm leaving just after my college exams in June and I can't wait. I always travel for a month but buy a twenty-two-day ticket – I like staying for two or three days in one place if I really like it. I'm going to spend ten days in Spain – I always spend three days in Barcelona because I love it and I've got friends there. I'm going to try and visit Portugal this year as well. And after that – who knows? I love the freedom of changing my plans at the last minute.

**Top tips:** Take some playing cards – it's a good way to pass the time and to make friends during long journeys. It's also a good idea to take some basic medicines – there's nothing worse than feeling ill on a train at 4 a.m.!

## Justine, 24, a photographer from London

I usually go InterRailing with my boyfriend in the early autumn when it's quieter. We already know southern Europe quite well so this year we're travelling through Belgium, the Netherlands and Germany to the Czech Republic. We're going to celebrate my birthday in Prague and then travel to Poland and back through Germany. It's best not to rush – a big mistake is to plan to visit too many places and then spend every day on the train.

**Top tips:** Always learn a few basic words in the language of each country you visit – I can say 'thank you' in nine languages! And don't forget a battery charger. InterRailing is no fun when your camera and mobile phone don't work!

## FACT BOX
### InterRail Global Pass

**Where can I use it?**
You can travel as much as you want in up to thirty European countries by train and on some ferries too (for example between Italy and Greece). You can't use the Pass to travel in your home country.

**How old do I have to be?**
Youth Passes are for people between the ages of 12 and 26. Adult Passes are for people over 26.

**How much does it cost?**
The most popular type of ticket gives you unlimited travel second class for 22 days and costs €309 for people under 26.
You can also buy cheaper tickets for 3–10 days.

# SPEAKING AND LISTENING

1 Do you take a guidebook when you go on holiday? What information can you get from a guidebook?

2 In pairs, quickly read the information and circle the attractions that are mentioned. Which places would you like to visit most? Why?

art gallery   cathedral   cinema   clubs
concert hall   museum   restaurants
shopping centre   stadium   theatre

**It's impossible to ever feel bored in Manchester – the cultural capital of the north of England.**

**The Museum of Science and Industry** (open daily 10–5; free) – a huge interactive museum where you can learn about the history of the world's first industrial city.

**Afflecks** (open daily) – three floors of small shops and cafés. The best place to buy alternative fashions, jewellery, CDs, posters and video games.

**The Lowry** (open daily; free) – a huge arts centre with two theatres, concert halls and exhibitions of art and photography.

**Manchester United Football Club Stadium Tour** (not open on match days; £20) – a fantastic day out for any football fan.

**Chinatown** – a lively district near the city centre, full of Chinese shops and restaurants.

**Deansgate Locks** – a district of old factories, now the best place in town to go clubbing!

3 [CD1.18] Listen and decide which places Will and Debbi finally decide to visit.

4 [CD1.18] Study Speak Out. Then listen again and <u>underline</u> the expressions you hear.

---

**SPEAK OUT** | Suggestions

| **Making suggestions** | **Rejecting a suggestion** |
|---|---|
| Let's (go to) … | I'm sorry but: |
| Do you fancy (going ) …? | it isn't really my cup of tea. |
| How about (visiting) …? | I'm not mad about … |
| We could (go) … | I'm not keen on … |
| | |
| **Agreeing to a suggestion** | |
| (That's a) good idea. | Why don't we (go to) … |
| (That) sounds good! | instead? |
| Yes./Sure./Why not? | |
| (That's) fine with me! | |

---

5 [CD1.19] Listen and repeat some of the phrases from Speak Out.

6 [CD1.20] Complete the dialogue with the phrases in the box. Then listen and repeat.

go for a walk   going to the theatre
go to the cinema   keen on   that sounds
about

**A** Do you fancy going clubbing tonight?
**B** I'm sorry but I'm not mad ¹_____ clubs.
**A** How about ²_____ ?
**B** Hmm, theatre tickets are expensive. Why don't we ³_____ instead? That new Tarantino film is on at the moment.
**A** I'm sorry but I'm not ⁴_____ Tarantino. We could just ⁵_____ down to the beach.
**B** ⁶_____ good!

7 In pairs, take turns to make and respond to suggestions.

1 **A** How about/go/theatre?
  **B** ☹ Why don't/visit/museum?
  **A** ☺
  How about going to the theatre?
  I'm sorry but I'm not keen on the theatre …

2 **A** fancy/go/shop?
  **B** ☺

3 **A** Let's/go sightsee/around the city.
  **B** ☹ Why don't/go/to the zoo?
  **A** ☺

4 **A** Why don't/go/country/Saturday?
  **B** ☺
  **A** How about/take/our bikes?
  **B** ☺

8 In pairs, roleplay the situation. Student A, look at page 123. Student B, look at page 123.

## VOCABULARY | Holidays

**1**  Think Back! **Write more words in gaps 1–9 in this advert.**

**2**  **Use the ideas from Exercise 1 (or your own) to invent your own dream holiday. Tell your partner about it.**

I'm going to visit …
I'm travelling there by … and I'm staying at a …
I'm leaving on … and staying for …
I'm going to …

### Mind the trap!

We arrive in a country/town.
We're arriving in England/London.

We arrive at a place/building.
We're arriving at Heathrow Airport/Victoria Station.

**3**  **Choose the correct answer.**

1 We have to be *on / at* the airport at half past eleven.
2 We're going *on / for* holiday for a fortnight.
3 I got these brochures at the travel *office / agent's*.
4 I'm *booking / arranging* a double room at the hotel.
5 Our flight is *cancelled / delayed*. It's leaving later this afternoon.
6 We're going swimming – don't forget your *sleeping bag / towel*!
7 She's arriving *to / in* Buenos Aires at midday.
8 We're landing *in / at* Schipol Airport.
9 We're going to stay *at / to* a youth hostel.
10 They're going to *shop / go shopping* tomorrow.
11 I can't find my rucksack. I'm going to the *lost property office / tourist information office*.

**4**  **Look at the photo. In pairs, answer the questions.**

1 What are the people doing?
2 Which country do you think the picture shows?
3 Would you like to have a holiday like this? Why?/Why not? Choose from these ideas.

stay active   boring   crowded   stimulating stressful   tiring   peace and quiet   relax get to know the local culture

4 Which foreign places do people from your country like to visit? Why?
5 Do you prefer places in your own country or abroad? Why?

# Dream Trips

THE TRAVEL AGENTS WHO CARE!

**Plan your dream trip!**

**Destination**
a city of your choice/
the coast of …/Lake …/
the … mountains/hills, etc.

**Travel**
on foot/by car/by motorbike/
[1]_____/[2]_____/[3]_____

**Accommodation**
at a campsite/[4]_____/[5]_____/
[6]_____

**Departure**
early tomorrow morning/on July 3rd …

**Length of stay**
for a (long weekend/fortnight/month, etc.)

**Activities**
sightseeing/sunbathing/snorkelling/climbing/
fishing/clubbing/hiking/[7]_____/[8]_____/
[9]_____

# WRITING | Formal email

**1** In pairs, read the advert and answer the questions.

**FIRST CLASS SCHOOL OF ENGLISH**

**Come to London and learn English!**

- courses all year
- all levels from Beginner to Advanced
- help with accommodation
- satisfied students from all over the world!

**www.1class.co.uk.net**

**1** Would you like to learn English in Britain during your school holidays? What are the advantages and disadvantages of courses like these?

**2** Does the advert give you enough information? What information is missing? Write a list of questions.

**2** Read Per's email. Are any of his questions similar to yours?

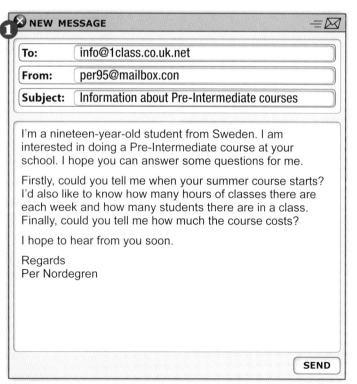

**NEW MESSAGE**

**To:** info@1class.co.uk.net

**From:** per95@mailbox.con

**Subject:** Information about Pre-Intermediate courses

I'm a nineteen-year-old student from Sweden. I am interested in doing a Pre-Intermediate course at your school. I hope you can answer some questions for me.

Firstly, could you tell me when your summer course starts? I'd also like to know how many hours of classes there are each week and how many students there are in a class. Finally, could you tell me how much the course costs?

I hope to hear from you soon.

Regards
Per Nordegren

**SEND**

**3** Read the email below and answer the questions about emails 1 and 2.

**1** Which email sounds formal and is similar to a letter? Which phrases suggest this?
**2** Which email sounds informal and is similar to a conversation?
**3** Who do we usually send formal emails to? Circle the correct answers.

- people we don't know
- friends and close family
- people we know very well
- businesses and institutions

**NEW MESSAGE**

**To:** blackcat7@mailbox.con

**From:** per95@mailbox.con

**Subject:** London?!

Hi Maria!

Thanks for your email. That's great news that we're both going to be at the same language school this summer. I'm so pleased – I'm really looking forward to seeing you again! ☺

I'm flying to London on July 15th and I'm staying with an English family in Crouch End. My course starts on July 18th (I'm in the Pre-Intermediate group). It's only twenty hours of classes a week – there's going to be a lot of time for sightseeing. ;)

What about you? When are you arriving? When does your course start? Write back and let me know!

Lots of love
Per xxx

**SEND**

**4** Look at the examples and answer questions 1–3 below.

**A Direct questions**
How many hours of classes <u>are there</u>?
How much <u>does it cost</u>?
When <u>does your course start</u>?

**B Indirect questions**
I'd like to know how many hours of classes <u>there are</u>.
Could you tell me how much <u>it costs</u>?
Could you tell me when <u>your course starts</u>?

**1** Which questions, A or B, sound less formal?
**2** Which questions don't use auxiliary verbs (*do/does*) and always have the verb at the end of the clause?
**3** What phrases are used to introduce indirect questions?

**5** Make indirect questions using the prompts.

1 What is your phone number?
Could you tell me _____ ?
2 Where do you live?
Could you tell me _____ ?
3 Where is the nearest youth hostel?
I'd like to know _____ .
4 What time are we arriving?
I'd like to know _____ .

**6** Read Maria's email to the school and compare it with Per's email in Exercise 2. Which email is better? Why?

⊗ NEW MESSAGE                    ☰ ✉

| To: | info@1class.co.uk.net |
|---|---|
| From: | blackcat7@mailbox.con |
| Subject: | Your School!! |

Hi guys

I'm a nineteen-year-old student from San Salvador.
My name's Maria. How do you do?

Perhaps I am going to come to your school (I love learning English – it's cool !☺) but I don't have enough information. How much is accommodation? Very expensive??? ☹
Are there any places on your Pre-Intermediate course?
How much free time do students have for sightseeing?
(I want to see London too!)

Write back quickly and tell me.

Bye for now!!!

Kisses
Maria

SEND

**7** In pairs, read Train Your Brain and correct Maria's email to the school. Use Per's email in Exercise 2 to help you.

**TRAIN YOUR BRAIN | Writing skills**

**Formal emails**

1 In the subject box, give a clear reason for writing your email.
2 Unlike a formal letter, you don't need a greeting if you don't know the person's name.
3 If you know the person's name, you can write *Dear* + name.
4 Say why you are writing your email in the first sentence.
5 Smileys (☺), exclamation marks (!), jokes and unimportant information aren't a good idea.
6 If you are asking for information try to use indirect questions (*Could you tell me …/ I'd like to know … + what/when/how/how much*, etc.).
7 End the email with *Best wishes/(Kind) regards*.

**8** In pairs, read the advert for a working holiday. Would you be interested in this kind of holiday? Why?/Why not?

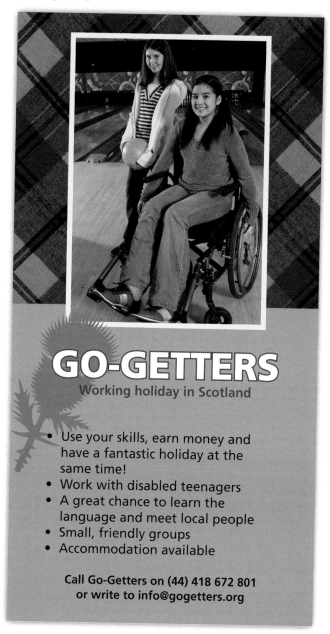

**GO-GETTERS**
Working holiday in Scotland

- Use your skills, earn money and have a fantastic holiday at the same time!
- Work with disabled teenagers
- A great chance to learn the language and meet local people
- Small, friendly groups
- Accommodation available

Call Go-Getters on (44) 418 672 801
or write to info@gogetters.org

**9** Write a formal email to Go-Getters asking for more information. Use Train Your Brain to help you.

- Introduce yourself and say why you are writing.
- Ask when the holiday starts and how long it lasts.
- Ask how much you can earn and how old you have to be.
- Say that you are expecting a reply and end in an appropriate way.

# VOCABULARY AND GRAMMAR

**1** Put the words from the box into five categories. Then add three more words from Units 1 and 2 to each group. (8 points)

snorkelling   laid-back   art gallery   train
battery charger   shopping centre
reserved   theatre   motorbike   modest
camping   money belt   ferry   sightseeing
penknife   passionate

personality adjectives: _____ , _____ ,
_____ , _____

means of transport: _____ , _____ ,
_____

holiday activities: _____ , _____ ,
_____

items for a holiday: _____ , _____ ,
_____

town attractions: _____ , _____ ,
_____

**2** Complete the sentences with the correct prepositions. (5 points)

1 Are you keen _____ skiing?
2 Who do you get _____ well with in your family?
3 Where do you prefer to stay: _____ a campsite or a youth hostel?
4 What do you do first when you arrive _____ a new city?
5 Which do you like better: travelling _____ train or bus?

**3** Complete the sentences with the correct form of the words in capital letters. (4 points)

1 It is usually a good idea to go on holiday for a _____ or longer. NIGHT
2 It rains so much here that you need to wear a _____ jacket very often. WATER
3 Charter planes usually take off and land at the most _____ times – either early in the morning or late at night. CONVENIENT
4 There are several good pizza restaurants in the _____ . NEIGHBOUR

**4** Complete the second sentence so that it has a similar meaning to the first sentence. Use the word in bold without changing it. (4 points)

1 Bill hates listening to rock music. **like**
Bill _____ rock music.
2 Shirley is watching TV at the moment. **not**
Shirley _____ her homework at the moment.
3 I'm always at school on time. **never**
I _____ for school.
4 I'm going to stay at home this summer. **not**
I'm _____ holiday this summer.

**5** Complete the email. For each gap choose the correct answer. (9 points)

> ⊗ NEW MESSAGE
>
> **To:** cilla2@mailbox.con
> **From:** rob46@mailbox.con
> **Subject:** Holiday photos
>
> Dear Cilla,
> Thank you for your email and the photos from your holiday in Spain. You ¹___ fantastic – really suntanned. I guess you ²___ getting brown.
> ³___ that our plan is to go to Spain too?! Mum and Dad ⁴___ our holiday. They ⁵___ a place somewhere in the south of Spain, but we ⁶___ to stay there all the time. We ⁷___ to visit some cities such as Seville as well.
> The weather is terrible at the moment. You know what the problem is – the rain! As you know I normally ⁸___ football on Wednesdays but this Wednesday I ⁹___ at home as there are so many grey clouds.
> Well, that's all for now. Hope to see you soon.
> Love
> Rob
>
> SEND

1 a looking   b are going to look   c look
2 a enjoy   b are enjoying   c enjoying
3 a Do you know
   b Are you knowing
   c Are you going to know
4 a are organising
   b organising
   c organise
5 a booking   b are going to book   c book
6 a don't plan
   b aren't going to plan
   c aren't planning
7 a want
   b are wanting
   c are going to want
8 a play   b am to play   c am playing
9 a stay   b am going to stay   c staying

# PRONUNCIATION

**6** **CD1.21** Listen to the words in the table and look at the word stress patterns. Now listen to the words in the box and put them in the correct column. Then listen, repeat and check.

| ●•• | •●• | ••●• |
|---|---|---|
| holiday | important | explanation |

convenient   nowadays   multilingual
classical   cathedral   optimistic   generous
reservation   frustrating   pessimistic
property   romantic

## LISTENING SKILLS

**7** CD1.22 **Listen. Are the statements true (T) or false (F)?** (5 points)

1 Jodie is packing for a holiday. ☐
2 She is going away in three days. ☐
3 Paula likes to make a list before she packs. ☐
4 Jodie is meeting her French boyfriend. ☐
5 She is taking three sweaters. ☐

## READING SKILLS

**8** **Read the text. Are the statements true (T) or false (F)?** (4 points)

1 About 400 million people speak English as their first language. ☐
2 In the USA the number of Spanish speakers is growing. ☐
3 Nowadays there are more and more languages in the world. ☐
4 English is definitely going to dominate the Internet even more in the future. ☐

**9** **Choose the best heading for the text.** (1 point)

a English in the world
b Languages around the world
c The language of the Internet

## SPEAKING SKILLS

**10** **Roleplay the conversation.**

On holiday in the UK you see an advert for a camping trip to Brighton. You and your friend want to go. Call the tourist office and ask for details.
**Student A**, make the call.
**Student B**, answer the call.

The following ideas may help you:
• Available places?
• Cost?
• Transport?
• What to do there?
• What to take?
• Other

## WRITING SKILLS

**11** **Follow the instructions and write an email.**

While visiting your family in Cardiff during your summer holiday, you read an article in the local press. In the article the local youth club invites young people to take part in a variety of activities. Unfortunately the article does not include enough information, so you decide to write an email to the youth club in which you:

• introduce yourself and ask if foreigners can participate in the advertised activities.
• write about your hobbies and express your interest in taking part in a certain activity.
• ask when the activities take place and how big the groups are.
• ask if you have to pay for participating in the activities and what you have to do to take part.

The importance of English as a global language is growing all the time. Of course, there are more native speakers of Chinese than of English – about a billion compared to about 400 million. But almost one and a quarter billion people across the world use English as a second or foreign language. And this number is getting bigger every year. English is the international language of politics, business, science, transport, advertising, the media and computers. For example, approximately seventy percent of websites are in English. Even in countries like Germany, almost ninety percent of research scientists use English as their working language every day.

There are some other languages which are gaining in popularity: the number of people who speak Arabic, Chinese or Portuguese in different countries is increasing too. Some languages like Urdu or Hindi are growing much faster than English. Even in the USA the fastest growing language is Spanish!

Not all languages are so successful, however. There are about 6,000 languages in the world but sadly many of them have an uncertain future. In fact, about twenty languages are disappearing every year.

Surprisingly, the Internet may offer a solution to this problem. Although it is true that English dominates the Internet, the number of websites in other languages is growing very quickly. With chat sites and messenger programs people can communicate more easily than before and in any language they know. So perhaps modern technology can help save some languages from dying out.

# Growing up

**Read, listen and talk about** school and education; growing up.
**Practise** the Past Simple and *used to* for past events; adjectives with *-ed/-ing* endings.
**Focus on** asking for permission; predicting in reading and listening.
**Write** a personal recollection.

## The best days of your life?

It was such a big day but I don't remember very much. It's not surprising – I was only five years old and it was a long time ago!

I walked to school with Mum and I cried all the way. I didn't want to go. I had a blue rucksack and a brand new pencil case. The playground was full of noisy, excited kids. Some of the children looked huge – I never knew that I was so small! Then a bell rang and everybody stopped running and went inside. How did they know what to do?

The classroom walls were yellow and there was a horrible smell of soap everywhere. There was also an aquarium with smelly fish in it. My teacher's name was Mrs Bell. ('What a funny name!' I thought.) She wasn't very strict but she spoke in a loud voice all the time. It was very strange.

I don't remember what we learnt that day. I think we sang songs and clapped a lot. Mrs Bell read us a story and we sat cross-legged on the floor. I was embarrassed because I didn't know how to do it!

'So, Kate, were you a good girl today?' Dad asked me later.
'I don't know!' I said.
'Was it fun?'
'No! And Mrs Bell said that we have to go back tomorrow!' I wasn't very happy.
'Did you make any new friends?'
'Yes, I did. I think ...'
'Did you learn anything?'
'No, I didn't! Dad! Why are you asking me all these questions? Didn't you go to school?'

# GRAMMAR AND READING

**1**  In pairs, answer the questions.

1 How old are children when they start school in your country?
2 Do you think this is too old/young? Why?

**2**  `CD1.23` Look at the photo and answer the questions. Use the ideas below to help you. Then read quickly and check your answers.

1 How old do you think the girl is?
2 What is the situation? How do you know?
3 How do you think she is feeling? Why?

primary school   school gates   playground
school uniform   say goodbye to
feel small/proud/anxious/excited/calm/scared/grown-up

## Work it out

**3**  `CD1.23` Read the text again and answer the questions.

1 Is Kate talking about a present or past event?
2 What are the two forms of the verb *to be* in the Past Simple?
3 Find four regular Past Simple verbs. What are their infinitives?
4 Find four irregular Past Simple verbs. What are their infinitives?

**4**  Complete the sentences.

| Present Simple | Past Simple |
|---|---|
| I walk to school.<br>I don't know how to do it.<br>Do you learn anything?<br>Yes, I do./No, I don't. | I ¹_____ to school.<br>I ²_____ know how to do it.<br>³_____ you learn anything?<br>Yes, I ⁴_____ ./No, I ⁵_____ . |

## Check it out

### Past Simple

We use the Past Simple to talk about things that started and finished in the past.

| | *to be* | Regular and irregular verbs |
|---|---|---|
| **Affirmative** | I was only five.<br>The walls were yellow. | The children looked huge.<br>I had a blue rucksack. |
| **Negative** | I wasn't very happy.<br>They weren't very strict. | I didn't want to go.<br>I didn't know how to do it. |
| **Questions** | Was it fun?<br>Yes, it was./No, it wasn't.<br>Were you a good girl? | Did you learn anything?<br>Yes, I did./No, I didn't.<br>How did they know what to do? |
| **Time expressions** | yesterday, last night/week/year/Saturday, when I was five,<br>ten years ago, in 2007/1999, one day/morning | |

**5**  Choose the irregular verb in each list and write its Past Simple form.

| | | | | |
|---|---|---|---|---|
| 1 play | look | start | think | _____ |
| 2 buy | decide | phone | work | _____ |
| 3 rain | talk | forget | shout | _____ |
| 4 listen | feel | visit | watch | _____ |
| 5 stay | hate | promise | wear | _____ |
| 6 live | give | invite | laugh | _____ |

**6**  `CD1.24` Listen and put the regular verbs in Exercise 5 in the correct column. Then practise saying them.

| /d/ | /t/ | /ɪd/ |
|---|---|---|
| played | looked | started |

**7**  Write the questions in the Past Simple. Then look at Kate's story again and answer them.

1 How old/be/Kate?
2 Kate/walk/to school/ on her own?
3 What/everybody/do/when the bell rang?
4 What colour/be/the walls?
5 What/be/Kate's teacher's name?
6 The teacher/be/strict?
7 The children/sing/songs?
8 Kate/enjoy/her first day at school?

**8**  In pairs, use time expressions from Check it out to answer the questions.

When did you last:
1 see your grandparents?
   I last saw my grandparents three weeks ago/in May.
2 check your email?
3 cook a meal?
4 go swimming?
5 study English for an hour?

**9**  `CD1.25` Listen to five teenagers talking about their first day at secondary school. Match speakers 1–5 with questions a–f. There is one extra question. Then listen again and check.

Speaker 1 ☐    Speaker 4 ☐
Speaker 2 ☐    Speaker 5 ☐
Speaker 3 ☐

a How did you spend your first day?
b Did you like your form tutor?
c Did you make any new friends?
d Did you arrive early?
e Were you scared before your first day?
f What did you wear?

**10**  Write a short description of your first day at secondary school. Follow the instructions.

• In pairs, answer questions a–f in Exercise 9. Make notes.
• Use your notes and the text in Exercise 3 to help you.

# READING

**1** Match the people with photographs A–D. What were they famous for? Use the verbs to complete the sentences about them.

propose   compose   paint   write

1 Agatha Christie _____ crime novels. ☐
2 Albert Einstein _____ the theory
   of relativity. ☐
3 Pablo Picasso _____ more than
   1,500 works. ☐
4 Beethoven _____ nine symphonies. ☐

**2** Look at the photos again and read the title of the text. What do you think the text is about?

**3** Read the first paragraph. What do you think the text is about now?

1 unhappy children ☐
2 people who had problems at school ☐
3 the effects of bad education ☐
4 successful people who had learning
   difficulties ☐

**4** Read the last paragraph only. Do you need to change your answer to Exercise 3?

**5** Look at Exercises 2–4 and complete points a–d in Train Your Brain.

---

**TRAIN YOUR BRAIN | Reading skills**

**Predicting**

You can make a text easier to understand by predicting what it is going to be about before you read it.
Always:
a   look at _____ .
b   read the _____ .
c   read the _____ paragraph of the text.
d   read the _____ paragraph of the text.

---

**6** CD1.26 Now read the whole text. Did you predict the subject correctly?

**7** Read the whole text again and match headings a–f with paragraphs 1–5. There's one heading you don't need.

a What is dyslexia? ☐
b Typical problems for children with
   dyslexia at school ☐
c How to help people with dyslexia ☐
d What some talented people had
   in common ☐
e Other famous people who had dyslexia ☐
f A person who had hidden talents ☐

**8** Find words or phrases in the text that mean the same as the words or phrases below.

a (para. 1) (v) stop going to
   school/university                    _drop out_
b (para. 2) (n) pupils in the same
   class at school                      _____
c (para. 3) (v) learn by heart          _____
d (para. 4) (n) a score which shows
   how good a piece of work is          _____
e (para. 4) (adj) unhappy because
   of poor results                      _____
f (para. 5) (adj) good at using your
   imagination                          _____

**9** Read the text again and choose the best answer.

1 The children in paragraph 1
   a had a difficult time at school.
   b had classmates who were stupid.
   c left school early.

2 Some famous writers, composers and
   inventors
   a were not very intelligent.
   b were surprised when they became
      successful.
   c had similar problems when they were
      children.

3 People with dyslexia
   a were probably born with the disability.
   b never knew about it.
   c can't remember anything.

4 Agatha Christie started writing because
   a her parents wanted her to.
   b she wanted to show her sister that she
      could write.
   c she wanted to leave school early.

5 The people mentioned in the last
   paragraph are
   a not geniuses.
   b crime writers like Agatha Christie.
   c well-known people who had problems
      with reading and writing.

**10** In pairs, answer the questions.

1 Do you remember where and when you
   learned to write? Was it easy?
2 Do you know anybody who is dyslexic?
   What problems do you/they have?
3 Was there anything you were bad at when
   you were younger but that you can do now?

A I couldn't swim when I was young but now
   I am quite a good swimmer.
B I didn't understand Chemistry when I was
   younger but now I'm quite good at it.

# Hidden talents

★★★★★★★★★★★★★★★★★★★★★★★★★★★★★★★★★★★★★★★★★★★★★★

**1**

They often didn't learn to read and write until they were older. Their parents often thought they were stupid and their friends laughed at them. Some of them hated their schooldays and decided to drop out of school as soon as possible. In short, they had unhappy schooldays.

**2**

Some of the world's greatest composers, writers and inventors had an unpleasant time at school like this. Later, when they became successful, nobody was more surprised than their old classmates. Were these people stupid? No, of course not! Some people believe that they had something in common – dyslexia.

**3**

Dyslexia is a learning disability which means that people have problems with reading and remembering written words. It is often difficult for them to memorise things. Studies show that people with dyslexia use a different part of their brain to read and remember. Experts think that the cause of dyslexia is genetic: probably somebody else in the family also had dyslexia. Statistically, about fifteen percent of people are dyslexic, but not everybody who has dyslexia knows about it.

**4**

Some people with dyslexia discover they have special, hidden talents but only when they are older. A good example is Agatha Christie, one of the most successful writers in history (two billion books published in forty-four languages!). At school she had problems with writing and often got bad marks for essays. Her parents were disappointed and wanted Agatha to leave school early. She only started writing because her older sister said Agatha couldn't do it! And even when she was already a famous crime writer, she sometimes felt embarrassed because she still couldn't spell.

**5**

There are many more examples of people like Agatha Christie: Albert Einstein, Leonardo da Vinci, Ludwig van Beethoven, Pablo Picasso, John Lennon, Thomas Edison … important and creative people who had problems with reading and writing when they were young. Of course, that doesn't mean that everybody with dyslexia is a genius, but it shows that sometimes people can be a lot more intelligent than they seem.

A

C

D

## SPEAKING

**1** In pairs, look at the photo and try and guess the answers to the questions.

1 Where are they?
2 What do you think the problem is?

**2** CD1.27 Listen to the conversation. Were your answers to Exercise 1 right?

**3** CD1.27 Listen again. Which things does the student want to borrow? Make a list.

**4** CD1.28 Study Speak Out. Then listen and <u>underline</u> the phrases you hear. Which of the speakers sounds rude? Why?

### SPEAK OUT | Permission

| Question | *Yes* | *No* + reason* |
|---|---|---|
| Can I borrow your dictionary? Is it OK if I smoke? | Yes, of course. Sure, no problem. | Sorry, you can't. I'm using it. I'm afraid not. It's not allowed. |
| Do you mind if I open the window? Do you mind if I turn the TV off? | No, please do. No, I don't mind. | I'm afraid I do. It's a bit cold. Yes, I do. I'm watching it. |

**5** CD1.29 Listen and repeat some of the phrases from Speak Out.

### Mind the trap!

Do you mind if I …? = Is it a problem for you if …?

If somebody asks you a question starting with *Do you mind if …?* and it isn't a problem, you should answer *No (= No, it isn't a problem.)*

Do you mind if I sit here? No, I don't./No, please do.

**6** In pairs, ask for permission. Choose from the ideas below.

A Is it OK if I take your chair?
B No, I'm sorry, you can't. I need it!

Can I …?   Is it OK if I …?
Do you mind if I …?

borrow your watch/your shoes/
some money …
use your glasses/dictionary/mobile phone …
ask you a question/for your phone number/ …
keep your pen/ …
visit you tonight

**7** In pairs, make a dialogue for each situation.

1 You have to phone home from a friend's house. You don't have a mobile phone.
2 The train is full. There is one free seat in the middle of a large family.
3 You need to leave class early today but there's a test in the last hour.
4 You are on a bus. It's very cold and the window is open.

# GRAMMAR AND LISTENING

**1** **CD1.30** Read and listen to the continuation of the conversation on page 28, and say which avatar, A or B, shows Katie when she was younger.

**Josh** You used to live in Leeds, didn't you?
**Katie** Yes, but …?
**Josh** You used to go to Wadley School.
**Katie** Sorry, do I know you?
**Josh** Your name's Katie, and your brother's called Gary, but you didn't use to call him Gary; you used to call him Gazza. Your parents had a shoe shop, but they sold it five years ago and moved to London.
**Katie** Wait a minute!
**Josh** You didn't use to be so slim. You used to wear lots of make-up and you used to have lots of piercings too.
**Katie** How do you know all this?
**Josh** You didn't use to have blonde hair, either.

## Work it out

**2** Read the sentences and tick the correct ones.

Katie used to wear lots of make-up.
**a** Katie wore make-up regularly in the past (but now she doesn't). ☐
**b** She only wore make-up one time. ☐

Katie didn't use to have blonde hair.
**a** Her hair was a different colour before. ☐
**b** Her hair was the same colour before. ☐

## Check it out

### used to

*Used to* expresses a regular habit or state in the past which doesn't happen any more. We can't use *used to* if something happened only once.

I used to wear glasses but now I don't need them.

She didn't use to have blonde hair but now she does.

Did you use to have long hair?
Yes, I did./No, I didn't.

**3** Correct the wrong sentences.

1 We used to wear school uniform.
2 He used to fail his Maths exam last Friday.
3 She didn't use to be so popular.
4 I used to forget to do my homework yesterday.
5 Did you use to cry a lot when you were little?
6 Last summer I used to break my leg.

**4** Use *used to/didn't use to* to write about the changes in Katie's life.

1 Katie lives in London now, but _____ .
2 Katie goes to university now, but _____ .
3 Katie's brother's name is Gary, but _____ .
4 Katie's slim now, but _____ .
5 Katie doesn't wear much make-up now, but _____ .
6 Her hair is blonde now, but _____ .

**5** **CD1.31** Say why you think Josh knows so much about Katie. Then listen and check.

**6** Complete sentences 1–5 with *used to/didn't use to* and the verbs below.

be (x2)   go (x2)   have   wear

1 Josh _____ in the same year as Gary.
2 Josh _____ swimming with Katie.
3 He _____ to her house to see her.
4 He _____ glasses, and he _____ spots.
5 He _____ good-looking, but he is now.

**7** In pairs, use the prompts to ask and answer about changes in your life in the last five years.

appearance/clothes/home/family/friends/school/likes and dislikes/free time

**A** Which video games did you use to play five years ago?
**B** I used to play Super Mario Bros all the time. What about you?
**A** I didn't use to play Super Mario Bros, but I used to play Zelda a lot.

**29**

## VOCABULARY | Adjectives with *-ing/-ed*

**1** Think Back! In pairs, add as many adjectives as you can to the lists.

| Adjectives with *-ing* endings | Adjectives with *-ed* endings |
|---|---|
| annoying | annoyed |
| disappointing | disappointed |
| embarrassing | embarrassed |
| frightening | frightened |

### Mind the trap!

If a thing, person or situation is … boring,
interesting,
annoying,

you feel … bored.
interested.
annoyed.

**2** Choose the correct answer.

1 I felt very *exciting / excited* before my first day at school.
2 I always think exams are very *tiring / tired*.
3 She felt *surprising / surprised* when she passed all her exams.
4 Our old textbook was a bit *boring / bored* …
5 … but I'm really *interesting / interested* in this one.
6 I was *amazing / amazed* that the others knew what to do.

**3** Complete the sentences. Make adjectives from the verbs in capital letters.

1 This school has lots of _____ pupils like me.  SATISFY
2 I was _____ at the words my uncle used.  SHOCK
3 Our team lost 3–0. It was a _____ result.  DISAPPOINT
4 I used to think tractors were _____ !  FASCINATE
5 That film is absolutely _____ .  TERRIFY
6 I got 12% in the Maths test. I felt so _____ .  EMBARRASS

**4** Answer the questions and tell your partner how you felt.

How did you feel:
• before your last English test?
• after your last English test?
• on your first day at school?
• on the day before the last school holidays?

I felt terrified before my last English test.

**5** In pairs, follow the instructions. Take turns to be Student A or Student B.

**Student A**
1 Choose one of the *-ed* adjectives from Exercise 1 and remember a moment when you felt like that.
2 Tell your partner the adjective you chose.

**Student B**
1 Ask your partner *yes/no* questions to find out where he/she was and why he/she felt that way.
2 You have only ten questions to find out the answer.

A Embarrassed.
B Were you at school? Did you make a mistake?

A

## LISTENING AND SPEAKING

**1** Look at photo A and try to answer the questions.

1 What do you think the situation is?
2 How are the people feeling? Why?

**2** CD1.32 Listen to Part 1 of the recording and check your answers to Exercise 1. Which words or phrases helped you decide if your answers were correct?

**3** In pairs, think about the situation. From your experience what do you think the people are going to say? Make a list.

**4** CD1.33 Listen to Part 2 of the recording and check your ideas from Exercise 3.

B

**5** CD1.33 Listen again and tick the expressions you hear.

1 How do you do? ☐

2 Do come in. ☐

3 How are you doing? ☐

4 Make yourself at home! ☐

5 Nice to meet you! ☐

6 What a surprise! ☐

7 Just call me … ☐

8 Take a seat. ☐

**6** In pairs, complete Train Your Brain with the words below. Look at Exercises 1–3 to help you.

key words   experience   situation

---

**TRAIN YOUR BRAIN | Listening skills**

**Predicting**

a Look at the pictures or photos to guess what the
¹_____ is in general.

b Listen for ²_____ to check your ideas.

c Think about the situation and use your
³_____ to try to guess what the people are
going to talk about.

---

**7** CD1.34 Look at photo B and use Train Your Brain to help you predict the answers to questions 1–4. Then listen to Part 3 of the recording and check.

1 What is the situation?
2 What are Simon's mum and Becky looking at?
3 How is Simon feeling? Why?
4 What do you think Simon's mum is talking about?

**8** CD1.34 Listen again. Are the statements true (T) or false (F)?

1 Simon used to go on holiday to the seaside. ☐
2 He used to have short hair. ☐
3 He used to love ice cream. ☐
4 Simon used to want to be a policeman. ☐
5 He stopped playing the piano. ☐
6 He used to play football. ☐

**9** Work in groups. Think about when you were a small child. Ask each other these questions.

1 Where did you use to go on holiday?
2 What was your favourite food?
3 How was your appearance different?
4 What did you want to be as an adult?
5 What musical instrument did you use to play?
6 What games/sports did you use to enjoy?

# Create and inspire

**Read, listen and talk about** artists and writers; music; inspiration.
**Practise** the Past Simple and Past Continuous; time expressions.
**Focus on** recounting past events; phrasal verbs.
**Write** informal emails.

## Eureka moments!

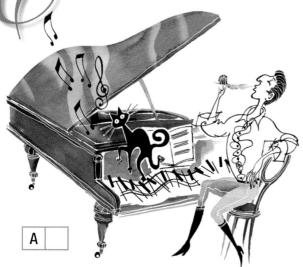

A

B

C

**1**

One day in the 1920s, the great American composer George Gershwin was travelling to a concert in Boston. While he was sitting alone on the train, he suddenly got the idea for his most famous work, *Rhapsody in Blue*. When you listen to the music today, you can clearly hear the train wheels and the whistle!

**2**

Night was falling and the moon was shining. Beethoven was walking around Vienna – he was looking for inspiration. He was passing a small house when he heard one of his compositions. Somebody was playing it on the piano but kept on making mistakes. Beethoven was intrigued and decided to find out who it was. He entered the house and realised that the girl at the piano was blind. He sat and played music to her for over an hour. Suddenly the moon appeared at the window. Beethoven was excited by the special atmosphere in the room and began to compose his famous *Moonlight Sonata*.

**3**

In the summer of 1837, the Polish composer Chopin was living in Paris. Late one evening he was composing alone in his music room. While he was sitting at the piano, a small kitten suddenly ran across the piano keys. Chopin liked the strange melody and he tried to write it down. In 1838, he published a new composition. The title? – *The Cat Waltz*!

# GRAMMAR AND LISTENING

**1** `CD2.1` Listen to these three pieces of music. Which one do you like best? Which adjectives could describe each piece?

*Rhapsody in Blue* by George Gershwin
*Moonlight Sonata* by Ludwig van Beethoven
*The Cat Waltz* by Fréderic Chopin

| exciting | boring | dramatic | mysterious |
| melodic | catchy | irritating | sentimental |

**2** `CD2.2` Read anecdotes 1–3 and match them to pictures A–C.

## Work it out

**3** Match sentences 1 and 2 with the uses of the Past Continuous, a or b.

1 Night was falling and the moon was shining.
2 Late one evening Chopin was composing in his music room.

a setting the scene at the beginning of a story
b saying that somebody was in the middle of an action at a particular time

**4** Look at the sentence and answer the questions.

While Gershwin **was travelling** by train, he suddenly **got** the idea for *Rhapsody in Blue*.

1 Did these actions happen
  a one after another?  b at the same time?
2 Which action was shorter and which tense do we use to talk about it?

## Check it out

### Past Continuous

We use the Past Continuous:

- to set the scene, often at the start of a story.
  Night was falling and the moon was shining.

- to talk about what was happening at a particular moment in the past.
  At ten o'clock he was composing in his music room.

- with the Past Simple to show that a long activity was interrupted by a short one.
  While/As he was sitting at the piano, a small kitten suddenly ran across the piano keys.
  He was passing a small house when he heard one of his compositions.

| **Affirmative** | I/He/She was listening.<br>We/You/They were listening. |
| **Negative** | I/He/She wasn't listening.<br>We/You/They weren't listening. |
| **Questions** | Was I/he/she listening?<br>Yes, I/he/she was./No, I/he/she wasn't.<br><br>Were you/we/they listening?<br>Yes, you/we/they were./<br>No, you/we/they weren't. |

**5** Look at the pictures and the texts in Exercise 2 again. Correct the sentences.

1 Gershwin was smoking a cigar.
2 Gershwin was travelling with friends to Boston.
3 Beethoven was walking around Vienna in the morning.
4 Somebody was playing one of Beethoven's compositions on the violin.
5 In 1837, Chopin was living in Warsaw.
6 Late in the evening, Chopin was reading in his music room.

**6** Complete the sentences with the correct form of the Past Simple or the Past Continuous.

It was a hot day in the summer of 1965. An unhappy young Colombian ¹_____ (drive) his car from Mexico City to Acapulco. As he ²_____ (cross) the desert, he ³_____ (come) up with the idea for a book. When he ⁴_____ (arrive) in Acapulco, he started writing the novel *One Hundred Years of Solitude*. Its author, Gabriel García Márquez ⁵_____ (win) the Nobel Prize for Literature in 1982.

**7** Complete the sentences. Use the Past Simple or the Past Continuous.

1 I _____ (read) my brother's diary when he suddenly _____ (come) into the room!
2 Where _____ you _____ (go) when I _____ (see) you last night?
3 When I _____ (wake) up this morning, it _____ (snow).
4 I _____ (drop) my mobile while I _____ (text) my friend.
5 _____ you_____ (sleep) when I _____ (phone) this morning?
6 He _____ (not look) where he _____ (go) and _____ (crash) into a tree.

**8** `CD2.3` Listen and write sentences with the Past Continuous and the Past Simple. Use the prompts below.

watch the football match   start to rain
robbers break into the house   sleep
have a bath   have a picnic   complain
play the guitar   have a good idea   ring

1 While he was watching the football match, his phone rang.

**9** What do you think your partner was doing at these times? Ask and check if your guesses were correct.

ten o'clock last night
six o'clock this morning
last Saturday at 8 p.m.

A Were you sleeping at ten o'clock last night?
B No, I wasn't. I was studying Chemistry!

# Finding your creative moments

Novelist Gavin Rhys talks about how he comes up with ideas ...

Mrs Rance, my old English teacher, once wrote on my report card, 'Gavin is a pleasant boy but has no imagination.' Perhaps she was right. Certainly, when I was sixteen, I found writing very stressful – my mind used to go blank in the middle of an essay because I didn't have any ideas. I'm sure Mrs Rance was surprised when I became a writer. The truth is that people work best in different conditions and I had to find out for myself the conditions that were most creative for me. The first thing is to find a place where you enjoy working. I used to do my homework lying on the floor. Nowadays I do all my writing at the kitchen table. The great short story writer Raymond Carver used to write while he was sitting in his car, parked in front of his apartment. Others find the noise and distractions of libraries or railway stations more inspiring than at a desk at home.

The next thing is to identify the time of day when you feel creative and can work without interruption. Toni Morrison, the American novelist, used to get up half an hour before dawn, light a candle and wait for the sun to come up before she got down to work. I prefer staying up to work when everyone else is asleep. The French writer, Henri d'Aguesseau, whose wife was always ten minutes late for dinner, used this time to write every evening. He kept on writing and a year later he finished his book (and it eventually became a bestseller!).

But what do you do when the ideas aren't coming? The most important thing is to stop concentrating on the problem and to do something else. I find my best ideas come to me when I'm chilling out in the bath. I'm not the only one – Benjamin Franklin did most of his writing in the bath and of course Archimedes solved a complicated problem while he was having a bath. There's a good reason why taking a break in the middle of your work is creative – when you relax it is easier for the right part of the brain (responsible for imaginative thinking) to come up with creative ideas. So it's official – relaxing is creative.

Another good time to come up with ideas, according to the scientists, is just after you wake up. At this time your brain is disorganised but the right part of the brain is still very active so you are open to all sorts of unusual ideas. So sometimes I wake up fifteen minutes early and just lie in bed and think – it can be very creative.

## DID YOU KNOW?

Scientists believe that people are twenty percent more creative when they are happy and relaxed. That's why some companies, such as Google, put table tennis tables in their offices.

**34**

## READING

**1** In pairs, describe the photo and answer the questions.

1 What do you think his job is? Why?
2 Where do you think he usually does his work?
3 What are the advantages and disadvantages of working/studying at home?

**2** Read the first and the last paragraph of the article, look at the title and decide what the article is about.

a How to write your first novel.
b The best age to be creative.
c Different ways to be more creative.

**3** Quickly read the article. Was your answer to Exercise 2 correct?

**4** CD2.4 Read the article again. Are the statements true (T) or false (F)?

1 Gavin used to find it hard to write essays. ☐
2 Raymond Carver used to write when he was travelling. ☐
3 Henri d'Aguesseau used to write while he was eating with his wife. ☐
4 D'Aguesseau's book was very successful. ☐
5 Having a clean body is very important for solving problems. ☐
6 The right side of the brain comes up with the most imaginative ideas. ☐
7 The right side of the brain isn't very active when you wake up. ☐

**5** Complete the sentences with the correct form of the words in capital letters.

1 I can't work in the school library – there are too many _____ .  DISTRACT
2 She was good at Chemistry so she decided to become a _____ .  SCIENCE
3 He's very _____ – he's terrible at planning his work.  ORGANISE
4 The written exam was fine but the speaking exam was very _____ .  STRESS
5 He's a very _____ young musician.  CREATE
6 People often stare at her because of her _____ clothes.  USUAL
7 I love Verdi – he was such an _____ composer.  IMAGINE

**6** In pairs, answer the questions.

1 Where do you work best? At home/in the library …? How well do you work when it's noisy and there are distractions?
2 What homework do you usually do first/last? Why?
3 Are you good at multi-tasking (doing several things at the same time)?
4 How do you relax when you've got a lot of work?

**7** Look at the photo on page 120 and follow the instructions.

## VOCABULARY | Phrasal verbs

**1** Think Back! Look at the article again. Complete these sentences with the correct verbs from the box.

chill   come   get   keep   stay   find

1 I'm really tired this morning – I _____ on making mistakes.
2 I'm trying to _____ up with an idea for my essay.
3 To _____ out more about our products, visit our website.
4 It's not a good idea to _____ up all night and study.
5 I usually _____ out by listening to music or phoning a friend.
6 I've got an important essay to write but I can't _____ down to it.

**2** Write the correct phrasal verb from Exercise 1 next to its definition.

a continue doing something; do something many times _____

b think of (an idea) _____

c get some information _____

d start working _____

e not go to bed _____

f [informal] relax _____

**3** Complete the sentences with a phrasal verb from Exercise 2 in the correct tense.

1 She _____ the idea for the book while she was travelling by train.
2 Martin's sleepy today – he _____ and chatted all night on the Internet.
3 We didn't do very much on our holiday – we usually just _____ on the beach.
4 We need to _____ how much the tickets cost – let's phone the theatre tomorrow.
5 My boss is really angry with me – I _____ coming to work late.
6 It was hard for me to _____ my schoolwork after the summer holidays.

**4** Choose three phrasal verbs from Exercise 2. Write your own sentence for each verb.

> This happened just before Christmas last year. I wasn't having a good day. First, I lost £20 on the bus. Then, I failed a Maths exam. And finally, my boyfriend left me! I was totally fed up; my life was a disaster! When I got home, I started playing about on the computer. After a while, I saw a video on YouTube. It showed a couple dancing. The woman was in a wheelchair but they were dancing beautifully and really enjoying themselves! I was amazed. It was totally inspiring! As I was watching, I realised two important things. First, if you really want to do something, you can do it. And second, I remembered how much I used to love dancing as a kid. So I stopped feeling sorry for myself and took up dancing seriously. I go to classes three times a week and I love it. I used to feel depressed all the time, but not any more. A video clip changed my life!

## SPEAKING AND LISTENING

**1** Look at the photo and answer the questions. Use the words below to help you.

1 What are the people doing?
2 Is it easier or more difficult for the woman? Why?
3 Are you interested in dancing? Why?/ Why not?

audience   disabled   move   partner
perform   turn   wheelchair

**2** **CD2.5** Read and listen to Caitlin's story and answer the questions.

1 When did it happen?
2 Why was she fed up?
3 What video clip did she see?
4 How did she feel when she saw it?
5 What did she learn from it?
6 How did it change her life?

**3** Underline the words and phrases in Speak Out that Caitlin uses in her story.

---

**SPEAK OUT** I Recounting a past event

Say when the story happened.
**It happened a few years ago./It was in [+ year]./ I was about … years old./I was in my first year of secondary school./This happened just before Christmas last year./I was visiting … .**

Use linking words to talk about each stage of the story.
**First/Then/After a while/Next/Finally/ The last thing I remember …**

Use the Past Continuous when two actions happened at the same time.
While **I was leaving** the house, I suddenly remembered that … .
As **I was watching**, I realised two important things.

Say how you felt.
**I was surprised/amazed/pleased/excited/fed up/…**

Find a good way to finish your story.
**I'll never forget that day.**
**It was the best day of my life.**
**… changed my life!**

---

**4** Add these time expressions for telling a story to the correct place in the table.

After that   Eventually   First   Later
Next   It happened two years ago
The first thing I saw   Finally   Then
The last thing I remember

| The beginning | The middle | The end |
|---|---|---|
| It was in 2001 | Afterwards | In the end |
| _____ | _____ | _____ |
| _____ | _____ | _____ |
| _____ | _____ | _____ |

**5** **CD2.6** Choose the adjective that best describes the speaker's feelings in each situation. Then listen and check your answers.

1 I started dancing around the room.
(excited / irritated / worried)
2 I had the best results in the class.
(embarrassed / pleased / silly)
3 Suddenly the plane started shaking.
(amazed / surprised / worried)

**6** Study Speak Out. Then choose from these ideas and tell a partner about a special time in your life. Before you begin, plan your story and look for the vocabulary you need.

Talk about a time when you …
• felt inspired by someone or something.
• suddenly had a good idea.
• got some good/bad news (exam results, a relationship, death of somebody famous …).
• were very lucky/unlucky.
• made a mistake.

# LISTENING

**1** In pairs, answer the questions.

- Who is your favourite poet?
- How much do you know about him/her?
- Who are the most famous poets in your country's literature? Do you like their poetry? Why?/Why not?

**2** Read the extract from Coleridge's biography. Why do you think he did NOT finish his famous poem?

## Samuel Taylor Coleridge

Samuel Taylor Coleridge was one of England's great poets. Born in 1772, he studied at Cambridge University but he gave up before the end of his studies. Together with his friend Wordsworth, Coleridge became one of the most important Romantic poets in England. One of Coleridge's most famous poems was *Kubla Khan* – a fantastic vision of an exotic land. Unfortunately, he never finished the poem. While he was writing it, somebody k

**3** CD2.7 Listen to the story. Was your prediction in Exercise 2 correct?

**4** CD2.7 In pairs, put the story in the correct order. Compare your answers with another pair. Then listen again and check.

**a** As he was listening to the stranger at the door, Coleridge began to forget his dream. ☐
**b** Coleridge decided to spend the night in a lonely farmhouse. ☐
**c** He didn't finish his poem. ☐
**d** He had an amazing dream while he was sleeping. ☐
**e** He wasn't feeling well and took some medicine at bedtime. ☐
**f** He read a book and fell asleep. ☐
**g** A stranger knocked at the door. ☐
**h** He began to write a poem about his dream. ☐

**5** In pairs, use the prompts below and appropriate past tenses to tell the story about Coleridge.

18th century, travel on his own, feel ill, take some medicine, read by the fire, fantastic dream, wonderful palace, write *Kubla Khan*, knock at the door, stranger from Porlock, nothing important, listen for an hour, feel irritated, remember very little, lose wonderful poem

**6** In pairs, complete the sentences and read them to your partner. Guess if your partner's sentences are true or false.

1 I was writing an essay when _____ .
2 While I was watching the most exciting part of my favourite programme _____ .
3 We were winning the game when _____ .
4 A friend was telling me something really important when _____ .
5 While I was trying to get to sleep _____ .
6 As we were driving to _____ .

# WRITING | Informal email

**1** Read the leaflet. Then answer the questions in pairs.

1 Which of these art forms is not present at the Mardale Festival?

cinema   dance   music   painting   poetry
photography   short stories   theatre

2 Which event do you think is the most interesting? Why?

3 When was the last time you went to an event similar to one of those in the leaflet? Who did you go with? Did you have a good time?

# The 7th Annual Mardale Arts Festival

## Friday 23 May

**6 p.m.   Strictly Dancing**
Learn to dance with the instructors from TV's Star Academy!

**9 p.m.   Robbie Wilson**
Rap star Robbie, back home for the first time in three years!

## Saturday 24 May

**6 p.m.   Words Matter!**
Marianne Scott reads her amazing poetry!

**9 p.m.   Battle of the Bands**
Six local bands fight for the prize of a week in a top recording studio!

## All weekend

**Art Exhibition**
The best of our young artists show off their work

**Classic movies**
Our choice of the best films ever made

**The Story Tree**
Write a fifty-word story and pin it to the tree. Great prizes!

**Jamming**
Bring your instrument and join in!

**Plus** … face painting, games, storytellers, clowns, street theatre and lots more!

**2** Look at emails 1–3 and fill in the subject boxes with subjects a–e. There are two extra subjects.

a Great news!
b Not too late
c Art exhibition
d Brilliant idea!
e Request for info

**1**
To: sid_strings@coolmail.con
From: paulwillow@pmail.con
Subject:

Hello Sid

I've got a great idea. Did you know there's a Battle of the Bands at the Mardale Arts Festival? It's a chance for your group to play live – you never know, you could win it! Write back soon and let me know what you think.

Hope you're well.

All the best.
Paul

SEND

**2**
To: mcp23@stargaze.con
From: jj@pmail.con
Subject:

Thanks for the email. It was good to hear from you!
I'd love to see your pictures – thanks for asking me.
I'll text you when I know what time I'm going to be there.

CU soon.

JJ

**3**
To: paulwillow@pmail.con
From: sid_strings@coolmail.con
Subject:

Hi Paul

I can't believe it! We won! ☺ We started really badly – first, Dee forgot to plug in his guitar, then KC got the lyrics wrong, and finally, Euan fell off his seat while he was doing his drum solo! But after that we were brilliant!

Thanks for the great idea – cheers.

Sid

SEND

**3** In pairs, study Train Your Brain and circle these things in emails 1–3.

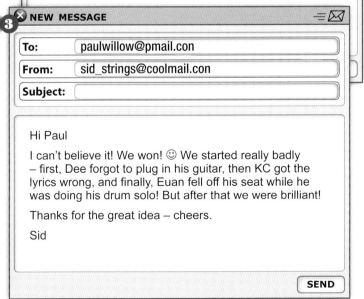

- a smiley
- an abbreviation
- a dash
- two greetings
- three endings

**TRAIN YOUR BRAIN | Writing skills**

**Informal emails**

1 Use an informal style like you do when you're speaking.
2 You can omit the greeting, but most people begin with *Hi (there)* or *Hello*.
3 You can use smileys ☺ and abbreviations (*See you = CU*) like in text messages.
4 Common endings are: *Bye/Cheers/See you soon/All the best/Best wishes/Love* + your name.
5 We often use dashes (–) to separate ideas.
6 Don't forget to fill in the subject box.

**4** Complete these phrases with one word in each gap. Then look at emails 1 and 2 again to check.

1 Write _____ soon.
2 Let me _____ what you think.
3 _____ you're well.
4 _____ the best.
5 Thanks _____ the email.
6 It was_____ to hear from you.
7 I'd _____ to see …
8 CU _____ .

**5** In pairs, rewrite this formal email as an informal email using phrases a–i. Look at page 121 to check.

a best wishes
b Hi Marianne
c want to come
d we'd love to see you there
e Write back soon –
f Do you want to …?
g send us your phone number
h a really cool festival
i let you know more about it

Subject: Mardale Arts Festival

Dear Ms Scott

I am writing to ask you whether you would like to take part in the Mardale Arts Festival on 23–24 May. It is one of the most prestigious arts festivals in the country, and we would love to welcome a poet of your talent to the event.

If you would like to perform at the festival, please reply to this email with a contact number and I will call you to give you further details.

I am looking forward to hearing from you.

Kind regards,
Jez Bodlin

SEND

**6** Choose from the subjects below and write two emails to your classmates. Use Train Your Brain and the phrases in Exercise 4 to help you. Reply to all the emails you receive.

- Mardale Arts Festival
- Want to go out?
- The weekend at last – any great ideas?
- Help! Homework problems!
- Let's have a party!
- You'll never guess what happened last night!
- Did you hear about …?

**39**

# VOCABULARY AND GRAMMAR

**1** Choose the correct words. (5 points)

1 The kids at school were running in the
*aquarium / playground / uniform.*
2 I used to be *annoyed / terrified / terrifying*
of my Maths teacher.
3 I lost the keys but *finally / first / next* I
found them in my pocket.
4 I passed my Physics exam. I felt really
*pleased / stupid / fascinated.*
5 I always feel very *calm / frightened / anxious*
before exams – I never worry about them.

**2** Complete the text with the correct form of
the phrasal verbs in the box. (6 points)

come up   find out   keep on   stay up
get down to   write down

I usually go to bed early, but yesterday I
¹_____ very late. I had to write a story for
my school magazine but before I ²_____
work it was 10 p.m. I was trying to ³_____
with a good idea. It wasn't easy. I ⁴_____
lots of ideas in my notebook, but they weren't
very good. I ⁵_____ thinking of stories from
films or books. Nothing original. Suddenly, I
heard a strange noise. I wanted to ⁶_____
what it was, so I turned the light off and looked
outside. It was only a cat but now I had an idea
for my story. I started writing.

**3** Change the words to complete the
sentences. (6 points)

1 Beethoven was a great _____ .   COMPOSE
2 The strongest friendships often
start in _____ school.   SECOND
3 The film was really _____ .   BORE
4 This is a very _____ story.   DRAMA
5 To be a writer, you need to have
a good _____ .   IMAGINE
6 We need to _____ a lot for
our next History test.   MEMORY

**4** Rewrite the sentences using the words in
capital letters so that they have the same
meaning as the original ones. (5 points)

1 Did the teachers punish the
children a lot?
_____ ?   STRICT
2 I'm a good student now, but I
wasn't before.
_____ .   USE
3 I went into the room. The man
was shouting.
_____ .   WHEN
4 I was writing the last answer.
The teacher told me to stop.
_____ .   WHILE
5 I passed all of my exams.
_____ .   FAIL

**5** Complete the sentences with the correct
form of the verbs in brackets. (8 points)

1 Her boyfriend _____ (can/not) come to
the party last night.
2 I don't remember exactly but I think there
_____ (be) about twenty-five students in
my class.
3 They _____ (record) their new album in
Los Angeles last month.
4 I _____ (not/revise) before my last exam
and I got a low mark.
5 _____ (you/make) many friends when
you were at primary school?
6 When I got to school, my classmates
_____ (write) an essay.
7 Why _____ (you/start) taking piano
lessons last month?
8 He fell off the stage when he _____
(perform) at a music festival.

# PRONUNCIATION

**6** [CD2.8] Read the words. In each group choose the
word that has a different vowel sound. Then listen,
repeat and check.

1 all / car / floor / more
2 first / shirt / start / work
3 bath / form / mark / guard
4 bored / door / turn / store
5 four / heard / sir / term
6 word / bar / heart / laugh

# LISTENING SKILLS

**7** [CD2.9] Listen to a radio programme about how
schools help their students to be more creative.
Match speakers 1–5 with statements a–f.
There is one extra statement. (5 points)

1 Vicky ☐   4 Jake ☐
2 Greg ☐   5 Brian ☐
3 Jessica ☐

a The school offers many after-school activities.
b The school doesn't have a timetable.
c The school helps students to participate
in competitions.
d The school receives free technological
equipment.
e The school organises meetings with
professionals.
f The school gives learners a lot of freedom.

## READING SKILLS

**8** Read the magazine article and choose the correct answers. (5 points)

1 The author of the article thinks that
   a many people cannot be creative.
   b creativity is only a myth.
   c creative people need help.
   d false ideas can limit creativity.

2 The author says that
   a physical exercise is good for your brain.
   b parrots are clever and creative.
   c other people's creations can help us create.
   d TV programmes can't give you inspiration.

3 Constructive criticism
   a can stop your friends from trying to create.
   b can help them become more creative.
   c is the same as brainstorming.
   d is never honest.

4 If you want to remember your ideas, write them down
   a immediately.
   b in the morning.
   c only if they're good.
   d if they came to you in a dream.

5 The author wrote the article
   a to show us that we're like parrots.
   b to tell us that we aren't creative.
   c to advise us how to be more creative.
   d to help us believe in ourselves.

## SPEAKING SKILLS

**9** Give a presentation about cultural events in your city to a group of English-speaking students. The following ideas may help you:

• Museums and art galleries
• Cinema and theatre
• Dance and music
• Festivals and concerts
• Literature and poetry reading
• Other

## WRITING SKILLS

**10** Follow the instructions and write an informal letter.

After attending a new school for a few weeks, you decide to write a letter to a friend from the USA. In the letter you:
• write what kind of school it is and describe it.
• mention one thing which makes your new school different from the school you used to go to and say if this is a good or a bad change.
• write your impressions of your new classmates and describe your form tutor.
• say how you are doing in the new school and what your favourite subjects are.

# Creative myths and tips

**Many people believe they cannot create anything. I don't agree. I think everyone can be creative. Unfortunately, there are some popular myths which stop people from showing their creativity. So let me try to help you become more creative.**

### Myth number 1: 'I am not creative.'

Many people say this but the truth is that we are all creative. That's what makes us different from parrots. They can say clever things but don't have original or imaginative ideas. People, on the other hand, have the power of imagination. The problem is that most of us don't use it enough. When we grow up, we learn to limit our creativity because we don't want to be different from other people.

**TIP** Brains, like bodies, need exercise to keep fit. So use your brain. Read books, go to the theatre or the cinema, listen to music and the radio, and be careful about which TV programmes you watch. You're sure to find some inspiration to help you create something original.

### Myth number 2: 'Honest hard criticism will help my friends improve their ideas.'

It's good to be honest, but if your criticism is too hard it will limit creative thinking and teach your friends to keep their ideas to themselves. Creative ideas are fragile. They need care, not kicking.

**TIP** Don't be too negative when you criticise your friends' ideas. It's not good for their confidence. Instead, offer gentle constructive criticism and use brainstorming to help your friends make their ideas even better.

### Myth number 3: 'I don't need a notebook. I always remember my ideas.'

Maybe. But I doubt it. Imagine in a dream you find the answer to a problem. But then you wake up, have breakfast, get dressed, go to school, and so on. Eventually, in the late afternoon you finally have time to think about the problem … and find that you can't remember the solution that came to you in your dream.

**TIP** Always carry a small notebook and a pen or pencil with you. That way, if you have an idea, you can quickly note it down. After reading your notes, it's possible you'll think that most of your ideas are silly. Don't worry, that's normal. What's important is that taking notes can help you keep your good ideas and become more creative.

# A place called home

**Read, listen and talk about** houses and homes.
**Practise** comparative and superlative of adjectives; relative pronouns.
**Focus on** describing photographs.
**Write** a description.

PROPERTIES OF DISTINCTION
www.verrallandco.con

Verrall and Co
ESTATE AGENTS

**DETACHED HOUSE IN THE SUBURBS**

£265,000

PROPERTIES OF DISTINCTIO
www.verrallandco.c

Verrall and Co
ESTATE AGENTS

**CITY CENTRE FLAT**

£350,000

## GRAMMAR AND LISTENING

**1** Look at the homes in the photos and tick the things you see.

hedge ☐   fence ☐   garage ☐   lawn ☐
skylight ☐   front door ☐   drive ☐
balcony ☐   letterbox ☐   chimney ☐

**2** Use the prompts below to think of reasons why the people in this family want to live in these places.

1 Dad wants to live in **a house in the suburbs** because _____ .
2 Ivy wants to live in **a city centre flat** because _____ .
3 Mum wants to live in **a country cottage** because _____ .

quiet   near the shops   spacious   garden
friendly neighbours   fun   inexpensive

**3** CD2.10 Read and listen to the dialogue to check your answers to Exercise 2.

**Dad** The detached house in the suburbs is the most spacious; it's got three bedrooms, a huge fitted kitchen, an attic, a basement, a garden …

**Ivy** There's a bigger flat for sale upstairs on the third floor. Why don't we buy that?

**Dad** Because it's the most expensive and it isn't big enough.

**Ivy** Why do you want to move to the suburbs? The centre's got shops and … it's the most interesting part of town!

**Dad** And the noisiest too. It's a lot quieter in the suburbs. Life is better there.

**Ivy** No, it isn't. It's worse! It's too far from all my friends. There's nothing to do there.

**Mum** Why don't we buy the country cottage! It isn't as expensive as the house and people are friendlier in the country. It's the nicest place to live.

**Ivy** No, it isn't. It's even more boring than the suburbs!

**5** Find comparative and superlative adjectives in the dialogue in Exercise 3 and add them to the box.

### Comparison of adjectives

| | Adjective | Comparative | Superlative |
|---|---|---|---|
| **One syllable** | quiet | 1 _____ | the quietest |
| | big | 2 _____ | the biggest |
| | nice | nicer | 3 _____ |
| **Two syllables ending in -y** | noisy | noisier | 4 _____ |
| | friendly | 5 _____ | the friendliest |
| **Two or more syllables** | boring | 6 _____ | the most boring |
| | expensive | more expensive | 7 _____ |
| **Irregular** | good | 8 _____ | the best |
| | bad | 9 _____ | the worst |
| | far | further | the furthest |

**Ways of comparing:** not as expensive (as) = cheaper (than)
too small = not big enough

**6** CD2.11 Complete the sentences with the comparatives or superlatives of the words in brackets. Then match speakers a–c with sentences 1–5. Listen and check.

a Ivy    b Mum    c Dad

1 It's _____ (far) from school so it means getting up _____ (early) and getting home _____ (late). ☐
2 The house is _____ (large), _____ (comfortable) and _____ (peaceful) than the flat. ☐
3 The cottage in the country is the _____ (peaceful) place to live. ☐
4 The country isn't the _____ (good) place to live. It's the _____ (bad)! ☐
5 Country people are _____ (fit) and _____ (healthy) than people in cities. ☐

**7** Use the words in brackets to change the sentences so that they are true for each speaker.

1 Ivy: 'The flat isn't as near the city centre as the house.' (than)
'The flat is nearer the city centre than the house.'
2 Dad: 'The centre isn't as noisy as the suburbs.' (than)
3 Ivy: 'The suburbs are more interesting than the centre.' (as)
4 Ivy: 'It's easier to get to school from the house in the suburbs.' (difficult)
5 Ivy: 'The country is as boring as the suburbs.' (most)
6 Mum: 'The flat is nicer than the cottage.' (as)
7 Ivy: 'The house isn't very far from the shops.' (too)
8 Dad: 'The centre is too quiet.' (enough)

**8** CD2.12 In pairs, decide where you think Ivy and her parents are going to move to. Then listen and check and say how Ivy feels about it.

**9** Work in groups and answer the questions. Then tell each other the advantages and disadvantages of your homes.

In your group who lives:
• in the centre of town/suburbs/country?
• closest to/furthest from school?
• in the noisiest/quietest part of town?
• in the most interesting district?

PROPERTIES OF DISTINCTION
www.verrallandco.con

PROPERTIES OF DISTINCTION
www.verrallandco.con

COUNTRY COTTAGE

£195,000

### Work it out

**4** Match sentences 1 and 2 with the sentences with the same meaning, a or b.

1 The house is **not as expensive as** the flat.
  a The house is **cheaper than** the flat.
  b The house isn't **cheaper than** the flat.

2 The flat is **too small**.
  a The flat is **big enough**.
  b The flat isn't **big enough**.

## GRAMMAR AND READING

**1** In pairs, look at the photo, read the email and answer questions 1–4.

1 Where is Nadine staying in New York?
2 What does she think of the district/her flatmate/the flat?
3 What does Nadine find unusual about the flat?
4 Why would you like/not like to live in this flat?

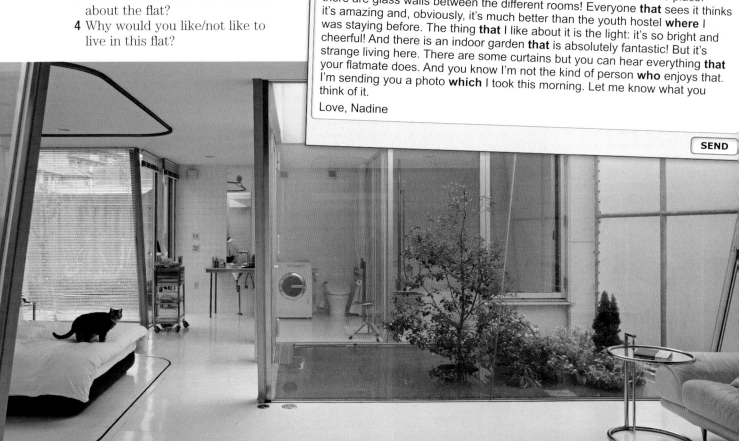

**NEW MESSAGE**

| To: | rosiebow@mailbox.con |
| From: | nadine25@mailbox.con |
| Subject: | USA trip day 8, New York City |

Hi Rosie

Do you remember Miki? The American girl **who** we met at Joel's party? The girl **whose** father is a writer? I met her for a coffee yesterday and she invited me to spend a few days in her apartment! It's on the Lower East Side – a great district **where** there are lots of cool shops and cafés.

Miki's great – she's just the kind of girl **that** you want to share a flat with and the flat is lovely. But there's one thing **which** is very odd about this place: there are glass walls between the different rooms! Everyone **that** sees it thinks it's amazing and, obviously, it's much better than the youth hostel **where** I was staying before. The thing **that** I like about it is the light: it's so bright and cheerful! And there is an indoor garden **that** is absolutely fantastic! But it's strange living here. There are some curtains but you can hear everything **that** your flatmate does. And you know I'm not the kind of person **who** enjoys that. I'm sending you a photo **which** I took this morning. Let me know what you think of it.

Love, Nadine

SEND

## Work it out

**2** Look at Nadine's email again and answer the questions.

Which of the words in bold refer to:
a people? _____ and _____
b possessions? _____
c objects or things? _____ and _____
d places? _____

**3** Look at sentences 1 and 2 and choose the correct answer, a or b.

1 I'm sending you a photo (**which**) I took this morning.
2 There's one thing **which** is very odd.

We can leave out *who/which/that* when they are followed by:
a a pronoun (*I, you, she, everybody* …) or a noun.
b a verb.

## Check it out

### Relative pronouns

*Who* and *that* refer to people.
She's the American girl who we met at Joel's party.
Everyone that sees it thinks it's amazing.

*Which* and *that* refer to objects and things.
There's one thing which is very odd about this place.
The thing that I like about it is the light.

*Whose* refers to possessions: people or things we have.
That's the girl whose father is a writer.

*Where* refers to places.
A district where there are lots of cool shops and cafés.

We can leave out *who/which/that* when they are followed by a noun or a pronoun.
Here is a photo I took this morning. =
Here is a photo which I took this morning.

**44**

**4** Choose the correct relative pronouns. Sometimes more than one answer is possible. Tick the sentences where you can leave out *who*, *which* or *that*.

1 That's the neighbour *that / who / which* lives upstairs. ☐
2 This is the key *which / who / where* you need to open the back door. ☐
3 This is a picture of the loft *which / where / that* I'm staying. ☐
4 This is the carpet *that / which / whose* I want to buy. ☐
5 That's the man *whose / who / that* flat we're renting. ☐
6 The guy *which / whose / who* you saw is my new flatmate. ☐
7 The flat *that / which / whose* we rented last year was very expensive. ☐

**5** Look at the email again and find five sentences with a relative pronoun you can leave out.

**6** CD2.13 Listen and complete the plan of the flat where Nadine is staying.

bathroom    Nadine's bedroom
kitchen and dining room    living room
cupboard    lavatory

**7** CD2.13 Listen again and look at the plan. Write the numbers of the rooms where you can find these things.

sink ☐     washbasin ☐
desk ☐     bookshelves ☐
freezer ☐     DVD player ☐
shower ☐     games console ☐
armchair ☐     vacuum cleaner ☐
wardrobe ☐     dishwasher ☐

**8** Write the missing relative pronouns. Then circle those which you can leave out.

1 This is an apartment _____ owner is an artist.
2 Do you see the computer _____ is on the desk?
3 It's one thing _____ I don't like sharing.
4 That's the market _____ I do my shopping.
5 The books belong to the girl _____ used to live here.

**9** Use the phrases in the box to complete the definitions.

use to clean the floor    keep clothes
lives with you    sells flats and houses
use to wash clothes    watch TV

1 A washing machine is a thing *you use to wash clothes* .
2 A living room is a place _____ .
3 A wardrobe is a place _____ .
4 Your flatmate is the person _____ .
5 An estate agent is a person _____ .
6 A vacuum cleaner is a thing _____ .

**10** Complete the sentences for you. Then, in pairs, compare your sentences.

1 _____ is the place where I usually hang out with my friends.
2 _____ is something that I don't understand.
3 _____ is the person whose opinion I trust the most.
4 _____ is the possession which is most important to me.
5 _____ is the person who makes me laugh the most.

(9) _____
(10) balcony
(11) Miki's bedroom
(8) _____
(5) _____
(2) hall
(7) indoor garden
(6) _____
(3) _____
(4) study

**45**

## Why do we build strange places?

There are many amazing buildings around the world. Perhaps some near where you live. But why do people build strange places? Why not just design buildings that are useful and <u>practical</u>?

One reason is that some of us like to be different. We can see that in the houses where we live and also in the clothes we wear. So perhaps it's not surprising that French fashion designer Pierre Cardin has a very special home: the **Bubble House** in the south of France. With its <u>round</u> windows, oval doors and curved walls some people say it looks more like a plant or an animal than a house. Others say that it is a place where aliens could live. However, even if you don't like it, you have to admit it's original.

Another reason for designing unusual buildings is to attract people's attention. One of the best examples is the **Kansas City Public Library** in Missouri, USA. The outside wall of the library looks like a row of enormous books. The message is clear: there are books in here. The people who <u>designed</u> the library asked local <u>residents</u> to choose the books that best represent their city. And now these giant books attract people to the library. So what's next? A café that looks like a coffee cup? A hotel in the shape of a bed? Or a baker's with walls of bread?

Some people want to use their buildings to communicate. Take, for example, businessman Daniel Czapiewski who <u>built</u> the **Upside Down House** in Szymbark, Poland. When you go inside, you walk on the <u>ceiling</u>. The furniture is on the <u>floor</u>, but the floor is above your head!

Although many people feel sick as they walk around the house, it is very popular with tourists. However, for Mr Czapiewski the house is more than a simple tourist attraction. He built it to protest about the state of the world; to say that we are running the world the wrong way.

Finally, some buildings are special because of their strange <u>location</u>: on a mountain top, in a lonely forest, or on a rocky island. Often the reason that people choose to build in such strange places is to find a quieter life; to escape the noise and violence of the world. Perhaps the best examples are the **Meteora monasteries**, which sit on top of spectacular rock columns in central Greece. Tourists are welcome at some times but the monasteries are still really peaceful places with the most wonderful views you can imagine. The only problem is to decide whose turn it is to go out to buy the bread.

# READING

**1** In pairs, look at photos A–D and say what types of buildings they are from the list below. Then read the article quickly to check.

church    library    monastery    museum
private home    shopping centre    station
theatre    tourist attraction

**2** CD2.14 Read the article again and match buildings A–D with the reasons for building them 1–5. There is one extra reason.

1 to enjoy peace and quiet ☐
2 to express an opinion ☐
3 to win a competition ☐
4 to show the owner's personality ☐
5 to tell people what's inside ☐

**3** Read the article again. Are the statements true (T), false (F) or is there no information (NI)?

1 The author of the article is an architect. ☐
2 The Bubble House is not a place where people can live. ☐
3 The people of Kansas City helped choose the books which decorate the library wall. ☐
4 A lot of people visit the Upside Down House. ☐
5 You can visit the Meteora monasteries at weekends. ☐

**4** Complete with the underlined words from the article.

1 Windows on ships are usually _____ .
2 Don't leave your clothes on the _____ .
3 It's a small room in the attic – my head hits the _____ .
4 Our town is a good _____ for your factory.
5 The _____ are angry the pub stays open until 2 a.m.
6 Old people find flats more _____ than houses with stairs.
7 They _____ the Eiffel Tower in under two years.
8 A famous architect _____ that building.

**5** In pairs, answer the questions.

1 Which of the four buildings is the strangest?
2 Which one would you most like to visit? Why?
3 What's the strangest building you know?

# VOCABULARY | Home

**1** Think Back! Put these words in the correct category in the table. Then, in groups, add other words you know to each category.

study    attic    fence    carpet    kettle
washing machine    hedge    vacuum cleaner
toilet    cupboard    balcony    curtains
garage    bookshelves    wardrobe    stairs
garden    freezer    basement

| Rooms/ places in the house | Furniture/ decorations | Appliances | Things outside the house |
|---|---|---|---|
| study | carpet | kettle | fence |
| | | | |
| | | | |

**2** Check the meaning of the new words and put them in the table in Exercise 1.

microwave    doorbell    stool    blinds
heater    rug    sofa    chest of drawers

**3** Use a dictionary to decide if these adjectives have a positive (+) or a negative (–) meaning. Some words can have both a positive and a negative meaning.

| Adjectives to describe homes | | |
|---|---|---|
| bright | original | roomy |
| practical | spacious | elegant |
| ugly | attractive | tasteless |
| comfortable | tiny | modern |
| tasteful | uncomfortable | cosy |

**4** CD2.15 Read the text on page 121 and choose the correct words. Then listen and check. What kind of room is the person describing?

**5** Write a description of your bedroom. Look at the text on page 121 to help you. Include the following information.

**Paragraph 1**
1 Do you like it? Why?/Why not?
2 Is the room big/comfortable/warm/bright enough?
3 What can you see from the window?

**Paragraph 2**
1 Do you have any decorations like pictures/ posters on the wall/door?
2 What kind of furniture/appliances are there in the room?

**Paragraph 3**
1 What do you do in your room?
2 What did you use to do there?

# SPEAKING

**1** In pairs, look at photos 1–3 and answer the questions.

1 What type of accommodation does each picture show? Choose from the ideas below.

> a semi-detached house    terraced houses
> a detached house    a cottage
> a block of flats

2 What type of accommodation do you think is:
- the most attractive?
- the most modern?
- the most comfortable?

3 What kind of accommodation is most common in your country?

4 What kind of home does your family live in?

**2** CD2.16 Listen and decide which photo in Exercise 1 the speaker is describing.

**3** Read the description on page 121 and answer the questions.

1 What does the speaker talk about first – small details or a summary of what the photo shows?

2 Which phrases does the speaker use to describe where something is in the photo?

3 Which tense does the speaker use to describe actions?

4 Does the speaker have a negative or a positive reaction to the photo? How do you know?

**4** Study Speak Out and check your answers to Exercise 3.

---

**SPEAK OUT** | Describing photos

Start by saying what the photo shows in general.
**The photo shows** a housing estate in a city.

Talk about what you can see in more detail. Use the following phrases to describe where things are:
**in the background/middle/foreground**
**at the bottom/top**
**on the right/left**

**In the foreground** there's a woman with a big rucksack.

Use the Present Continuous to describe what people are doing.
**She's wearing** a sun hat and **she's walking**.

Use phrases like *perhaps*, *probably*, *(it/there) might be* and *looks like* + noun if you are making a guess.
**It might be** somewhere in Europe.
**There might be** a playground in the background.
**Perhaps** they're coming back from school.
She **looks like** a typical tourist.
It's **probably** a great place to live.

Use *looks/seems* + adjective to show how you feel about the photo.
It **looks/seems** quite **attractive/horrible/relaxed**.

---

**5** Look at photo 1. What does the photo show in general?

48

**6** **CD2.17** Look at photo 1 again and complete the missing phrases. Sometimes more than one answer is possible. Then listen and check.

1 _____ there's a little boy on a bike.
2 _____ there are some people who are chatting in the street.
3 _____ there might be a parked car.
4 _____ there's a big hill with a farm on it.

## Mind the trap!

Usually when we describe what we can see in general we use the words *a* and *some*.

On the right a woman is talking on a mobile phone.
There are some cars and a bus in the background.

But when we talk about something for the second time we use *the*.

There's a small cottage in the background.
The cottage looks very attractive.

**7** What else can you say about photo 1? Answer the questions.

1 Can you guess which country or place the people are in? Why do you think so?
2 Which adjectives describe the scene best for you? Choose three from the list.

attractive   bright   pleasant   nice   relaxed   boring
colourful   horrible   quiet   ugly

**8** In pairs, follow the instructions. Student A, look at photo 2 on this page. Student B, look at the photo on page 123.

- Look at **Speak Out** and make notes on what you are going to say. Use the text on page 121 to help you.
- Describe your picture to your partner.

**9** Complete the sentences to make them true about a typical home in your country. Then compare your answers with a partner.

1 People in my country usually live in a _____ .
2 The typical home has got _____ bedrooms.
3 Most homes are rather _____ and _____ .
4 Most people _____ a garage.
5 Nearly everybody has got a TV, a _____ and _____ .

# Good food!

**Read, listen and talk about** food; diets; lifestyles.
**Practise** countable and uncountable nouns; quantifiers; articles with singular countable nouns.
**Focus on** complaining and apologising; dealing with new words in listening, word stress.
**Write** a letter of complaint.

## BOOKS

### Hungry Planet

Photographer Peter Menzel and author Faith D'Alusio visited thirty families around the world to find out what people eat. The result is 'Hungry Planet'. In our first look at the book we analyse the food that two very different families eat in one week.

The Mendozas of Todos Santos, Guatemala

**A**

They eat too many sweet things; there's too much sugar in their diet: there's a packet of biscuits, some cake and a lot of chocolate bars. They drink quite a lot of fruit juice, but there isn't much fresh fruit although there are some apples and grapes and one or two oranges. There aren't many vegetables either.

**B**

They don't eat much meat, just some chicken and there isn't any fish either, but they do eat a lot of eggs. There aren't many packaged snacks, just a few bags of tortilla chips and a little chocolate, and there aren't any fizzy drinks at all. There are a lot of fresh vegetables and fruit, especially tomatoes, carrots, bananas, pineapples, green beans and avocados.

The Baintons of Collingbourne Ducis, Great Britain

# GRAMMAR AND VOCABULARY

**1** Look at the photos, read texts A and B and answer the questions.

1 What is 'Hungry Planet'?
2 Which text, A or B, corresponds to each of the families?
3 Which family do you think has the healthier diet?
4 Which diet would you prefer to eat? Why?

**2** **CD2.18** In pairs, tick the food and drink that you can see in the photo of the Mendozas. Use a dictionary if you need to. Then listen and repeat.

oil ☐   wine ☐   prawns ☐   tea ☐
flour ☐   yoghurt ☐   rice ☐   beans ☐
carrots ☐   beer ☐   butter ☐   beef ☐
chicken ☐   bacon ☐   red peppers ☐
tuna ☐   coffee ☐   mineral water ☐
eggs ☐   cheese ☐   brussels sprouts ☐
ham ☐   onions ☐   breakfast cereals ☐

**3** In pairs, put the words from Exercise 2 in the categories in the table. Then add as many words as you can.

| Fruit and vegetables | Meat and fish | Dairy | Drinks | Other |
|---|---|---|---|---|
| apples | sausages | ice cream | fruit juice | sugar |

## Work it out

**4** Look at texts A and B again and answer the questions.

1 Which of the underlined nouns are uncountable? Circle them.
2 Are these uncountable nouns singular or plural?

**5** Look at the words in bold in the article and answer the questions.

1 Which of these words or phrases are used with both countable and uncountable nouns?
2 Which of these words or phrases are only used with uncountable nouns?
3 Which of these words or phrases are only used with countable nouns?
4 Which four phrases mean *some but not a lot*?

## Check it out

### Quantifiers

**Countable nouns**

| Are there any eggs? | How many eggs are there? |
|---|---|

There are too many
There are a lot of
There are some                              eggs.
There aren't many/There are a few
There aren't any

**Uncountable nouns**

| Is there any cheese? | How much cheese is there? |
|---|---|

There is too much
There is a lot of
There is some                              cheese.
There isn't much /There is a little
There isn't any

**6** **CD2.19** Choose the correct words. Use Check it out to help you. Then guess which country the family comes from. Listen and check.

A Are there ¹*any / some* dairy products in their diet?
B Yes. They don't eat ²*any / some* cheese but there are ³*any / some* eggs and ⁴*a little / a few* milk and yoghurt.
A What about fruit?
B They don't eat much fresh fruit: there aren't ⁵*any / some* oranges, just a watermelon and ⁶*a little / a few* strawberries.
A How ⁷*much / many* meat and fish do they eat?
B Well, they eat ⁸*a few / a lot of* seafood. Some people might think they eat ⁹*too much / too many*, but fish is good for you. They don't eat ¹⁰*much / any* meat, just ¹¹*some / a few* beef and pork, but they eat ¹²*a lot of / much* noodles and rice. Perhaps there are ¹³*too much / too many* packets and tins, but there aren't ¹⁴*some / many* sweet things, so in general, it's a very healthy diet.

**7** Work in pairs. Student A, look at page 123. Student B, look at page 124.

**8** Use the phrases from the fact boxes in Exercise 7 to write sentences about your family's diet.

**9** In groups, find out about each other's diets. Use the prompts below.

In your group who has:
• the healthiest diet?
• the sweetest tooth?

A How much fruit/convenience food do you eat?
B I eat too much/too many/a lot of/a little/ a few ...

A Do you eat a lot of vegetables/chocolate/ dairy/meat?
B I don't eat much/many/any ...

**51**

## READING

**1** In pairs, look at the graph and answer the questions.

1 Which country has the largest/smallest percentage of vegetarians?
2 Are any of the figures surprising? If so, which?
3 How popular is vegetarianism in your country, in your opinion?

**2** In pairs, use a dictionary to check the words below. Then answer the questions.

cereals   seeds   nuts   insects   beans   roots

1 Which of these things are part of people's diets in your country?
2 Which of these things would you not like to try?

**3** CD2.20 Read the article and choose the best answer.

1 Millions of years ago our ancestors
  a moved from the savannah to central Africa.
  b mostly ate seeds.
  c ate fruit and vegetables that nobody eats today.
  d didn't eat meat very often.

2 The Aborigines are an example of people
  a who recently changed their diets.
  b who have a lot of meat in their diets.
  c who don't eat much meat.
  d whose diets are similar to the Aztec and Inca diets.

3 In the nineteenth century people started eating more meat because
  a technology helped the price of meat to fall.
  b it became fashionable to eat the same things every day.
  c a lot of people bought fridges and freezers.
  d farmers started keeping more animals.

4 Some people don't eat meat today because they
  a believe their health is better without meat.
  b were born in the 1960s.
  c read books by George Bernard Shaw.
  d want to save money.

5 It is true to say that
  a there are more vegetarians than people who eat meat in most countries.
  b the number of vegetarians in the world is growing.
  c vegetarianism is less fashionable than in the 1960s.
  d many people try to eat meat less often.

6 The main idea of the article is that
  a people across the world today have different diets.
  b killing animals is wrong.
  c in many countries people don't eat meat.
  d most of us eat more meat than people in the past.

**4** Work in pairs. Are you a vegetarian? Why?/Why not? Use the ideas below to help you.

• Eating meat is natural/wrong/against my beliefs.
• Meat is tasty/good for you/makes you strong.
• Vegetarian food is delicious/healthy/not filling/boring/expensive.
• I only eat fish/chicken/turkey/pork/beef/lamb.
• I'm trying to cut down on how much/many … I eat.

**52**

FEATURES

**Numbers of vegetarians in selected countries**

Figures for 2008

% of population who do not eat meat

India 40%
Italy 10%
Germany 9%
UK 6%
USA 3.8%
Croatia 3.7%
Australia 3%
Czech Republic 1.5%
Poland 0.8%

Country

# Was Fred Flintstone a vegetarian?

Some anthropologists now think that
for millions of years man's diet was more
than eighty percent vegetarian.
Alan Vega investigates …

Twenty-four million years ago when our ancestors lived in the tropical forests of central Africa they probably ate plants and fruit and from time to time a few insects. When these prehistoric people started to travel north into the savannah their diet changed too, and they began to eat a lot of seeds and other plant material. And this is probably how man lived for the next twenty-two million years, eating roots, seeds, fruit, nuts, vegetables and occasionally a little meat.

How do we know? One important clue is our teeth. Just like animals which eat plants, humans have teeth called molars (these are the large, flat teeth at the back of our mouths) which we need to break down hard food such as seeds. Archaeologists can also tell us about diets of the past.

The Aztecs and Incas ate a lot of cereals, beans and fruit and not much meat at all. In classical India most people didn't eat meat and the Japanese were mainly vegetarian until a few generations ago. The main food of the slaves who built the Pyramids was boiled onions! Even today, some societies whose lifestyles are unchanged (like the Aborigines of Western Australia) still have mostly vegetarian diets.

During the nineteenth century people in western countries suddenly began to eat a lot more meat. New methods of keeping and killing animals, better transport and new inventions like fridges and freezers meant that meat was suddenly cheaper for ordinary people. It was probably at this time that the typical western meal that millions of people eat every day – meat, potatoes and vegetables – was born.

Also during the nineteenth century, the vegetarian movement started in Europe and the USA. But it was only in the 1960s that more and more people in the west decided to give up meat in their diets. So why do people choose to be vegetarian? Many people decide to become vegetarian for personal reasons. First of all, some people think that it is healthier not to eat meat. Others believe that it is cruel to eat animals. The Irish writer George Bernard Shaw once said, 'Animals are my friends – and I don't eat my friends.' Finally, there are some people who think that growing food for cows and pigs to eat is not very economical and bad for the environment. Today vegetarianism is more and more popular across the world. But in most countries people who never eat meat are still a very small percentage of the population.

## LISTENING

**1** CD2.21 Listen to the radio programme. Don't worry if you don't understand all the words. Choose the correct option, a or b.

The main topic of the programme is why
a fast food is bad for us.
b many people choose to eat fast food.

**2** CD2.22 Listen and think about the context these words are used in. Then decide what part of speech each word is – noun (n), verb (v) or adjective (a).

1 greasy ☐
2 substantial ☐
3 gut ☐
4 munch ☐

**3** CD2.23 What do you think the words in Exercise 2 mean? Listen out for clues before or after the words. Then, in pairs, choose the best definitions.

1 greasy
A with a lot of vitamins
B with a lot of fat or oil

2 substantial
A very big
B very small

3 gut
A where food goes in our bodies after it leaves the stomach
B the part of the brain which controls how hungry we feel

4 munch
A drink quickly
B eat slowly

**4** Read the sentences in Train Your Brain. Fill in the missing words. Look at Exercises 2 and 3 to help you.

---

**TRAIN YOUR BRAIN** | Listening skills

**Dealing with new words**

When you hear a word which you don't understand:
1 Analyse the context in which the word is used to decide what _____ it is.
2 Listen out for clues _____ or _____ the word to help you guess the meaning.

---

**5** CD2.24 Listen to the rest of the programme and try and guess the meanings of the words below. Use Train Your Brain to help you.

loathe   mug   peckish   nutritious

**6** CD2.24 Compare your answers to Exercise 5 with a partner. Listen again. Then check your answers in a dictionary.

## VOCABULARY | Food

**1** In pairs, look at the photos and answer the questions.

  1 Which of the places in the photos is the best place to:
  • have something to eat with friends after watching a film?
  • take somebody on a romantic first date?
  • take a friend from abroad for an evening meal?
  2 Do you often eat out? What kind of places do you like going to?

**2** CD2.25 Listen and match conversations 1–3 with photos A–C.

  1 ☐    2 ☐    3 ☐

**3** CD2.25 Check you understand the words in the list. Use a dictionary if you need to. Then listen again and tick the items you hear.

  a burger and milkshake ☐    a sandwich ☐
  goulash ☐    apple pie and ice cream ☐
  a cappuccino ☐    garlic bread ☐
  lasagne ☐    chicken curry with rice ☐
  fish and chips ☐    a cream cake ☐
  chocolate cake ☐    pizza ☐    salad ☐
  spaghetti Bolognese ☐    tomato soup ☐
  steak and chips ☐

**4** In pairs, look again at the list in Exercise 3 and answer the questions.

  1 Which things are often served as starters/desserts/main courses?
  2 Which things are suitable for someone who is a vegetarian?
  3 Which things are not suitable for somebody on a diet?
  4 Which things are/aren't popular in your country?

**5** Match the words with their opposite meanings. Use a dictionary if you need to.

  1 sweet ☐        a unhealthy
  2 spicy ☐        b stale
  3 low fat ☐      c tasteless
  4 healthy ☐      d mild
  5 delicious ☐    e bitter
  6 fresh ☐        f greasy

---

### TRAIN YOUR BRAIN | Dictionary skills

**Word stress**

If you are unsure about which syllable has the main stress, a dictionary can help you. The ' symbol comes before the syllable with the main stress.

**café** /ˈkæfeɪ/ *n* [C] **1** a small restaurant where you can buy drinks and simple meals
**avocado** /ˌævəˈkɑːdəʊ/ *n* [C,U] a dark green, oval fruit which is pale green inside and is not sweet

---

**6** CD2.26 Use a dictionary and mark the main stress in these words. Then listen and practise saying them.

  kebab  lemonade  margarine  menu
  pizza  spaghetti  dessert  recipe  melon

# SPEAKING

**1** In pairs, look at the picture. Do you think this is a good place to eat out? Why?/Why not?

**2** Match sentences a–e with speech bubbles 1–5 in the picture.

a The music's too loud! ☐
b It isn't hot enough. And what is this doing here? ☐
c It's the wrong order! We didn't ask for this! ☐
d Ow! ☐
e There's a mistake in the bill! ☐

**3** CD2.27 Study Speak Out. Then listen and <u>underline</u> the apologies you hear.

---

**SPEAK OUT** | Complaints and apologies

**Complaints**

| Excuse me, I'm sorry but … | it's very/too … . it isn't … enough./It isn't very … . it isn't working properly. there's a mistake (in the bill/order). it's the wrong order. you forgot to … . |
|---|---|

**Apologies**

| I'm (really) sorry, … | about that. I didn't mean to … . it was an accident. I completely forgot. it was rather stupid of me. I didn't realise. I … by mistake. |
|---|---|

---

**4** CD2.28 Listen and repeat some of the phrases from Speak Out.

**5** In pairs, write a complaint for each situation. Use Speak Out to help you.

1 You lent your friend your MP3 player. He gave it back and now it doesn't play. *I'm sorry, but my MP3 player isn't working properly.*
2 Your friend promised to phone you. You waited all evening but he didn't phone.
3 You bought a sandwich. The bread is very stale.
4 You ordered a ham and mushroom pizza. The waitress brings you a tuna and pineapple pizza.

**6** Match the complaints from Exercise 5 with the apologies. Then practise the dialogues in pairs.

a I'm very sorry about your order. It was very careless of me. ☐
b I'm sorry – it wasn't my fault. My brother was on the phone all evening. ☐
c I'm sorry. I dropped it – it was an accident! ☐
d I'm very sorry. I gave you an old one by mistake. ☐

---

**Mind the trap!**

If somebody apologises to you first, we usually accept the apology by saying *That's OK!* or *Never mind*.

I'm sorry I'm late.   Never mind./No problem.

Oh! I'm really sorry. It was an accident.
That's OK!/It doesn't matter.

---

**7** In pairs, write a short dialogue for these situations. Then practise your dialogues.

1 You bought a hotdog from the college canteen. It isn't very hot and there's no ketchup in it.
2 You borrowed your friend's laptop computer. Now it's got a virus and it doesn't work.

Dear Sir/ Madam,

(1) I am writing to complain about the quality of the service and the food at your pizzeria.

(2) My girlfriend and I ordered a cheese and tomato pizza and a cheese and salami pizza at 8.15 last night. The girl who answered the phone told us to wait half an hour for the pizzas to arrive. Unfortunately the pizzas did not arrive until 9.50 p.m., 95 minutes later. To make matters worse, when we woke up this morning we were both feeling very ill. Neither of us could go to work today because we both had terrible stomach pains. We are certain that the pizzas are to blame.

(3) I feel that you should improve the quality of your service. It is unacceptable that customers have to wait so long for their orders. More importantly, I also think you should check the freshness of your ingredients.

(4) I believe I should receive a refund of £7.50 and an apology. If I do not receive a satisfactory reply, I am afraid that I am going to contact the local media about this matter. I look forward to your reply.

Yours faithfully,

Declan Brown

## WRITING | Letter of complaint

**1** In pairs, look at the photo and answer the questions.

1 Where are the couple? What are they doing?
2 How do you think they are feeling? Why?

**2** CD2.29 In your opinion, what is the best way to complain about bad food/service? Choose from the ideas below. Then listen and check what the couple decide to do.

- Write a letter asking for a refund/an apology/ compensation
- Contact the media/local newspaper
- Write a negative review on the Internet

**3** Read the letter of complaint and answer the questions.

1 What are Declan's two complaints?
2 What two suggestions does he make to the restaurant to improve its service?
3 What two things does he want from the company as compensation?

**4** In pairs, look at Declan's letter again and match paragraphs 1–4 with their contents a–d.

a Suggestions about how the company can improve its service. ☐
b The reason for writing. ☐
c What went wrong and the problems it caused you. ☐
d The type of compensation you expect. ☐

**5** Match the underlined expressions in Declan's letter with ideas 1–4.

1 there was also another problem
2 something went wrong/was disappointing
3 you expect the company to write back to you
4 you refuse to tolerate the situation

**②**

**A** ☐
I believe I should receive ¹_____ refund for £5.60. I enclose ²_____ receipt from March 2nd and I look forward to your reply.

**B** ☐
Unfortunately, when I tried to eat my sandwiches at lunchtime, I found they were completely inedible. Later, at home I noticed ¹_____ sell-by date of ²_____ cheese was February 9th, over three weeks ago.

**C** ☐
Dear Sir/Madam

**D** ☐
To make matters worse, I also noticed that ¹_____ carton of milk and ²_____ yoghurt were also past their sell-by dates.

**E** ☐
Yours faithfully

**F** ☐
I am writing to complain about ¹_____ freshness of some of the products which you sell in your supermarkets.

**G** ☐
I think that you should check that there are no other out-of-date food products in ¹_____ store. It is unacceptable that you have dairy products on sale that are several weeks past their sell-by dates.

**H** ☐
Last Saturday (March 2nd) I bought ¹_____ tube of 'Tuba Cheese' from ²_____ Harrow Road branch of your supermarket. I used ³_____ cheese this morning to make sandwiches for my packed lunch.

# TUBA CHEESE
## The best cheese in the world – in a tube!

---

**6** Study **Train Your Brain**. Then quickly read letter 2 and in pairs put sections A–H in the correct order 1–8.

> **TRAIN YOUR BRAIN** | Writing skills
>
> **Letter of complaint**
>
> **1** In the first paragraph give your reason for writing. (*I am writing to complain about …*)
> **2** In the next paragraph, say what went wrong and mention the problems you had. (*Unfortunately …/ To make matters worse …*)
> **3** In a new paragraph, give suggestions about how the company can improve its service (*I feel that you should improve/change/make sure/check … / It's unacceptable that …*)
> **4** At the end say what you want the company to do as compensation. (*I believe I should receive a refund for …/an apology*)
> **5** Start/end your letter in a formal way. (*Dear Sir/ Madam, I look forward to your reply, Yours faithfully*)

**7** How would you say the highlighted words in letter 2 in your language? Use a dictionary to help you.

## Work it out

**8** Study rules 1 and 2 and choose the correct words 1–7 in the examples. Then complete the gaps in letter 2 with *a/an* or *the*.

### Articles with singular countable nouns

**1** We use **a/an** when we are talking about one person/ thing for the first time. But when we mention the same person/thing again we use **the**.
We ordered ¹*a / the* sandwich and ²*a / the* hamburger. ³*A / The* sandwich was stale and ⁴*a / the* hamburger was cold.

**2** We also use **the** when it is clear from the context that we are talking about one specific person or thing. ⁵*A / The* girl who answered ⁶*a / the* phone said ⁷*a / the* manager wasn't there.

**9** Read the situation and write a letter of complaint, taking care with articles and using **Train Your Brain** to help you.

You invited a friend/partner to a rather expensive restaurant with a very good reputation. The food was excellent but the service was terrible.

Write a letter of complaint to the restaurant manager in which you:
- say why you are writing and mention when you visited the restaurant
- explain how the waiter ignored you for forty minutes and how you and your friend/partner were very disappointed
- mention that the music was too loud and that there was a mistake in the bill
- make a suggestion about what the manager should do and ask for an apology

# VOCABULARY AND GRAMMAR

**1** Complete the crossword and find the
secret message. (6.5 points)

1 uses electricity and keeps you warm
2 a place for your books
3 a comfortable chair
4 something you cover the floor with
5 quicker than a bath
6 You can keep your clothes in a chest of … .
7 a room at the bottom of the house
8 a fence made of plants
9 a seat with no back
10 where you wash your hands
11 a place in a flat where you can stand outside
12 where smoke comes out of the roof
13 where you can find ice cream

**2** Look at the food items in the box and
answer the questions. (6.5 points)

cabbage   crisps   pork   cheese   beef
fruit juice   sausages   beans   tea
chips   broccoli   wine   butter

Which of the food items:
1 are drinks? _____ , _____ ,
_____
2 can vegetarians NOT eat? _____ ,
_____ , _____
3 are vegetables? _____ , _____ ,
_____
4 come from potatoes? _____ , _____
5 are milk products? _____ , _____

**3** Choose the correct words. (4 points)

1 Martha has a lot of *tasteful / tasty /
spacious* furniture.
2 I love my flat – it's small but *uncomfortable /
tiny / cosy*.
3 The bread is *stale / spicy / fresh* – we need
to buy some more.
4 My pie wasn't very *greasy / filling /
delicious* – I still felt hungry afterwards.

**4** Complete the second sentence so that it
has a similar meaning to the first sentence.
Use the word in bold without changing it. (5 points)

1 I haven't had a worse day in my life.  **the**
It was _____ of my life.
2 Maggie is prettier than Kate.  **as**
Kate _____ Maggie.
3 There's only a little money in the drawer.
**much**
There _____ in the drawer.
4 My flat isn't big enough to invite people
for dinner.  **small**
My flat _____ to invite people for dinner.
5 There isn't one café in this part of town.  **any**
There _____ in this part of town.

**5** Complete the text. For each gap choose the
correct answer. (8 points)

Windsor is the ¹____ inhabited castle in the
world with nearly 1,000 years of royal history.
Today, it is one of the Queen's official homes.
When she is staying at the castle, a flag flies
above the White Tower.

In 1992, there was a terrible fire ²____ destroyed
more than 100 rooms in the castle. However, only
five years later the castle was open to the public
again – and it was just ³____ beautiful as before.

Windsor is one of ⁴____ popular tourist
attractions in the UK – there are about one
million people ⁵____ visit it each year. Only the
Tower of London and Edinburgh Castle receive
⁶____ visitors than Windsor Castle. There is a
website ⁷____ you can buy tickets, and when
you get to the castle, there are many guides
⁸____ job it is to explain the fascinating history
of this marvellous castle.

1 **a** largest   **b** larger   **c** large
2 **a** where   **b** whose   **c** which
3 **a** as   **b** more   **c** most
4 **a** more   **b** most   **c** the most
5 **a** which   **b** whose   **c** who
6 **a** more   **b** most   **c** much
7 **a** where   **b** whose   **c** which
8 **a** where   **b** whose   **c** which

# PRONUNCIATION

**6** **CD2.30** Listen to the words and circle the letters that
you don't hear. Then listen again and repeat.

answer   business   cupboard   daughter
every   half   grandmother   island   lamb
neighbour   sandwich   Wednesday

## READING SKILLS

**7** Match headings 1–5 below with
paragraphs A–D. There is one extra heading. (4 points)

1 Two houses, one address ☐
2 Not just a home ☐
3 The future of Downing Street ☐
4 Surprisingly modest ☐
5 Saved! ☐

**8** Read the text and match numbers 1–6
with letters a–g. There is an extra letter
you do not need. (6 points)

## 10 DOWNING STREET

Number 10 Downing Street, the home of the British
Prime Minister, is probably one of [1]_____ . In most
countries, the head of a government lives in a large
mansion or even a palace so it's often a surprise to
visitors that the Prime Minister's home looks like a
modest terraced house in a rather [2]_____ . But what's
really behind the elegant black-brick walls and the
tasteful front door?

First of all, 10 Downing Street is enormous [3]_____ . It
is actually two buildings which share the same address.
At the front in Downing Street is the famous terraced
house that we all know from photographs. This modest
residence dates from 1683 and behind it is a splendid
mansion which tourists never see. King George II gave
this larger house to Sir Robert Walpole, the first Prime
Minister, in 1733 and it was then that the two
buildings became one address, 10 Downing Street.
But most Prime Ministers after Walpole chose to live
in their own houses, [4]_____ . In fact, at the beginning of
the nineteenth century, the houses in Downing Street
were in poor condition and the area had a bad
reputation for crime.

It was only really in the twentieth century that
Downing Street became the traditional address of the
Prime Minister. In the 1960s the house was in a
terrible state so there were discussions about [5]_____ .
But, in the end, everyone agreed that the building is an
icon and the government decided to renovate it with
original materials.

The Prime Minister's home is actually only a small part
of the building – some rooms on the third floor. The
other rooms are offices and conference rooms where
the Prime Minister works and meets with [6]_____ .

a and has more than 60 rooms
b the most important members of the
government and foreign leaders
c that he built himself
d the most famous addresses in the world
e knocking down the house and building a
new one
f which were more comfortable
g ordinary street in the centre of London

## SPEAKING SKILLS

**9** Look at the two photos and compare them.
Include the points below.

- The differences between the places where
the people are celebrating
- Why the people met in these places
- The atmosphere in both places
- The clothes that people in the photos are
wearing

## WRITING SKILLS

**10** Follow the instructions and write a formal letter.

During a summer language course in the UK,
you are staying in a hostel. Unfortunately you
don't like the place and decide to write to
the Director of Studies to complain about the
situation. Write a letter in which you:
- introduce yourself and give your reason
for writing.
- mention two negative things about the place
and justify your opinion.
- ask for help and suggest a new type of
accommodation.
- write about two qualities that the new place
should have and explain why it is important
for you.

# Looking ahead

**Read, listen and talk about** future predictions; technology and the environment.
**Practise** *going to* and *will* for predictions; the First Conditional.
**Focus on** probability and inference; listening for specific information.
**Write** a leaflet.

13TH JUNE, 7:50

I'**m going to** be late for my exam!
It'**s going to** be another terrible day!

13TH JUNE, 8:40

Oh no! It'**s going to** rain!

**A**    **Friday June 13th**

After a cloudy start, it **will** be dry and warm.
Temperatures 24–26°C.

**B**       **GEMINI**   **May 22nd–June 21st**
Friday 13th **will** be a day of pleasant surprises. With Pluto
around you'll want to slow down and enjoy yourself!

**C**    **Maths**   *1B*
*I'm sure Luke **won't have** any problems in
passing his Maths exam in June but he has
to believe in himself more!*   *J Barnard*

**French**   *2A*
*Luke is working hard and is making good
progress.*   *A Thorpe*

## GRAMMAR AND LISTENING

**1** Match texts A–C about June 13th, the day of Luke's
Maths exam, with text types 1–3. Are they optimistic
or pessimistic?

1 A horoscope ☐
2 A school report ☐
3 A weather forecast ☐

**2** Look at the photos and read the captions. Is Luke
optimistic or pessimistic about June 13th?

### Work it out

**3** Match sentences 1 and 2 with definitions a or b.

1 Look at the weather! I'm going to get wet.
2 I'm sure that Luke will pass his exam
   in June.

a An opinion, belief or guess about the future.
b A confident prediction about the future when
  we can see now what is certain to happen next.

**4** Look at these sentences from the photos.
Match Luke's predictions 1–3 with the evidence
he uses a–c.

1 It's going to rain! ☐
2 I'm going to be late for my exam! ☐
3 I'm not going to pass! ☐

a I don't know any of the answers!
b I can see dark clouds!
c It's twenty to nine!

**60**

I don't know any of these answers! **I'm not going to** pass!

13TH JUNE, 9:05

## Check it out

### Future predictions

We use *going to* when we can **see (or hear) now** what is certain to happen next so we are quite sure about our prediction.

**I'm not going to pass** this exam. (I don't know any of these answers!)
Oh no! **It's going to rain.** (I can see the clouds.)

We use *will/won't* for what we **believe** will happen in the future. Often we are only guessing.

The forecast says it **won't rain** at the weekend.
Don't worry. I'm sure you**'ll find** a job soon.

**5** Read the situations and write a sentence with *going to*. Use the verbs below.

miss   fall   faint   be (x2)   crash

1 Megan is looking very pale.
  She _____ .
2 Jackie starts school at 9 a.m. It's 8.50 and she's still washing her hair.
  She _____ late.
3 The road is very wet and the car is driving too fast.
  It _____ .
4 Philip's running to the bus stop. His shoelaces are undone.
  He _____ .
5 Tom's train is leaving at 7.30. It's 7.28 and he's queuing for his ticket.
  He _____ his train.
6 There's a terrible mess in the kitchen. My parents are coming home in a few minutes.
  They _____ very angry.

**6** Choose the correct answers.

1 Experts believe that in 2030, the world's population *will / is going to* be eight billion.
2 The coach is very hot and crowded. It *will / is going to* be a very uncomfortable journey!
3 That waiter is carrying too much. He *will / is going to* drop those glasses!
4 I think that travelling by plane *will / is going to* be cheaper in the future.
5 Do you think that people *will / are going to* live on the moon in the future?
6 It's getting colder and colder. *It will / is going to* snow tonight.

**7** CD3.1 Listen to the fortune teller and complete her predictions 1–4. In groups, try and guess what will happen in Eve's life.

**1** You will be in a place with a lot of _____ , Eve.

**2** Somebody from below will _____ .

**3** There's a tall young man who you'll be _____ to see.

**4** He will _____ your money.

A I think she'll go to the seaside.
B I think a guy will rescue her at the swimming pool.

**8** CD3.2 Listen to the end of the story. Were any of your predictions correct? What was the explanation for 1–3?

1 the place with a lot of water?
2 the person from below?
3 the man interested in the money?

**61**

# A BRAVE NEW WORLD?

The second half of the twentieth century shines with fantastic promises. Here our panel of Associated Press experts look ahead to the dawn of the twenty-first century ...

## TRANSPORT

Flying will be as normal as travelling by car or train. Large aeroplanes (perhaps with atomic engines) may fly at more than 1,000 miles[1] an hour. In 2000 we will be able to fly around the world in one day – we will be neighbours with everyone else on Earth. We will use radio-controlled missiles to deliver letters and parcels across the world. It is possible that hybrid car-planes will be popular.

## MEDIA AND COMMUNICATIONS

By 2000, a small man-made planet will circle Earth, 400 miles up. It will get its power from the sun and perhaps we will use it to reflect radar or television signals around the world.

3-D colour television will be very common by 2000. A small gadget will project realistic pictures on the living room wall and the images will almost seem alive. Films will still be popular and almost all of them will be in colour. Westerns, musicals and historical films will still be with us. There certainly won't be so many cinemas in our towns – it is possible that people one day will pay to watch films in the comfort of their living rooms. Radio stations probably won't exist because nobody will want programmes without pictures. Telephones will use radio signals so it will be possible to use them even outside the home.

## HEALTH

A cure for cancer will exist and we will probably no longer suffer from common illnesses like colds and flu. Women will live on average to eighty years of age and men to seventy-five. People will be taller and slimmer than they are today thanks to a balanced diet of vitamins and proteins. Women, especially, will look very different. The average woman of the year 2000 will be more than six feet[2] tall and wear a size eleven[3] shoe.

## READING AND SPEAKING

1 In pairs, look at the picture. Which year or decade do you think it shows?

2 Quickly read the article and check your prediction to Exercise 1. Underline sentences in the text which seem to predict these things.

| | |
|---|---|
| 1957 | Sputnik 1 (first artificial satellite) |
| 1969 | first flight of Tupolev Tu-144, first supersonic passenger plane (maximum speed 2,500 km/hr) |
| 1973 | first practical mobile phone conversation |
| 1976 | first VHS home video recorders; 1996 – first DVD players |
| 2008 | US life expectancy: men 75, women 81 (1950 average 69) |

3 In pairs, answer the questions.

Which of the ideas in the text
1 turned out to be completely unrealistic?
2 didn't come true but, in your opinion, are still a good idea?

4 CD3.3 Read the article again. Are the statements true (T) or false (F)?

1 The world will seem smaller because of faster planes. ☐
2 Television sets will no longer exist. ☐
3 People will still enjoy the same types of film as they did in the 1950s. ☐
4 We won't go to the cinema so often. ☐
5 People won't be fat at the start of the twenty-first century. ☐
6 There will be no teachers in schools. ☐

## EDUCATION AND WORK

In the future science and technology will be the key subjects at school and TV will replace teachers in some subjects. More young people will go to university. As for jobs, people will definitely work shorter hours than today (perhaps just twenty hours a week) and women will definitely have top jobs in finance, business and government. A woman might even be president.

---

¹10 miles = 16 kilometres
²1 foot = 30 centimetres
³size 11 = size 45

---

**5** Match 1–6 with their synonyms a–f.

1 engine
2 key
3 man-made
4 power
5 replace
6 suffer from

a artificial
b motor
c energy
d be ill with
e most important
f take the place of

**6** Study Speak Out. <u>Underline</u> examples of each expression in the article.

---

### SPEAK OUT | Probability

**Very likely**
Computers **will definitely be/certainly be** cheaper in the future.

**Likely**
Mobile phones **will probably be** cheaper in the future.

**Possible**
**Perhaps** air travel **will be** cheaper in the future.
**It is possible that** air travel **will be** cheaper in the future.
Air travel **may be/might be** cheaper in the future.

**Unlikely**
Cars **probably won't be** cheaper in the future.

**Very unlikely**
Petrol **definitely won't be/certainly won't be** cheaper in the future.

---

**7** CD3.4 Listen and repeat some of the phrases from Speak Out.

**8** CD3.5 Listen and complete the predictions. Which prediction is most certain? Then listen again and match the predictions with explanations a–d.

1 People will _____ stop wearing glasses in the future. ☐
2 _____ people will be more interested in religion in 2025. ☐
3 It will _____ be more common for retired people to study something new. ☐
4 People will _____ travel more in the future. ☐

a People will live longer and have more free time.
b Laser technology will be cheap.
c People will be bored with technology.
d Air travel will be cheaper.

---

### Mind the trap!

When you make a negative prediction with *think*, use the negative form of *think* and not of *will*:

I don't think it will rain.  NOT  I think it won't rain.

---

**9** In pairs, decide if the predictions below will come true in your country in the next thirty years. Use the expressions from Speak Out.

1 People will stop using their cars.
2 Banknotes and coins won't exist.
3 Most people will work from home.
4 Newspapers will only exist on the Internet.

I don't think that people will stop using their cars.

**10** Work in groups. What are the chances that you will do these things before your thirtieth birthday?

• have children        • have a good job
• get married          • go and live abroad
• own a car            • start your own company

I think I'll definitely have children before my thirtieth birthday.

# GRAMMAR AND WRITING

**1** Read the two election leaflets and answer the questions.

Which party wants to:
1 spend less on defence?
2 lower taxes?
3 make electricity cheaper?
4 improve public transport?

**2** In pairs, say which of the parties' ideas you like/ dislike and why.

A I think it's a good idea to increase/ protect/reduce/create/encourage …
B I think it's wrong to help/cut/invest in/ spend more on …

## Work it out

**3** Look at the sentence and answer the questions.

If we win, we will reduce the price of petrol.

1 Does the speaker think it is possible/realistic that they will win?
2 Which tense is used after *if*?
3 Which tense is used in the other part of the sentence?

## Check it out

### The First Conditional

We use the First Conditional to talk about a realistic situation that will/might happen in the future.

**The condition**        **The result**
*If* + Present Simple,     *will* + infinitive

If we win, we will spend more on public transport.
If we don't win, the economy won't get better.

**4** Find other examples of the First Conditional in the leaflets in Exercise 1.

**5** Complete the sentences with the correct form of the verbs in brackets.

1 People _____ (switch) to public transport if we _____ (increase) road tax.
2 The air _____ (get) cleaner if people _____ (switch) to public transport.
3 People _____ (be) healthier if the air _____ (get) cleaner.
4 If we _____ (not reduce) taxes, there _____ (be) more unemployment.
5 If there _____ (be) more unemployment, people _____ (not have) so much money.
6 If people _____ (not have) so much money, they _____ (spend) less.

**6** Complete the sentences. Then compare your answers with a partner.

1 If I get some money for my birthday, I _____ .
2 I'll earn a lot of money if _____ .
3 I'll be surprised if _____ .
4 I'll be really disappointed if _____ .
5 I _____ if I pass all my exams this summer.
6 My English won't get better if _____ .
7 If _____ , I'll be really pleased.

**7** In pairs, ask and answer about what you will do in these situations.

• there's nothing interesting on TV tonight
• you can't fall asleep tonight
• there's a 24-hour electricity cut tomorrow
• the weather's good at the weekend
• the weather's terrible at the weekend
• there's a big class test on Monday morning

A What will you do if there's nothing interesting on TV tonight?
B I'll chat online or play a video game.

**8** In groups, write an election leaflet for a student party at your school. Use the leaflets in Exercise 1 and the ideas below to help you.

If we win/don't win, we will/won't …
If you vote/don't vote for us, we will/ won't …

• **improve**
  the appearance of …/the snack bar

• **get rid of**
  the cloakroom/the rules about …
  school uniforms/punishments for …

• **introduce**
  a better choice of …/exams on …
  new rules about …

• **change**
  the rules about …/the timetable

• **spend money on**
  decorating the …
  more computers/sports facilities

• **reduce/increase**
  the number of tests/students/teachers
  the price of …

• **open**
  an Internet café/a second-hand shop

**9** Invent a name for your party and present your ideas to the class. Then vote for the party with the best ideas.

# Vote for the INDEPENDENT DEMOCRATS

## ID'S PROMISES TO YOU!

★ Public transport is a waste of money. If we win on June 9, we will reduce the price of petrol. Travelling by car will be cheaper.

★ ID believes in opportunities for our young people. We will spend more on education if you vote for us.

★ We will cut taxes and create thousands of new jobs. If we don't win, unemployment will get worse.

★ Cheap electricity will help the economy, so we will build more nuclear power stations if we win.

## VOTE FOR ID ON JUNE 9!
### 'Putting you first!'

# EGO
## ECOLOGY AND GREEN OPPOSITION

### EGO'S KEY PLANS

- The army is an expensive luxury. We will cut military spending if we win the election.

- Our environment is in danger. We promise to protect wildlife, invest in renewable energies like solar and wind power and encourage everyone to recycle.. If you vote for **EGO**, the environment will be safe.

- Air pollution is a major problem. If we win, we will increase taxes on road users and spend more on public transport: the key to cleaner air.

## WE CAN MAKE THE FUTURE BETTER ON JUNE 9 VOTE EGO

## VOCABULARY | Ecology

**1** In pairs, circle the things which are good for the environment and <u>underline</u> those which are harmful.

ride bikes   drive cars   travel by plane
use public transport   sort domestic waste
replant forests   recycle paper
drive to huge shopping centres
use bottle banks

**2** Match headings a–g with points 1–7 in the leaflet.

a Cut down on waste! ☐
b Buy more local products ☐
c Lower unemployment, more leisure time ☐
d No more noise and air pollution ☐
e Renewable energies ☐
f Slowing down climate change ☐
g The end of acid rain ☐

# A BRIGHT GREEN FUTURE

1 Our cities will be cleaner and quieter: there will be no cars; only bikes, public transport and pedestrians.

2 We will do our shopping in local shops and transport fewer things over long distances.

3 We will recycle more and throw out less rubbish.

4 People will work shorter hours so there will be more jobs.

5 Solar panels, wind farms and wave power will provide clean energy for our factories and homes.

6 The trees in our forests and the fish in our rivers will be healthy.

7 Less pollution means temperatures will stop rising.

If we don't act soon, our way of life will not survive climate change. But if we make the right decisions now, we will have a bright green future!

Visit us at brightgreen.dom to find out ways you can help.

**3** In pairs, answer the questions.

1 Do you think the future that the leaflet describes is optimistic or pessimistic? Is it realistic or unrealistic?
2 Which ideas in the leaflet do you like/dislike?

**4** For questions 1–5 ~~cross out~~ the verb that does NOT collocate with the nouns. Use a dictionary to help you.

1 destroy   help   protect   survive
**the environment**

2 cut   increase   recycle   reduce
**pollution**

3 protect   recycle   reduce   sort
**domestic waste**

4 help   protect   save   switch to
**wildlife**

5 invest in   lower   produce   switch to
**renewable energy**

**5** CD3.6 Listen and match speakers 1–5 with statements a–f. There is one extra statement.

a I don't know much about climate change. ☐
b I have a brilliant plan to stop climate change. ☐
c There is nothing we can do to stop climate change now. ☐
d We will find a technological solution to climate change. ☐
e It's not necessary to do anything to stop climate change. ☐
f We have to do everything we can to stop climate change. ☐

**6** In pairs, describe the photo and answer the questions. Use the phrases in Exercises 1 and 4 to help you.

1 Where is the person? What is she doing? Why?
2 What do you do to help the environment?
3 Which ways of helping the environment do you think are most effective?

# 'The machine of flying fire will trouble ... the great chief.'

Nostradamus, The Centuries published 1568.

## LISTENING

**1** You are going to hear the story of Nostradamus. Do you know anything about him? In pairs, answer the questions.

1 In which century did Nostradamus live?
2 What is he famous for?

**2** Read the gapped text and decide what kind of information you need to complete gaps 1–7.

A date/year ☐ ☐
A number ☐ ☐ ☐
A noun ☐
An adjective ☐

## The Life of Nostradamus

His real name was Michel de Nostredame. Nostradamus was born in ¹ _____ in southern France. He had ² _____ brothers. As a boy he was interested in Maths and Astrology, but finally decided to study ³ _____ at Montpellier University. He completed his studies in ⁴ _____ and married a woman from a ⁵ _____ family. They had ⁶ _____ children. He started making his famous predictions when he was ⁷ _____ years old.

**3** **CD3.7** Listen to Part 1 of the recording and complete the text in Exercise 2. Don't worry if you don't complete all the gaps the first time you listen.

**4** **CD3.7** Did you hear all the information you needed? Circle any uncompleted gaps and listen again to complete the missing information.

**5** In pairs, put the advice in Train Your Brain in the correct order. Look at Exercises 2–4 to help you.

---

**TRAIN YOUR BRAIN** | Listening skills

**Finding specific information**

a Mark or underline any gaps that you didn't hear the first time. Then listen again. ☐
b Look at the gaps in the table or text and decide what kind of information is missing – dates, names, places, numbers, etc. ☐
c Listen and try to complete the missing information. Don't panic if you don't hear everything the first time. ☐

---

**6** **CD3.8** Before you listen to Part 2 of the recording, use Train Your Brain to prepare yourself for filling in the gaps in the text below. Then listen and check.

## The Books of Nostradamus

To begin with, Nostradamus started making predictions about the next ¹ _____ months. He published his first almanac in ² _____ .These almanacs were very ³ _____ so Nostradamus decided to make predictions for several centuries into the future. He wrote in several different languages: French, Latin, Greek and ⁴ _____ . He needed ⁵ _____ years to finish his work. Nostradamus died in ⁶ _____ and the finished book was published ⁷ _____ years after his death.

**7** **CD3.9** Listen to Part 3 of the recording and choose the sentence which best summarises Mary's views.

a Nostradamus was wrong because he only wrote negative predictions.
b The predictions are interesting but I don't really believe them.
c Nostradamus correctly predicted events that really happened, such as wars and revolutions.

**8** In groups, play at being Nostradamus! Make five predictions about your town/school/country for the next ten years. Show them to another group and see if they agree with your predictions.

**67**

# Jobseekers

**Read, listen and talk** about jobs and work.
**Practise** verb patterns.
**Focus on** reading for specific information; taking and leaving messages.
**Write** a covering letter (for a job).

**CAREER QUIZ**

## WHAT IS THE BEST JOB FOR YOU?

**Try our personality test!** } For each pair of sentences choose the one that best describes you.

**1**
A I <u>enjoy</u> studying for exams with a friend.
B I <u>like</u> studying for exams on my own.

**2**
A I'm good at remembering facts and information.
B I find it easy to remember jokes and funny stories.

**3**
A I always <u>hope</u> to get top marks at school.
B I <u>love</u> helping friends with their problems.

**4**
A When I <u>decide</u> to do something, I always do it.
B I often change my mind about the best thing to do.

**5**
A I <u>must</u> finish my work before I think about going to a party.
B I <u>can</u> always find time to enjoy myself – even if I have a lot of things to do.

**6**
A I <u>want</u> to use my practical knowledge in my future career.
B I <u>would like</u> to use my imagination and my creativity in my future career.

**7**
A When I'm in a group, I <u>hate</u> being the centre of attention.
B When I'm in a group, I <u>need</u> to be the leader.

**8**
A I <u>start</u> feeling bored when I don't have new experiences or meet new people.
B I <u>avoid</u> being in new situations if possible.

## GRAMMAR AND READING

**1** Check you know the jobs below. Then say which jobs you can see in the photos.

1 librarian, therapist, priest, accountant, scientist, nurse
2 engineer, computer programmer, pilot, police officer, doctor, architect
3 psychologist, writer, translator, fashion designer, teacher, musician
4 insurance agent, lawyer, judge, salesperson, businessman/woman, marketing manager
5 company director, banker, politician, TV presenter, reporter, actor

**2** Think Back! In pairs, compare the jobs in Exercise 1. Which ones, in your opinion, are:

• the hardest/easiest?
• the most stressful?
• the most interesting?
• the best/worst paid?

A I think doctors have the most stressful job.
B No, it's more stressful to be a police officer.

**3** CD3.10 Do the personality test and check your score on page 121. Do you agree with the results?

**6** CD3.11 Complete the sentences with the correct form of the verbs in brackets. Then listen and check.

'I can't ¹_____ (believe) it! I passed all my exams! I really don't know how I managed ²_____ (pass) Maths. Now I need ³_____ (decide) what to study at university. The problem is that I don't know what I want ⁴_____ (do). A few months ago I decided ⁵_____ (study) Biology, but now I'm not sure. It seems ⁶_____ (be) difficult to find a job as a biologist. I suppose I could ⁷_____ (become) a doctor, but it must ⁸_____ (be) a very stressful job. My mum says you can learn ⁹_____ (enjoy) anything, but I wouldn't like ¹⁰_____ (work) in a hospital. I enjoy ¹¹_____ (work) with people. I don't like ¹²_____ (do) the same thing every day. I don't mind ¹³_____ (get) up early. I love ¹⁴_____ (travel) and I prefer ¹⁵_____ (work) outside. Oh, and I can't stand ¹⁶_____ (talk) on the phone for a long time. What's the best job for me?'

**7** Work in pairs. What's the best job for the girl in Exercise 6?

**8** CD3.12 Listen to the three conversations and match the speakers with the jobs.

artist   police officer   musician
politician   firefighter   TV presenter

1 Mr Jones    _____
2 John        _____
3 Marilyn     _____

## Work it out

**4** Match the form of the verb a–c that comes after the underlined verbs in sentences 1–3.

1 *to* + infinitive ☐
2 *-ing* form ☐
3 infinitive without *to* ☐

a A teacher should be patient.
b She promised to work harder.
c I prefer working on my own.

**5** Complete the table with the underlined verbs from the personality test.

**Verb patterns**

**Verbs followed by *-ing* form:**
prefer, miss, stop, practise, not mind, can't stand,
_____ , _____ , _____ , _____ , _____ , _____

**Verbs followed by *to* + infinitive:**
agree, learn, manage, offer, promise, seem, wish,
_____ , _____ , _____ , _____ , _____

**Verbs followed by infinitive without *to*:**
could, might, should, _____ , _____

**9** CD3.12 Complete the statements with the infinitive or *-ing* form of the verbs in brackets. Then listen again and match them with speakers a–c.

1 I love _____ (write) songs.
2 I can't stand _____ (have) a routine.
3 I enjoy _____ (be) the centre of attention.
4 I don't mind _____ (wear) a uniform.
5 I hope _____ (get) the chance to play.
6 I'd like _____ (help) people.
7 I can _____ (do) things for people.

a Mr Jones ☐ ☐
b John ☐ ☐ ☐
c Marilyn ☐ ☐

**10** In pairs, write five true and five false sentences about yourself. Use verbs from Exercise 5. Read your sentences to your partner. Guess which ones are true.

A I would like to be a musician.
B I think that's true./That's definitely false!

# READING AND VOCABULARY

**1** In pairs, use the prompts below to say why you would/wouldn't like these jobs.

- vet
- video games tester
- taster in a chocolate factory
- Formula 1 driver
- gardener
- model

work outside    nine-to-five routine
commute to work    earn a good/bad salary
holidays    travel    do something useful
dangerous/fun/boring    good/bad for your health

**2** Read the text quickly. Which sentence best describes the general idea of the text?

**a** The text describes a man who has a wonderful job.
**b** The text describes a wonderful job that a man won in a competition.

**3** Match paragraphs 1–4 with the headings a–f. There are two extra headings.

**a** A job for life
**b** Island Paradise
**c** Finding the perfect candidate
**d** A waste of money
**e** Everyone's a winner!
**f** A stress-free job?

**4** Read the questions. <u>Underline</u> the key words in the questions which can help you find the answers.

1 What is Ben's job?
2 What does he have to do in his job?
3 How much does he get paid?
4 How long is Ben going to work on the island?
5 Why do tourists come to Hamilton Island?
6 How easy was it for Ben to get the job?
7 How does Ben feel about his job now?

**5** Look at the words you <u>underlined</u> in Exercise 4. <u>Underline</u> the same words or similar ideas in the text.

**6** Read before and after the key words and expressions in the text to answer the questions in Exercise 4.

**7** Complete the sentences in Train Your Brain with the words and phrases below. Look at Exercises 2–6 to help you.

- underline
- the main idea
- similar ideas
- before and after

> **TRAIN YOUR BRAIN | Reading skills**
>
> **Finding specific information**
>
> 1 Read the text once quickly to get ___ of what it's about.
> 2 Read each question carefully and ___ the key words.
> 3 Look for the key words or ___ in the text.
> 4 Read ___ the key words to find the answer to the question.

**8** **CD3.13** Read the text again and use the advice in Train Your Brain to answer these questions.

1 What benefits does Ben's job offer?
2 How easy is it to get to Hamilton Island?
3 How did Ben apply for the job?
4 What did the candidates have to do in the final interview?
5 Why did *Tourism Queensland* give Ben the job?
6 What jobs did Ben have before this one?
7 Why are the organisers pleased with the results of the competition?

**9** Find words and phrases 1–10 in the text and check their meaning. Then use them to complete sentences a–e.

1 earn
2 break
3 salary
4 turn up
5 contract
6 full-time
7 interview
8 employers
9 permanent
10 application

**a** I don't _____ enough money. I need a bigger _____ .
**b** It's not a hard job. We can _____ late and we get a half-hour _____ at 11.
**c** Is this job _____ or temporary? Part-time or _____ ?
**d** Her _____ were happy with  her work so they offered her a new _____ .
**e** I sent in my _____ and I got an _____ straightaway.

**10** In pairs, answer the questions.

1 Would you like to have Ben Southall's job? Why?/Why not?
2 What would you like to do when you leave school?
3 Would you like to have an exciting job? Why?/Why not? If so, which one?

Ben Southall

**1**  Ben Southall is the caretaker of a tropical island. His job involves swimming, relaxing, making friends with the local people, exploring other islands and having a good time.

He also has to write a blog and take photos and videos of the island to show the world what a wonderful place it is. It's a full-time job, but he can turn up for work when he wants to and choose to have a break any time he feels tired. He earns a monthly salary of £12,500 – twelve times more than the UK minimum wage. His free beach home has three bedrooms, a private pool and wonderful views. And when he needs to get around the island he has an electric golf buggy. It's a dream job except for one thing. It isn't permanent. Ben's contract is only for six months.

*It's a dream job except for one thing.*

*It isn't permanent.*

**2**  The job was the prize in a competition that Ben's employers, *Tourism Queensland*, organised to attract tourists to the Great Barrier Reef. Ben's new home, Hamilton Island, is in the Whitsunday Islands in Queensland, north-eastern Australia. It is a beautiful island very near the Great Barrier Reef Marine Park. It also has the largest airport in the area and frequent ferries to the mainland. So it is the perfect place for tourists to stay when they want to visit the wonders of the Great Barrier Reef.

**3**  To get the job Ben had to win a competition with almost 35,000 applicants from over 200 countries. In his application video he said he loved travelling and adventure and enjoyed talking to people. He included pictures of himself trekking in Africa, riding an ostrich, bungee jumping, scuba diving and kissing a giraffe.

The job interview for the sixteen finalists in the competition took place on the island and lasted for four days. They had to answer questions and show they could snorkel, swim, organise barbecues and write entertaining blogs. Ben managed to impress the organisers with his imagination, his energy, his ability to deal with difficult situations and his love for Queensland.

**4**  Ben, who is thirty-four years old and comes from Hampshire in the UK, used to work as a tour guide in Africa and as a charity worker. He is, of course, delighted that he won the competition and is absolutely certain that he has the best job in the world. However, Ben is not the only winner. The competition cost *Tourism Queensland* 1.7 million Australian dollars to organise. But the publicity it brought to the region was worth over 110 million Australian dollars!

# VOCABULARY | Work

**1** Think Back! Add suffixes to these words to form jobs. Which suffixes do we add to nouns and which to verbs?

| NOUNS | | VERBS | |
|---|---|---|---|
| 1 art – | artist | 1 act – | actor |
| 2 library – | ___ | 2 design – | ___ |
| 3 music – | ___ | 3 direct – | ___ |
| 4 politics – | ___ | 4 manage – | ___ |
| 5 psychology – ___ | | 5 programme – ___ | |
| 6 science – | ___ | 6 report – | ___ |
| 7 therapy – | ___ | 7 translate – | ___ |

**2** Read the sentences and underline the other adjective + preposition phrases. What verb form do we use after prepositions: the infinitive or the *-ing* form?

> **Sara**  I'm very <u>fond of</u> reading and I'm keen on using foreign languages.

> **Max**  I'm comfortable with playing in front of large audiences and I'm used to travelling.

> **Lucy**  I'm interested in helping people with their problems and I'm good at giving advice.

> **Jon**  I'm mad about working with computers but I get bored with being on my own.

**3** Which of the jobs in Exercise 1 do you think would be the most suitable for the four people in Exercise 2? Discuss with a partner.

**4** In groups, follow the instructions.

- Use the phrases from Exercise 2 to write three sentences about yourself.
- Read your sentences to the rest of the group. Who is the most similar to you in your group?

## Mind the trap!

*Job* and *work* have different meanings.

*Job* refers to a specific task or occupation. It is a countable noun.

As soon as I graduate, I'm going to start looking for a job.

*Work* refers to something more general. It is usually uncountable.

I can't go out tonight. I've got too much work to do.

**5** Complete these sentences with *work* or *job*.

1 Too much _____ and not enough fun can cause stress.
2 My ideal _____ is one where I could work outside with a group of friends.
3 Well done! You did a good _____ with my computer. It's really fast now.
4 Hard _____ never killed anybody.
5 If you're not busy right now, I have a _____ for you. Can you peel the potatoes?
6 I like _____ – it fascinates me, especially when other people are doing it.

**6** Look at cartoons A and B and choose the two captions for each cartoon. Then say which caption you think is funnier for each cartoon.

1 'It's a fantastic CV.  We're very interested in meeting the person who wrote it.'
2 'I'm looking for temporary work.'
3 'I see that you're good at using a computer.'
4 'I'm keen on working outside.'

## LISTENING AND SPEAKING

**1** In pairs, describe the photo and answer the questions.

    1 What is the situation?
    2 How do you think the people are feeling? Why?
    3 Do you get nervous before an interview or oral exams? Why?

**2** **CD3.14** Listen to Part 1 of the recording and answer the questions.

    1 What job is Rachel phoning about?
    2 What does Jacob's flatmate Lily think he should do?
    3 What message, A or B, does Jacob leave for Rachel?

**A**

Rachel –

Jacob Pearce phoned.
He'll call back
later.

**B**

Rachel

Jacob Pearce phoned.
He has an exam on Thursday
and can't come to the
interview.

Can you phone him back?

**3** **CD3.15** Listen to Part 2 of the recording. What time is Jacob's interview now?

**4** **CD3.16** Listen to Part 3 of the recording. Does Jacob feel confident about the interview? Why?/Why not?

**5** **CD3.17** In pairs, study Speak Out and try to put the conversation below in order. Then listen and check.

| SPEAK OUT \| Taking and leaving messages |
| --- |
| **A** Hello? |
| **B** Hello. Can/Could I speak to X, please? |
| **A** I'm sorry. He/She isn't here. Can I take a message? |

| **B** No, its OK thanks. I'll call back later. | Yes, please. Can/Could you tell him/her that (*name*) phoned and (*message*) …? |
| --- | --- |
| | Can you ask him/her to (phone me back)? |

| **A** OK. I'll tell him/her. Goodbye. |
| --- |

    a That's brilliant news. I'll let him know. Goodbye. ☐
    b Hello, good morning. Could I speak to Jacob Pearce, please? ☐
    c Yes, please. Can you tell him that Rachel Stephens called again and I'm happy to tell him that he's got the job, starting on Monday. Can you ask him to phone me back? ☐
    d Hello, 605782 ☐
    e I'm sorry, but Jacob's out again at the moment. Can I take a message? ☐

**6** **CD3.18** Listen and repeat some of the phrases from Speak Out.

**7** In pairs, use Speak Out to roleplay the conversation. Student A, look at page 123. Student B, look at page 124.

**73**

SEARCH www.actongazette.con/jobs

**ACTON GAZETTE**   HOME | NEWS | JOBS | CONTACT

## TEEN JOBS

ⓘ **NEW**

### PART-TIME TOUR GUIDES

FOR LOCAL TOURIST BUREAU
TO SHOW SMALL GROUPS
AROUND LONDON

- **Excellent working conditions**
- **Must be over eighteen years old**
- **Ideal for students**

To Apply
- Write to:
  **West Acton Travel,
  19 Acton High Street,
  London W3 5YQ**
- or click **Apply Online.**

**APPLY ONLINE**

---

45 Western Avenue
Acton
London
W3  5YQ

22nd May 2020

West Acton Travel
19 Acton High Street
London W3 5YQ

Dear Sir/Madam,

**❶** I am writing to apply for the job of part-time tour guide, [1] <u>which I saw</u> in last Friday's *Acton Gazette* (19th May).

**❷** I am a nineteen-year-old student at Hammersmith College. [2] <u>I am currently</u> studying for an NVQ in Travel and Tourism and I recently [3] <u>did</u> a course in Local History at the college. I am also fluent in French and [4] <u>have a good knowledge of</u> Italian. [5] <u>I also have</u> a qualification in First Aid.

**❸** [6] <u>I believe</u> I am a [7] <u>good</u> candidate for the job because I am interested in working in the tourism industry and I am keen on London and its history. [8] <u>In addition to this,</u> I feel I am mature, responsible, [9] <u>outgoing</u> and have a good sense of humour.

**❹** [10] <u>I enclose</u> a recent photo and my application form. I look forward to your reply.
Yours faithfully,

*Lauren Cole*
Lauren Cole

---

## WRITING | Covering letter

**1** In pairs, look at the job advert and tick any skills, qualities or qualifications that could be useful for this job. Why are they useful?

- an interest in local history ☐
- a good knowledge of foreign languages ☐
- sociable ☐
- a swimming certificate ☐
- a good sense of humour ☐
- a qualification in First Aid ☐
- mature ☐
- enjoy taking risks ☐
- good at singing ☐
- an interest in politics ☐
- a good knowledge of computers ☐
- a driving licence ☐

**2** Read the covering letter. Which things from Exercise 1 are in the letter? Do you think Lauren is a good candidate for the job? Why?/Why not?

**3** Look at the letter again. Put missing information a–d in gaps 1–4 in the letter plan.

    **a** character and personal qualities
    **b** current studies or job
    **c** other things you are sending with your letter
    **d** where you saw the advert

    Paragraph 1  reason for writing/job title/
               ¹ _____

    Paragraph 2  age/ ² _____/other qualifications
               or skills

    Paragraph 3  why you are a good candidate/
               ³ _____

    Paragraph 4  ⁴ _____/hope for a reply

**4** Match phrases a–j with similar phrases 1–10 in the letter.

    **a** In my opinion
    **b** am proficient in
    **c** I am sending … with this letter
    **d** which appeared
    **e** What's more
    **f** completed
    **g** At the moment I am
    **h** strong
    **i** Additionally, I have
    **j** sociable

**5** Study Train Your Brain and check your answers to Exercises 3 and 4.

---

**TRAIN YOUR BRAIN** | *Writing skills*

**Covering letter (for a job)**

These are formal letters. Write *Dear Sir/Madam* and end with *Yours faithfully* (if you know the person's name write *Dear Mr/Ms …* and end with *Yours sincerely*).
**Mention:**

- Why you are writing (*I am applying for …*), the job title and where you saw the ad (*…which appeared in last week's paper/on the Internet*)
- Your current studies or job (*I am currently studying/ working for …*), other qualifications or skills (*Additionally, I am proficient in French*) and perhaps your age
- Why you are a good person for the job (*In my opinion, I am a strong candidate because I am interested in/ keen on/enjoy*). Include positive personal qualities (*What's more, I believe I am hard-working, outgoing, motivated …*)
- Any other documents you are sending with your letter (*I enclose …*) and that you hope for a reply (*I look forward to hearing from you*)

---

## Mind the trap!

We usually use *a/an* with jobs.

She's a translator/a scientist/an engineer.
NOT ~~She's engineer.~~

But with the phrase *I am writing to apply for the job* (*post/position*) *of* we don't usually use an article.

I'm writing to apply for the post of ~~a~~ gardener.

**6** You find these job adverts in a newspaper. Make a list of skills, qualifications or personal qualities which could be useful, using Exercise 1 to help you.

### ACTON LOCAL NEWSPAPER VACANCIES

**TESDA SUPERMARKET REQUIRES MATURE YOUNG ADULTS TO WORK AS DELIVERY DRIVERS**

- The job involves delivering groceries to our customers' homes.
- Must be motivated and physically fit.
- Hours: Weekends and evenings. <u>Clean driving licence is essential</u>

### THE ACTON HERALD

### JOB VACANCIES

**VIP STAFFING** NEEDS PART-TIME NANNIES FOR THE SUMMER HOLIDAYS.

- Must like children!
- Foreign languages, the ability to play a musical instrument and a driving licence is an advantage.
- Basic cooking skills required.
- <u>Ideal for students.</u>

<u>Must be aged sixteen or over</u>

**7** Write a job application letter using Train Your Brain to help you. Mention these points:

- the job you are applying for and where you found the ad
- your age and what you are currently doing
- any other skills and qualities that make you a good candidate
- mention that you are expecting a reply

**8** In groups, follow the instructions.

    **1** Join a group with students who applied for <u>the same job</u> as you.
    **2** Read the covering letters from a group who applied for <u>a different job.</u>
    **3** Look at Train Your Brain, and check the letters.
    **4** Choose the best candidate for the job.

## VOCABULARY AND GRAMMAR

**1** Complete the text with the correct form of the words in brackets. (7 points)

### Not sure what to do after school? Read on …

#### What are you like?

- Good with language?

- An analytical mind?

- The creative type?

- Good with numbers?

- Good in front of cameras?

- A practical mind?

- Want to help people?

#### You could be a/an …

__writer__ (write)
or _____ (translate)

_____ (law)
or _____ (psychology)

_____ (art)
or _____ (music)

_____ (account)
or _____ (sale)

TV _____ (report)
or _____ (act)

_____ (engine)
or _____ (science)

_____ (politics)
or _____ (therapy)

### Want to know more? Come to the Careers guidance meeting – 3 p.m.

**2** Complete the second sentence so that it has a similar meaning to the first sentence. Use the word in bold without changing it. (5 points)

1 I think swimming is more fun than cycling.
**prefer**
I _____ to cycling.
2 I will go for a walk if it is sunny.
**rains**
If _____ go for a walk.
3 It is quite likely that I will get the job.
**probably**
I _____ get the job.
4 Steve doesn't like working hard.
**keen**
Steve _____ working hard.
5 Stella and John don't usually work at weekends.
**avoid**
Stella and John _____ at weekends.

**3** Read the sentences and choose the correct words. (6 points)

1 This *energy / power / atomic* station uses only renewable energy.
2 I live far away from my office. I need to *commute / apply / turn up* every day.
3 The Greens want to *reduce / improve / increase* the number of recycling plants.
4 To *survive / replant / protect* our planet, we must cut pollution.
5 I *can't stand / don't mind / am fond of* my job. It's too stressful!
6 My parents care about ecology so they sort *petrol / environment / rubbish*.

**4** Complete the sentences. Use *will* or *going to* and the verbs in the box. (6 points)

| ask | be | crash | look | rise | use |
|---|---|---|---|---|---|

1 Oh no! Look at that plane! It _____ !
2 In 2030 everyone _____ solar power in their homes.
3 I'm fed up with my job. I _____ for a new one.
4 Experts say sea levels _____ by about 25 cm this century.
5 Don't worry. I really don't think you _____ unemployed for ever!
6 Sssh! This is a key moment in the film. He _____ her to marry him.

**5** Complete the sentences with the correct form of the verbs in brackets. (6 points)

1 If you _____ (do) that again, I _____ (tell) the others.
2 Soon you _____ (not have) any money left if you _____ (buy) so many gadgets.
3 If the government _____ (not invest) in public transport, our roads _____ (get) too crowded.
4 The boss _____ (talk) to her if she _____ (forget) her uniform again.
5 _____ (you call) me if the train _____ (be) late?
6 It _____ (not work) if you _____ (not switch) it on.

## PRONUNCIATION

**6** [CD3.19] Listen and put the words in the box in the correct column. Then listen, repeat and check.

| /dʒ/ | /ʃ/ | /tʃ/ |
|---|---|---|
| danger | pollution | virtual |

bridge   cheaper   elections   engineer
fashion   future   insurance   jeans
kitchen   social

## LISTENING SKILLS

**7** **CD3.20** Listen and choose the correct answers. (5 points)

1 Sonia Jefferson is a
  a guest at the meeting.
  b teacher.
  c student who is going to leave school.

2 Sonia thinks that being a tour guide is
  a always stressful.
  b sometimes boring.
  c very interesting, but sometimes difficult.

3 To become a tour guide you must
  a be an expert in history and geography.
  b learn some facts about the places you visit.
  c have a degree in tourism.

4 As a tour guide you also need to
  a know everything about First Aid.
  b speak a minimum of two foreign languages.
  c have a pilot's licence.

5 Sonia recommends the job of tour guide for people who want to
  a have a routine at work.
  b earn a lot of money.
  c have fun and adventure.

## READING SKILLS

**8** Read the text. Match headings a–f with paragraphs 1–5. There is one extra heading. (5 points)

  a Keep cool and win!
  b Mirror, mirror on the wall
  c Read minds to detect crime
  d Wearing your doctor
  e What is *Nextfest*?
  f Our mechanical friend

## SPEAKING SKILLS

**9** Discuss in groups. Do you think these things will happen in the future?

1 You will win an Oscar one day.
2 Your country's football team will win the next World Cup.
3 You will get a part-time job in the next year.
4 A meteor will destroy the planet this year.
5 You will fall in love before Christmas.

## WRITING SKILLS

### Are you interested in helping the environment?

★ **Would you like to save animals from extinction?**
★ **Then why not work for SOS for the Earth – the UK's most dynamic ecological group.**
★ **We're looking for young people to work part-time for our organisation.**

Send your application and a covering letter to our Director: Mr Henry Jones before the end of the month.

**10** Follow the instructions and write a formal letter.

You are attending a school in the UK as part of a student exchange programme. You see this announcement on the noticeboard. Write a letter to the organisation applying for a job. Include the following points:
• your reasons for joining the *SOS for the Earth* organisation.
• the personal experience in protecting the environment you have had so far.
• the area of environmental protection that you are most interested in and why.

Begin your letter like this:
Dear Mr Jones,

# Want to see the future?

by Maggie Shiels

**1** ☐

*Nextfest* is an extraordinary exhibition where you can meet the most innovative minds and discover new technology from around the world and see the things that will change the way we live, work and play in the future. For example, …

**2** ☐

*Brainball* is a computer game with a difference: if you're too competitive, you lose. The more relaxed you are, the better you play. *Brainball* measures your alpha waves and the person who is the most relaxed can push the ball to the other side and win. I'm sure it will be a popular game with yoga experts and stressed parents everywhere.

**3** ☐

If you're keen on fashion, *Nextfest* can show you the clothes of the future; fabrics which you can change by downloading styles from the web, clothes which look after your health and a biometric suit which monitors your body and gives you medicine when you need it.

**4** ☐

Another success is a humanoid robot which can walk, turn, climb up and down stairs – and even dance. *Asimo* mimics human movement and is friendly-looking. Its maker, Honda, believes it will be a big help to blind or elderly people and to those who can't get out of bed.

**5** ☐

Detectives will love brain fingerprinting. It is a technology which reads minds by measuring brain waves and your responses to words or images. It is the perfect way to decide who is a terrorist and who is not or who is responsible for a crime and who isn't.

If you want to see the future, come to *Nextfest*. It's open all this week at the State Science Exhibition Centre.

# Friends and family

Read, listen and talk about love and relationships.
Practise the Present Perfect; phrasal verbs.
Focus on agreeing and disagreeing.
Write text messages.

## GRAMMAR AND READING

**1** Look at the photo. What do you think is happening?

**2** CD3.21 Listen and read. Then decide who the people are.

| | | | |
|---|---|---|---|
| 1 Barbara | ☐ | a | Ian's gran |
| 2 Margaret | ☐ | b | Ian's father |
| 3 Monica | ☐ | c | Ian's mother |
| 4 Eddy | ☐ | d | Ian's girlfriend |

**Part 1**

**Barbara** Ian, you haven't eaten very much. Is anything wrong?

**Ian** I've got something to tell you. Monica and I have decided to get married.

**Barbara** Oh, that's … nice!

**Eddy** Have you decided on the date <u>yet</u>?

**Ian** No, we haven't. But I've <u>already</u> bought a ring for her!

**Margaret** That's great news! I'm so happy.

**Ian** Thanks, Gran.

**Part 2**

**Eddy** Ian has done a lot of stupid things in his life, but this is crazy! Monica hasn't finished college <u>yet</u>! Have you <u>ever</u> heard of such a thing?

**Barbara** I've never been so shocked! They only met five months ago! How come he's got enough money for a ring? He's <u>just</u> started his first job.

**Margaret** Excuse me, but haven't you forgotten something, you two? How old were you when you got married? Twenty – the same age as Ian. And you didn't have any money, did you?

**3** In pairs, answer the questions.

1 Are Ian's parents happy that he has decided to get married?
2 Who seems to understand Ian the best?

## Work it out

**4** Read the sentences and tick the correct rules.

Monica and I **have decided** to get married.
Ian **has done** a lot of stupid things in his life.
They **met** five months ago.

We use the Present Perfect to talk about:
- news and recent activities. ☐
- past actions if we say when they happened. ☐
- past actions if we don't say exactly when they happened. ☐

**5** Look at how words a–d are used in the dialogue and match them with their uses 1–4.

a already ☐   c just ☐
b ever ☐   d yet ☐

1 in affirmative sentences to mean *very recently*
2 in affirmative sentences to say something happened earlier than expected
3 in negative sentences to say something has not happened (but it may soon), or in questions to ask if something has happened
4 in questions, it means *any time before now*

## Check it out

### Present Perfect

We use the Present Perfect to talk about:
- news and recent activities.
We *'ve decided* to get married.
- finished actions in the past if we don't say exactly when they happened.
Ian *has done* a lot of stupid things in his life.

**Affirmative** I/You/We/They *have ('ve) gone*.
He/She *has ('s) gone*.

**Negative** I/You/We/They *have not (haven't) gone*.
He/She *has not (hasn't) gone*.

**Questions** *Have* I/you/we/they *gone*?
Yes, I/you/we/they *have*.
No, I/you/we/they *haven't*.
*Has* he/she *gone*?
Yes, he/she *has*.
No, he/she *hasn't*.

Time adverbials used with the Present Perfect:
*Already* and *just* in the affirmative; *ever* in questions; *yet* in the negative and in questions.

### Mind the trap!

We do not use the Present Perfect with time expressions which refer to a finished period, e.g. *last week, a year ago*.

They *met* yesterday. NOT They ~~have met~~ yesterday.

**6** **CD3.22** Listen and number the verbs in the order you hear them. Repeat the pronunciation of the Past Participles.

decided  told  read  done  taken
finished  met  bought  gone  eaten
happened  had  heard  forgotten  been

**7** **CD3.23** Complete the dialogue with the correct form of the verbs in brackets. Use the Past Simple or the Present Perfect. Then listen and check.

A ¹_____ you _____ (hear) the news? Ian and Monica ²_____ (decide) to get married.
B No way! ³_____ he _____ (tell) his parents yet?
A Yes, he ⁴_____ (tell) them last night.
B When ⁵_____ they ____ (meet)?
A They ⁶_____ (meet) at my party on New Year's Eve.
B ⁷_____ she ____ (finish) college?
A No, she ⁸_____ (not/finish) yet, but he ⁹_____ (already/find) a job. He ¹⁰_____ (start) work last month.

**8** **CD3.24** Complete the dialogue with the words below. Then listen and check.

already  ever  just (x2)  yet (x3)

Monica  Well, have you told your parents ¹_____?
Ian  Yes – I've ²_____ told them! Gran's really pleased but my parents aren't too happy.
Monica  Oh dear. I'm so glad that my parents have ³_____ accepted the idea.
Ian  I'd really like to see you. Have you finished your work ⁴_____?
Monica  No, I haven't finished it ⁵_____. Have you ⁶_____ felt that you just can't concentrate?
Ian  Hold on a minute …
Margaret  Sorry to interrupt. I've ⁷_____ talked to your mum and dad and everything's going to be OK.
Ian  Thanks, Gran! Did you hear that?
Monica  Yes, I did. Listen – I'll do my work tomorrow. We need to celebrate!

**9** In pairs, use the ideas below to interview your partner.

Have you ever …
- meet/anyone famous?
- feel/love at first sight?
- get/really angry with a friend?
- go/on a blind date?
- fall/in love with a place you visited?
A Have you ever met anyone famous?
B Yes, I have. I met … in a supermarket last week!
A I've never met anyone famous.

# GRAMMAR AND SPEAKING

**1** Are there any bands from the 1980s or earlier who are still popular in your country? What hits can you remember? Do you like them?

**2** In pairs, look at the photo and answer the questions. Use the ideas to help you.

1 What can you say about the people? Are they in their teens/twenties/forties?
2 What kind of relationship do you think they have? How do you know?

- best of friends/like brothers/a gang/mates/colleagues
- annoyed/comfortable with/tired of/jealous of each other
- argue/enjoy/hate spending time together/have a good relationship/have a lot in common

**3** CD3.25 Listen and read the article to see if your predictions in Exercise 2 were correct.

## Work it out

**4** Look at the article again and complete these sentences.

1 The band have been friends for over _____ years.
2 They haven't had a hit since _____ .

**5** Look at the sentences in Exercise 4 and choose the correct answers.

a We use the *Past Simple / Present Perfect* to talk about situations which began in the past and continue now.
b We use *since / for* to say when the situation started.
c We use *since / for* to say how long this situation has been true.

# Tinnitus   INTERVIEW!  MUSIC

Rock group Tinnitus, who had big hits in the 1980s with *Take My Love* and *Feel*, are back! Helen Todd spoke to the band ...

**DOWNLOAD!** 80s stars Tinnitus are back!
*Photograph (left–right):* Martin (drums), Brian (bass, vocals), Tony (guitar)

| | |
|---|---|
| HT | How did the band start? |
| Brian | Well, I've played the guitar since my seventh birthday. I met Tony and Martin at secondary school in 1977 and we became best mates. We all liked the same music so I taught Tony how to play the guitar and Tinnitus was born. |
| Tony | *You* taught *me* the guitar? You're joking, right? |
| HT | You've been friends for over thirty years. Have you ever fallen out? |
| Brian | Yes, of course we have. We're like brothers – and we fight like brothers. Actually, Martin has left the band five times – but he always comes back. |
| HT | Really? Is that true, Martin? |
| Martin | ... |
| Brian | Er, Martin isn't speaking to us today. |
| Tony | He hasn't spoken to anyone for five days. |
| HT | You haven't had a big hit since 1995. Is that a problem? |
| Brian | Actually, we've had two singles in the Top 100 since 1995 and our *Greatest Hits* album has been number 39 for the last three weeks. |
| Tony | And a lot of people still come to our concerts. Even young people. They know all the words. |
| HT | What are you doing at the moment? |
| Brian | We've just finished our winter tour of English seaside towns and we've recorded ten new songs since the start of the year. |
| HT | You're almost fifty now. Aren't you too old for this? |
| Brian | Sorry, we have to finish now. We're playing a concert in a few minutes. Er, has anyone seen my wig? ∎ |

- Tinnitus are playing in the car park at Folly Park Shopping Centre at 11 a.m. on Saturday

## Check it out

### Present Perfect

- We use the Present Perfect to talk about situations that began in the past and continue now.
- We often use *since* to say when the situation started or *for* to say how long this situation has been true.
  They haven't had a hit *since 1995*.
  They haven't had a hit *for* over *fifteen years*.

## Mind the trap!

We don't use the Present Simple tense to talk about situations that began in the past and continue to the present.

*I have lived* **here for four years.**
NOT  *I live* **here for four years.**

**6** Read the article again and answer the questions. Use the Present Perfect and *for/since*.

1 How long has Brian played the guitar?
2 How long has he known Tony and Martin?
3 How long has the drummer not spoken?
4 How long has their record been at number 39 in the charts?

**7** Read these sentences and answer the questions.

1 Leo was my boyfriend for five years.
  Ian has been my boyfriend for five months.
  – *Who is my boyfriend?*
2 Pat has lived here for ten days.
  Pam lived here for ten years.
  – *Who still lives here?*

**8** In pairs, make sentences with *for* or *since* and the phrases in the box. Say if your partner's sentences are true or false.

| | | |
|---|---|---|
| 7 o'clock | ten minutes | Tuesday |
| 1st January | a long time | last night |
| a week | 2009 | ages  I was … years old |

A I've had my watch for ages.
B True.
A No, false. I've had it since Christmas!

**9** In pairs, answer the questions about yourself. Then interview your partner.

How long have you:
1 been a student at this school/college?
2 known your best friend?
3 lived in your house/flat?
4 liked your favourite band/artist?
5 had your mobile phone/this book?

A How long have you been a student at this school?
B I've been here for two years.

## VOCABULARY | Relationships

**1** Match the phrasal verbs in sentences 1–6 with the definitions a–f. Use a dictionary if you need to.

1 He's **fallen out with** his girlfriend. They're not talking to each other any more.
2 She's the most popular girl in the class. She **gets on with** everyone.
3 He's clever, good-looking and generous. I'd love to **go out with** him.
4 Oh no! My parents want me to **look after** my baby brother on Friday night.
5 I **split up with** Jim because we were always arguing.
6 He's my friend and I'll always **stand by** him – even when he's wrong.

a to take care of ☐
b to have a serious argument ☐
c continue to be loyal ☐
d to have a good relationship with someone ☐
e to end a romantic relationship with someone ☐
f to have a romantic relationship with someone ☐

**2** Complete sentences a–d with the correct forms of the phrasal verbs in Exercise 1.

a I ¹_____ my girlfriend really well. It's the perfect relationship.
b Have you heard? Nicole ²_____ Tom. He's depressed because she's the best girl he's ever ³_____ with.
c She always ⁴_____ him, even when he went to prison.
d I ⁵_____ my mum again. We're not talking to each other! She wants to ⁶_____ me all the time. It's ridiculous! I'm not a baby!

**3**  CD3.26  In pairs, listen to the speakers and choose the people they are speaking about.

Speaker 1  his *girlfriend / sister*
Speaker 2  her *sister / mother*
Speaker 3  his *girlfriend / mother*

**4** In pairs, talk about your relationships. Use these phrases and the phrasal verbs from Exercise 1.

- She's very unfair/so easy to talk to/got a great sense of humour.
- She trusts me/gives me a lot of freedom/ irritates me.
- We have a lot (nothing) in common.
- We're comfortable with/jealous of each other/ the best of friends.
- I used to get on with her really well.

A I get on really well with my dad. He …

**81**

## READING

**1** CD3.27 In pairs, complete the song lyrics with the words below. Listen and check. Then say who you think the man is singing about.

alone   darkness   stay   too long   warm
wonder (v)

### Bill Withers – Ain't no sunshine (when she's gone)

There ain't no sunshine when she's gone.
It's not ¹_____ when she's away,
There ain't no sunshine when she's gone,
And she's always gone ²_____
Anytime she goes away.

I ³_____ this time where she's gone.
I wonder if she's gone to ⁴_____ .

There ain't no sunshine when she's gone,
And this house just ain't no home
Anytime she goes away.

And I know, I know, I know, I know …
I've got to leave the young thing ⁵_____ .
There ain't no sunshine when she's gone.

There ain't no sunshine when she's gone.
Only ⁶_____ every day.
There ain't no sunshine when she's gone,
And this house just ain't no home
Anytime she goes away.

**2** Read the song lyrics again and choose the best answers.

1 When the woman is not there, the man feels:
   **a** sad   **b** happy   **c** angry
2 Does the man know where the woman has gone?
   **a** yes   **b** no   **c** he's not sure
3 Does he think she's going to come back?
   **a** yes   **b** no   **c** he's not sure

**3** CD3.28 Read the story. Are these statements about the song, the story or both?

1 The woman has gone away.
2 The woman is working in another country.
3 The man knows he has to leave the woman alone.
4 He is sad without the woman.
5 He knows where the woman is.
6 He is afraid she may never come back.

### Sunshine

In a poor district near Lima a young man steps out of his home – a tiny house with a plastic roof. He looks up at the early morning sky. Another day with no sunshine. The weather has been terrible recently. He can't remember the last time he saw the sun. Heavy grey clouds fill the sky and his heart feels cold with sadness. There's no sunshine when she's gone, he thinks. There's only darkness every day. And she hasn't called for so long. He wonders if she's gone for ever. He tries to imagine life without her. What if she stays over there in Madrid cleaning the houses of the rich? ¹ He turns as he hears a noise; one of the children is waking up. ² They miss her so much. The house just isn't a home without her. Every day they ask him, 'When is Mamá coming home?' And what can he say? 'One day. Soon, my baby.' 'And why isn't ³ she here, Papá?' Why? Because ⁴ they need the money, and there are no jobs, and ⁵ over there she can earn in a day what you earn ⁶ here in a month. It isn't easy to feed five hungry children. But it isn't easy for them to live without their mother, either.

**4** Read the story again. Are the statements true (T) or false (F)?

1 This is a story about a poor family. ☐
2 The man hasn't talked to his wife for a long time. ☐
3 He doesn't know what job she has in Madrid. ☐
4 The children have forgotten about their mother. ☐
5 The man sends his children to work. ☐
6 At the end of the story, the woman comes home. ☐

**5** In pairs, decide which of the people in the story said these statements. Then compare your answers with another pair.

**1** Wake up! Mamá has come home.

**2** I've just come from the airport.

**3** We've missed you so much.

**4** Have you brought me a present?

**5** I've earned enough money. We can move away from here.

**6** I've taken them to school every day all the time you've been away.

**7** I've been away for two years, but now I'm here to stay.

**6** Match the underlined words 1–7 in the text with the people or places they refer to a–g.

a the man ☐
b Verónica ☐
c the family ☐
d in Madrid ☐
e his wife ☐
f the children ☐
g in Lima ☐

**7** In pairs, choose ONE of the topics below and tell your partner about it.

• Someone you know who has gone to another country to find work.
• A situation where you felt very homesick.
• A time when you missed someone very badly.

He sighs. Time to wake them up and get them ready for school. He knows many people who send their children to work, to wash cars or to beg, but she has always said that her children must get an education. But it's hard. He misses her, too. He misses her smile, her voice, the songs she sings even when things look black. And he knows she loves him. But why hasn't she called? Perhaps she's forgotten them. Perhaps she's decided to stay there. Perhaps she's found someone else. He feels like crying, but he can't. Not in front of the children.

A dog starts barking. He turns back to the house to start another day. Suddenly, a ray of sunshine breaks through the clouds and lights up the doorway just as Verónica steps through the door. He feels the warm sun on his back. The little girl has just woken up and is rubbing sleep from her eyes. [7] She looks so like her mother. She yawns and he hears her mother's voice. He hears his name, 'Nacho! Nacho!' Is Verónica speaking? Behind him he hears footsteps. He turns round. The sun is too bright and he can't see clearly. He puts his hand up to his eyes, and then thinks, 'I haven't woken up! I'm still dreaming!' But then Verónica shouts out, 'Mamá!' And he knows that sometimes dreams come true.

## SPEAKING AND LISTENING

**1** Work in pairs. How recently have you done these things? Answer with *never, not for a long time, recently.*

- do the washing-up
- do the vacuuming
- do the cooking
- set/clear the table
- make your bed
- tidy your room
- go out with your parents
- have an argument with your parents
- have a good talk with your parents

A Have you done the washing-up recently?
B Yes, I did it last night. I always do it.

**2** CD3.29 Listen and answer the questions.

1 Why is Jane upset?
2 Why does Ethan think she is wrong to be upset?
3 What does Ruby suggest?
4 What does Jane want to do?
5 What do her friends think of that?

**3** CD3.29 Who says sentences 1–6: Jane (J), Ruby (R) or Ethan (E)? Listen and check.

1 If you ask me, you're lucky. ☐
2 What do you think? ☐
3 I see what you mean, but I'm not sure I agree with you. ☐
4 Personally, I think you need to have a good talk with your parents. ☐
5 Oh come on! You can't be serious! ☐
6 That's right! ☐

**4** Complete Speak Out with the <u>underlined</u> expressions from Exercise 3.

| SPEAK OUT | Expressing opinion | |
|---|---|
| **Agreeing** | **Asking for opinions** |
| I totally agree. That's a good point. 1 _____ . | Do you agree? Don't you think ...? 2 _____ . |
| **Disagreeing** | **Expressing opinion** |
| (weak) That's true, but ... 3 _____ . | In my opinion, ... 5 _____ . |
| (strong) I'm sorry, I totally disagree. 4 _____ . | It seems to me ... 6 _____ . |

**5** CD3.30 Listen and repeat some of the phrases from Speak Out.

**6** CD3.31 Choose the correct phrases in the conversations. Listen and check your answers. Then act out the dialogues in pairs.

1 A Do you agree that teenagers watch too much TV?
B *That's a good point. / You can't be serious!* If you ask me, adults watch more TV than teenagers!

2 A Do you think that it's important for parents and children to talk to each other?
B *I see what you mean. / Do you agree?* – it's true talking can help your relationship – but it depends what you talk about.

3 A Don't you think that if you live in your parents' house, you have to do what your parents say?
B I totally disagree. *Personally, I think / That's right* my parents are my friends, not my bosses.

4 A *Don't you think / That's true, but* it's good if teenagers help with the housework?
B *I totally agree. / I totally disagree.* I think it's everyone's responsibility to help at home.

**7** Choose four topics from the sentences. In pairs discuss the topics. Use Speak Out to help you.

- Good parents control when their teenage children go out and who they go out with.
- It's wrong for parents to stop their teenage children from wearing the clothes they like or getting piercings or tattoos.
- Going out with your parents is embarrassing.
- It's a good idea for someone with a job to pay rent to their parents.
- It's better to study in a different town and live with other students, e.g. in a hall of residence, than it is to study in your home town and live with your family.

## LISTENING AND WRITING

**1** CD3.32 In pairs, look at the photos and answer the questions. Then listen and check your predictions to questions 1 and 2.

1 How does the girl feel in photo A?
2 What do you think has happened?
3 How does the girl feel in photo B?
4 What do you think has happened?

**2** CD3.32 Read sentences 1–6. Are the statements true (T) or false (F)? Then listen again and check.

1 Jimmy is Carol's boyfriend. ☐
2 Carol calls Darren to invite him to a party. ☐
3 Carol's worried because she hasn't seen Jimmy recently. ☐
4 She hasn't really tried to contact him. ☐
5 She thinks he may be ill. ☐
6 Jimmy went to the shopping centre with Carol's best friend, Lily. ☐

**3** Read text messages 1–3 and choose the correct meaning of these abbreviations.

1 u   under / you     4 @   and / at
2 w   what / with     5 CU  see you / queue
3 gr8 great / green    6 2   to / toe

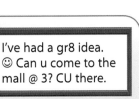

**4** In pairs, read the messages from Exercise 3 again and decide who sent them. Then say why you think Jimmy hasn't been in touch with Carol.

Jimmy ☐     Darren ☐     Carol ☐

**5** Read messages 4–6 below and match them with the senders and receivers a–c. Did you guess correctly what Jimmy was doing?

a Jimmy sent it to Darren. ☐
b Carol sent it to Jimmy. ☐
c Lily sent it to Jimmy. ☐

**6** Choose the correct meanings of the abbreviations in the messages above.

1 mins   minutes / months
2 IMO    in my opinion / I must object
3 Fri    friend / Friday
4 B      but / be
5 thanx  than anyone / thanks
6 4      for / fear
7 n      and / no
8 H & K  hot and cold / hugs and kisses

**7** In groups of four, use the abbreviations above and the ideas below to write a text message to each person in your group. Reply to all the messages you get.

- I've just _____ .
- I've finally _____ .
- I haven't _____ yet.
- Have you _____ yet?

# What's on?

Read, listen and talk about the media.
Practise the Passive.
Focus on taking part in a conversation; listening for gist.
Write short notes/messages.

## GRAMMAR AND VOCABULARY

**1** In pairs, answer the questions.

1 When do you usually watch TV?
2 How many hours of TV do you usually watch a week?
3 Do you think you watch too much TV?

**2** Look at the types of TV programmes in the box. Think of a programme in your country for each type.

soap operas   documentaries   talk shows
comedy series   game/quiz shows   debates
talent shows   cartoons   reality shows
sports programmes   news programmes

**3** CD3.33 Do the quiz in groups. Then listen and check.

# TV QUIZ

Try our quiz and see how much you know about the world of TV

**1** Which is the most popular of these TV programmes?
(It is watched by up to one billion people.)

A BBC World News
B The Eurovision Song Contest
C Formula 1 car racing
D English Premier League football

**2** Adverts are not shown on which of these TV channels?

A Fox
B The BBC
C Eurosport
D CNN

**3** Which TV family was created by Matt Groening in 1987?

A The Flintstones
B The Sopranos
C The Simpsons
D The Addams

**4** The first televised Olympic Games were broadcast from ___ in 1936.

A the USA
B Germany
C the UK
D Italy

**5** The Teletubbies' conversations have been translated into ___ languages.

A 45
B 30
C 15
D 0 (they don't talk)

**6** Which of these TV shows has been made in more countries (over 100)?

A Big Brother
B Strictly Come Dancing
C (Britain)'s Got Talent
D Who Wants To Be A Millionaire?

## Work it out

**4** Look at the Passive and Active versions of the sentences and choose the correct answer in the rule.

| Passive | Active |
|---|---|
| English football is watched by 1.2 billion people every week. | 1.2 billion people watch English football every week. |
| The Simpsons cartoon series was created by Matt Groening in 1987. | Matt Groening created The Simpsons cartoon series in 1987. |
| This show has been made in more than 100 countries. | They have made this show in more than 100 countries. |

We use the *Active / Passive* when the action is more important than the people who do it.

**5** Look at the verbs in the Passive sentences in Exercise 4 and complete the rules with the words in the box.

am/is/are   has been/have been   was/were

We form:
**1** the Present Simple Passive with _____ and the Past Participle.
**2** the Past Simple Passive with _____ and the Past Participle.
**3** the Present Perfect Passive with _____ and the Past Participle.

## Check it out

**The Passive**

We use the Passive when the action is more important than the people who do it. We often use the word *by* before the person who does the action.

We form the Passive with the verb *to be* and the Past Participle.

Adverts are not shown on the BBC. (Present Simple)
When was *The Simpsons* cartoon series created? (Past Simple)
It has been translated into 45 languages. (Present Perfect)

**6** In pairs, choose the correct form in each question. Then try to answer them.

**1** Pokemon and Hello Kitty *make / are made* in the same country. Which country is it?
**2** Many TV series *have made / have been made* about doctors. Can you name one?
**3** Which brothers *created / were created* Bugs Bunny and Daffy Duck?
**4** Which song contest *has seen / has been seen* on European TV every year since 1956?
**5** Which TV channel *played / was played* its first music video in New York in 1981?
**6** Miley Stewart *also knows / is also known* as a famous singer. What's the singer's name?

**7** Complete the facts about soap operas with the correct Passive form of the verbs in brackets.

The name 'soap opera' [1]_____ (give) to early radio and TV series because adverts for soap [2]_____ (include) in the programmes. Today the word 'soap' [3]_____ (often/use) instead of soap opera. The British soap *Coronation Street* [4]_____ (broadcast) every week since 1960. Since the 1970s many soaps such as *Neighbours* and *Home and Away* [5]_____ (make) in Australia. Latin American soaps ('telenovelas') are very popular: they [6]_____ (watch) by over two billion people around the world.

**8** Complete each sentence using the Passive so that it means the same as the sentence above it. Then say which TV show is being described.

**1** They first made this quiz show in the UK in 1998.
This quiz show _____ .
**2** They give the winners large cash prizes.
Large cash prizes _____ .
**3** They have turned the show into a board game.
The show _____ .
**4** At first, in the UK they asked the contestants up to fifteen questions.
At first in the UK _____ .
**5** Since 2007 they have asked the contestants only twelve questions.
Since 2007 _____ .
**6** We know the show for the question 'is that your final answer?'.
The show _____ .

**9** In pairs, answer the questions.

**1** What's your favourite TV programme? What time is it shown? On which channel? Where and when was it made? What else do you know about it?
**2** In your opinion, what are the best/worst/most popular TV programmes that have ever been made in your country? Why?

## READING

**1** In pairs, check you understand these types of films. Use a dictionary if you need to. Can you think of an example for each type?

science fiction    (psychological) thriller    fantasy    horror
(historical) drama    action    (romantic) comedy    cartoon

**2** In pairs, discuss how often you go to the cinema and what type of films you like or dislike. Use the words in Exercise 1.

**3** Look at the photos in pairs. What do you know about the actors or any of the films?

**4** CD3.34 Read the article and match films A–D with sentences 1–6.

Which film(s) …
1 wasn't a big commercial success? ☐
2 won several prizes? ☐ ☐
3 was an adaptation of an earlier film? ☐
4 was very funny? ☐
5 got positive reviews? ☐ ☐ ☐
6 was a fantasy film? ☐ ☐

**5** Read the statements. Are they true (T) or false (F)?

1 Johnny Depp left school early. ☐
2 After *Edward Scissorhands* he stopped playing unusual characters. ☐
3 Penelope Cruz was in her teens when she worked on TV. ☐
4 Orlando Bloom was still at drama school when he played Legolas. ☐
5 *Bend It Like Beckham* wasn't Keira Knightley's first film. ☐
6 Her image changed after *Bend It Like Beckham*. ☐

**6** Match words 1–5 from the article with their synonyms a–e.

1 eccentric (A)      ☐    **a** dramatic
2 modest (B)         ☐    **b** strange, unusual
3 spectacular (C)    ☐    **c** positive, warm
4 major (C)          ☐    **d** small
5 enthusiastic (D)   ☐    **e** important

**7** Match the underlined words or phrases in the article with definitions 1–6.

1 A film which is seen by a lot of people at the cinema.
2 An exciting action that looks dangerous.
3 Someone who tells the actors in a film what to do.
4 The story in a film, book, etc.
5 A short part of a film in which the action stays in one place.
6 Conversation which is written for a film.

**8** Tell your partner about the last film you enjoyed. Use the ideas below.

- *It's a comedy/* …
- … starred in the film/played the part of …
- It was *directed by* … /*made in* …
- The film takes place in *the future/France/ the nineteenth century/* …
- The plot is about …
- The dialogue is/soundtrack is/special effects are/ (battle) scenes are *great/spectacular* …
- It got *good/enthusiastic/negative* reviews.

# The Big Break

Every actor dreams of getting their first big break – a major film that makes them a star. Tim Collins looks back at the moment four young actors suddenly became Hollywood superstars.

**A**

**Edward Scissorhands**
**(1990 – Johnny Depp)**

Johnny Depp dropped out of school to become
a rock musician and he only became an actor by
accident when he was introduced to Nicolas Cage by
his wife. He started working as a TV actor and quickly
became a teen idol, a status which he hated. In 1990
he was offered the lead role in Tim Burton's *Edward
Scissorhands*, a fantasy film. Twenty-seven-year-old
Depp played Edward, an artificial man with scissors
for hands who ends up living in suburban America.
The film was a <u>box office hit</u> and got very positive
reviews. People started to take Depp seriously as
an actor and since then he has continued to play
eccentric, memorable characters.

**B**

**Vanilla Sky**
**(2001 – Penelope Cruz)**

Penelope Cruz trained as a ballet dancer in Madrid
before working as a TV presenter and finally, at the
age of eighteen, acting in films. In one of her first
Spanish films, Cruz played the part of Sofia in *Open
Your Eyes*, a psychological thriller about a man
who has disorienting experiences after a car crash.
Five years later, American <u>director</u> Cameron Crowe
remade the film as *Vanilla Sky* and Cruz was given the
chance to play Sofia again. Although *Vanilla Sky* got
terrible reviews and was only a modest commercial
success, it was seen by many more people than the
Spanish version (Tom Cruise starred in the Hollywood
film). Cruz, who speaks four languages, quickly
became a global superstar.

**C**

**The Lord of the Rings:**
**The Fellowship of the Ring**
**(2001 – Orlando Bloom)**

As a child, Orlando was encouraged by his mother to
take drama classes and he eventually studied at
London's Guildhall School, one of the UK's top drama
schools. Two days after graduating, he was given the
role of Legolas in *The Fellowship of the Ring*, the first
of the three *Lord of the Rings* fantasy films. As
Legolas, Bloom had to perform many <u>stunts</u> during
battle <u>scenes</u> and he even broke a bone after falling
off a horse. The film was praised by critics, especially
for its spectacular special effects, and won four
Oscars. Bloom went from being an unknown
twenty-four-year-old actor to a well-known celebrity.
He has continued to appear in major films such as
*Pirates of the Caribbean*.

**D**

**Bend It Like Beckham**
**(2002 – Keira Knightley)**

Keira Knightley grew up in London and began her
acting career on TV in her teens. Her first film role was
in the science-fiction epic *Star Wars Episode I*.
However, it was her role in the British comedy *Bend It
Like Beckham* that made her a star. Today Keira is
famous for her glamorous roles in *Pirates of the
Caribbean* and *Pride and Prejudice*, but in the 2002
film she played an ordinary teenage girl. The <u>plot</u>
follows the friendship between Jess, a football-mad
Sikh girl and Jules, played by Knightley, who both
dream of becoming professional footballers. With its
amusing <u>dialogue</u> and happy ending the film was a
big hit, received enthusiastic reviews and won several
international awards.

# SPEAKING

**1** In pairs, look at the photo and answer the questions.

- What is the woman in this photo doing?
- What kind of things can we buy online?
- Do you think this is a good way to buy things? Why?/Why not?

**2** [CD4.1] Listen to the radio phone-in programme and choose the correct answers.

**1** The caller is worried because her daughter
a spends too much time with her friends.
b is always on her computer.
c buys things online.

**2** The presenter thinks the caller
a is worrying about nothing.
b is right to worry.
c should stop her daughter shopping online.

**3** [CD4.1] Study Speak Out. Then listen again and <u>underline</u> the expressions you hear.

---

**SPEAK OUT | Conversations**

| **Asking for explanation** | **Asking for repetition** |
|---|---|
| • I'm not sure I understand. What do you mean? <br> • What do you mean by *encryption*? | • I'm sorry, I didn't catch what you said. Could you say it again, please? <br> • Could you repeat that, please? |
| **Hesitation** | **Politely interrupting** |
| • Well, you see, the thing is … <br> • I'm not sure really. <br> • Let me think … | • That's very/really interesting, but … <br> • That's true, but … <br> • I'd just like to say … <br> • Excuse me, can I just say … |

---

**4** [CD4.2] Listen and repeat some of the phrases from Speak Out.

**5** [CD4.3] Listen and choose the best replies.

**1** a Could you repeat that, please?
b How shall I put it?
**2** a That's true, but will that help?
b What do you mean by DDR memory?
**3** a Can I just say something?
b I'm not sure really.
**4** a Excuse me, I'd just like to say …
b Well, you see, the thing is …

**6** [CD4.4] In pairs, complete the dialogue with phrases from Speak Out. Then listen and compare.

**A** Newspapers could disappear because of the Internet and 24-hour news channels …
**B** [1](Interrupt) I don't like reading on a screen. And what about public transport?
**A** [2](Ask for an explanation)
**B** I mean, it's easy to read a paper on a bus, but the Internet isn't so practical, is it?
**A** [3](Hesitate) computers are getting smaller and you can access the Internet with …
**B** [4](Ask for repetition)
**A** Yes, I said you can connect to the Internet with your mobile phone.
**B** [5](Hesitate) OK, the *paper* versions of newspapers don't have much future, but did you know that over a million people read *The Guardian*'s website in only one day?

**7** Act out the dialogue from Exercise 6 with appropriate intonation.

**8** In groups of four, discuss the statement. Use Speak Out and the vocabulary below.

'Computers are bad for young people.'

---
social networking sites (Facebook, etc.)
online shopping    blog    download    virus
search engine (Google)    online games
upload    research (Wikipedia)    Internet
---

**90**

# LISTENING

**1** In pairs, answer the questions.

- When/Where/How often do you listen to the radio?
- What is your favourite radio station?
- Look at the types of radio programmes below. Which ones do you often/sometimes/never listen to?

local news    phone-ins    world news
comedy programmes    radio dramas
travel report    celebrity gossip
entertainment guide    discussions/debates
the weather    sports news

**2** CD4.5 Listen and choose the kind of radio programme this is. Don't worry if you don't understand everything.

- celebrity gossip    • local news
- entertainment guide

**3** In pairs, choose the key phrase in each pair which helped you decide what kind of programme you listened to.

1 some more news / the Hollywood star
2 was arrested / there's a hot story
3 getting a divorce / three months ago
4 this year's hit movie / fed up with their relationship
5 famous people / local comedy star

**4** CD4.5 Listen again and choose the main idea of what the presenter says.

a Matt Dawson was arrested.
b Matt and Lynette's marriage is in difficulty.
c Lynette is going out with Jasper Kale.

**5** Read Train Your Brain. Look at Exercises 2–4 and choose the correct answers.

---

**TRAIN YOUR BRAIN** | Listening skills

**Understanding the main ideas**

1 It *is / isn't* important to understand the context.
2 *Try / Don't try* to understand everything.
3 Listen for *key phrases / every detail* to help you understand the main idea.

---

**6** CD4.6 Listen and decide what type of radio report this is. What key words and phrases helped you decide?

**7** CD4.6 Listen again and choose the main idea of the report. Use Train Your Brain to help you.

a This week the weather has been bad.
b The weather will be good this weekend.
c Sunday is a good day for a picnic.

# VOCABULARY | The media

**1** Think Back! In pairs, add as many words as you can to each category in two minutes. Then compare your answers with another pair.

- **TV**
  broadcast, …
- **Radio**
  phone-in show, …
- **The Internet**
  download, …
- **Cinema**
  director, …

**2** In pairs, use the pronunciation chart on page 142 to understand words 1–6. Then match them with definitions a–f.

1 /ˈdɒkjəmentəriː/ ☐
2 /ˌentəˈteɪnmənt/ ☐
3 /ˈbrɔːdkɑːst/ ☐
4 /ˌsaɪəns ˈfɪkʃən/ ☐
5 /fəˈtɒɡrɑːfə/ ☐
6 /ˈdʒɜːnəlɪsts/ ☐

a a person who takes photos professionally
b an informative and educational programme
c the people who write stories in newspapers
d to send out radio or TV programmes
e stories about events in the future
f films, programmes or performances that amuse people

**3** Look at the list of sections in newspapers and magazines and tick those which offer entertainment more than news.

- TV guide ☐
- what's on ☐
- crossword ☐
- fashion tips ☐
- sports pages ☐
- cartoon strip ☐
- gossip column ☐
- readers' letters ☐
- weather forecast ☐
- international news ☐

**4** Complete sentences 1–6 so they are true for you. Then compare your answers with a partner's answers.

1 I find out what's happening in the world through *radio/newspapers/TV/the Internet/ my friends*.
2 The first section I turn to in a newspaper is the _____ .
3 The section I never read is the _____ .
4 The name of my favourite *newspaper/ magazine* is _____ . It is a *daily/ weekly/monthly* publication. I like it because _____ .
5 The name of my favourite *TV channel/ radio station* is _____ . I like it because _____ .
6 My three favourite websites are _____ . I like them because _____ .

# WRITING | Notes and messages

**1** Read the email. Where is Pete inviting Rachel to go on Saturday? Who else is he inviting?

**NEW MESSAGE**

| To: | Rachel@mail2.uk |
| From: | Pete88@magic.con |
| Subject: | Saturday night! |

Hi Rachel,

I hope you're well. Do you remember that competition I entered? Well, I won four free tickets to the Odeon cinema!

There's a new horror film on there. Tammi's seen it and she says it's great, really scary. Do you fancy going to see it tonight?

It starts at 7.30 p.m. so if you can make it, let's meet in the café at seven. I'm inviting Mark and Vicky as well.

I hope you can come – please phone if there's a problem.

Best wishes,
Pete

**SEND**

**2** Read Pete's note to Vicky below. Which words does he eliminate to make these sentences shorter?

> I've got four free tickets for a horror film tonight.
> Do you want to go?
> The film starts at 7:30.
> Why don't you meet me in the café at 7?
> I'm inviting Rachel and Mark too.
> I hope you can come.
> Could you phone me if you can't make it?

**3** In pairs, compare the email and the note in Exercises 1 and 2. Tick things from the email which are NOT in the note.

1 The name of the person Pete is writing to. ☐
2 Greetings and polite expressions –
   Hi …, I hope you're well. ☐
3 The time the film starts. ☐
4 The place and the time to meet. ☐
5 The fact that a friend likes the film. ☐
6 The other people he's inviting. ☐

**4** Look at Exercises 2 and 3 again and complete the guidelines in Train Your Brain with the examples 1–4.

1 *do, have*, etc.
2 *I, you, my*, etc.
3 *time/place of meeting*, etc.
4 *Dear …, How are you?, Best wishes*, etc.

---

## TRAIN YOUR BRAIN | Writing skills

**Notes and messages**

1 In short messages we don't usually write:
   • greetings and polite expressions like ᵃ_____ .
   • unimportant information.
2 We often leave out:
   • pronouns like ᵇ_____ at the start of sentences.
     ~~I~~ hope you can come.
   • auxiliary verbs like ᶜ_____ at the start of sentences.
     ~~Do you~~ fancy … ?
   • the definite article (*the*)
     ~~The~~ play starts …
3 We often use the Imperative in short notes.
   *Phone if you can't come.*
4 We must write the important details of the message like ᵈ_____ .

---

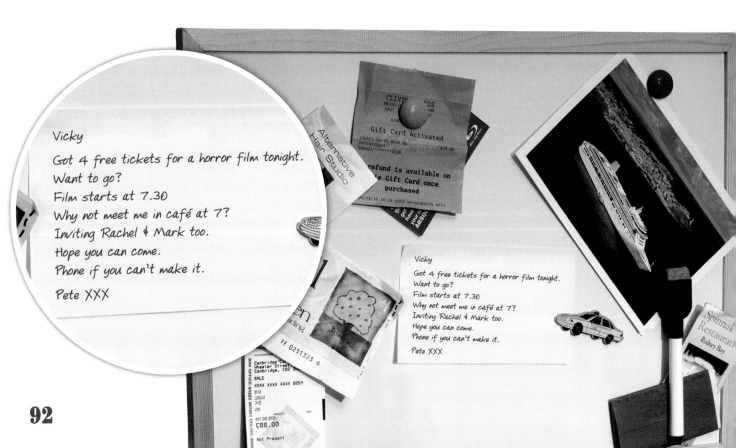

Vicky

Got 4 free tickets for a horror film tonight.
Want to go?
Film starts at 7.30
Why not meet me in café at 7?
Inviting Rachel & Mark too.
Hope you can come.
Phone if you can't make it.

Pete XXX

**5** In pairs, read short notes 1–4 and match them with the places a–d where they were left.

   **a** on a fridge in a typical kitchen ☐
   **b** on a door in a student flat ☐
   **c** on a desk in an office ☐
   **d** on a computer screen ☐

**6** Use these words to rewrite the four messages in Exercise 5 in full sentences.

   **1** I've/I'll be/Your/is
   **2** My/I/the
   **3** I/I'll/the
   **4** I've/I

**7** How many words can you remove from each sentence without changing the meaning?

   **1** I'll see you outside the cinema at eight.
   **2** I'm going to the club tonight. Do you want to come?
   **3** Are you going home on Friday?
   **4** Do you fancy watching *Heroes* tonight?
   **5** I'm arriving at the station at half six. Please wait under the clock.

**8** In pairs, read Vicky's reply to Pete. Cross out any unnecessary words or phrases. Look at page 121 and compare your answers.

**9** Write a short note inviting a friend to a *film/play/concert/art show/club*. Use Train Your Brain and the Speak Out on page 18 to help you.

   • Say where you are inviting him/her.
   • Suggest a time and a place to meet.
   • Suggest something you could do afterwards.
   • Mention how your partner can contact you if there is a problem.

**10** Exchange your note from Exercise 9 with a partner, and write a reply. Use Speak Out on page 18 to help you.

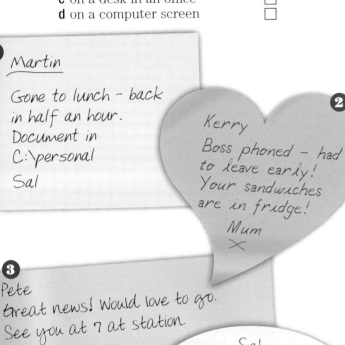

**1**

Martin

Gone to lunch – back in half an hour.
Document in C:\personal

Sal

**2**

Kerry
Boss phoned – had to leave early!
Your sandwiches are in fridge!
Mum
X

**3**

Pete
Great news! Would love to go.
See you at 7 at station.
Mark

**4**

Sal
Borrowed your dictionary.
Hope you don't mind.
Rachel

Dear Pete,

How's it going?
I am meeting my 19-year-old cousin from Bolton in Racey's on Saturday evening so I'm afraid I can't go with you, Mark and Rachel.
What a pity – I haven't been to the cinema for ages.
Anyway, do you want to meet for a coffee on Sunday at about 3 o'clock?

I will be upstairs in Toni's café.
Don't forget to let me know if there are any problems or if you can't come.

Best wishes,
Vicky XXX

## VOCABULARY AND GRAMMAR

**1** Complete the dialogue. For each gap write one word. **(6 points)**

**Kate** Have you ever fallen in love with someone that your parents didn't get [1]_____ with?

**Tina** Yes, last year I had a terrible [2]_____ with them because of my boyfriend. I really fell [3]_____ with them! We even stopped talking! Fortunately, I [4]_____ up with him after a few weeks. We never really had a good [5]_____ , anyway. By the way, have you heard the news? Gary and Jill are getting [6]_____ . The wedding's next month.

**Kate** No way! I don't think it's going to work. They're too young.

**2** Complete the article using the words in the box. **(8 points)**

radio stations   broadcast   music videos
news   weather   channels   TV guide
soap opera

# TAKE YOUR TV WITH YOU

Mobile phones are quickly becoming our main source of entertainment and information. Apart from the standard phone functions, they offer users many other options: we can watch [1]_____ of our favourite singers, read the [2]_____ from all over the world, check the [3]_____ forecast for the next day, and listen to countless [4]_____ in different languages. Now we can even watch our favourite [5]_____ on a mobile phone screen. They are [6]_____ in special short versions, called *mobisodes*, which last about thirty seconds each. Who knows, maybe soon there will be so many TV [7]_____ that offer this service that we will need a special [8]_____ just for our mobile phones.

**3** Complete the second sentence so that it has a similar meaning to the first sentence. Use the word in bold without changing it. **(4 points)**

**1** The last time I spoke to her was in 1998. **not**
I have _____ 1998.

**2** They print most newspapers in Nigeria in English. **are**
Most newspapers in Nigeria _____ in English.

**3** We ate in that restaurant last month. **already**
We _____ in that restaurant.

**4** Lucy is going to tell Mark tomorrow. **yet**
Lucy _____ .

**4** Read the conversation. For each gap choose the correct answer. **(7 points)**

**Dawn** Hey, Karen! Congratulations! I hear you [1]_____ in love! Tell me all about it! How long have [2]_____ him? Where [3]_____ meet?

**Karen** We [4]_____ at a nightclub last Saturday, so we have been together [5]_____ almost a week now. He's perfect – so handsome and intelligent! Anyway, what has changed in your life [6]_____ I last saw you?

**Dawn** Well … I've [7]_____ started a new job. It's great.

| | | |
|---|---|---|
| **1 a** fall | **b** have fallen | **c** been fallen |
| **2 a** you know | **b** did know | **c** you known |
| **3 a** do you | **b** did you | **c** were you |
| **4 a** met | **b** have met | **c** were meeting |
| **5 a** for | **b** since | **c** from |
| **6 a** for | **b** since | **c** ago |
| **7 a** yet | **b** since | **c** just |

**5** Complete the sentences so that they have the same meaning as the original ones. **(5 points)**

**1** They got married in 1983 and they're still married today.
They've _____ .

**2** We last went out together four months ago.
We haven't _____ .

**3** They published the first edition of *The Guardian* in 1821.
The first edition of *The Guardian* _____ .

**4** About 400,000 people buy *The Guardian* every day.
*The Guardian* _____ .

**5** We do not accept bad language on this website.
Bad language _____ .

## PRONUNCIATION

**6** **CD4.7** Listen and put the words in the box in the correct column. Then listen, repeat and check.

| /aɪ/ | /eɪ/ | /ɔɪ/ |
|---|---|---|
| blind | baby | noise |
| | | |
| | | |

boyfriend   campaign   cyclist   daily
engaged   enjoy   game   online   point
site   sunshine   voice

## LISTENING SKILLS

**7** CD4.8 Listen and complete gaps 2–9 with one word each.          (8 points)

The word 'tag' means [1] '_nickname_' .
The speaker's own tag is [2] '_____' .
A lot of people think that graffiti looks [3] _____ .
Some paintings in caves are over [4] _____ thousand years old.
The graffiti discovered in Pompeii gives us information about [5] _____ life at that time.
Graffiti makes it easier to understand the [6] _____ of old civilisations.
Modern graffiti is used for expressing [7] _____ messages.
Graffiti like 'TC was here' is not very [8] _____ .
Graffiti is an art form which you don't have to [9] _____ for.

## READING SKILLS

**8** Read the two texts below, then choose the correct answer about each text.          (2 points)

### Waterworld (1995)
This science-fiction film starred Kevin Costner, who was also the film's producer. There were many problems during the making of the film: the expensive 1,000 ton set was destroyed by a hurricane, and there were some unlucky accidents in which actors, including Costner, were almost killed. The film finally cost $175 million to make but only earned $88 million at the US box office.

**1 What do we know about Kevin Costner?**
Kevin Costner
**a** was in danger while making the film.
**b** got a lot of money for the film.
**c** starred in the film and directed it.
**d** destroyed the set of the film.

### Pirates of the Caribbean: At World's End (2007)
This action film was the third film in the Pirates of the Caribbean trilogy. *At World's End* was filmed in seventeen different locations, including Niagara Falls, the Bahamas, the Caribbean and Hawaii, which made it very expensive to make. The computer-generated special effects also helped make it the most expensive Hollywood film ever made.

**2 Why was the film special?**
It was special because
**a** it had special effects.
**b** it was filmed in seventeen cities.
**c** it cost a record sum of money.
**d** it used exotic locations.

## SPEAKING SKILLS

**9** Describe the photo. The following ideas may help you:

- Location
- People (clothes, appearance, etc.)
- Relationship between the people
- Situation
- Atmosphere
- Other

**10** What do you sometimes argue with your friends about?

## WRITING SKILLS

**11** Follow the instructions and write a message.

A friend invites you to a party. Unfortunately you are busy that day. Write a short message in which you:
- thank her for the invitation.
- apologise and explain why you can't go.
- suggest meeting the week after the party.

> Having a party at my place.
> Saturday at 9.
> Want to come?
> Bring a friend.
> Hope you can make it.
>
> Sally

# It's criminal!

**Read, listen and talk about** crime.
**Practise** the Past Perfect; Reported speech.
**Focus on** dealing with new words in reading; expressing feelings.
**Write** a notice for a lost item.

## CRIMINAL GAFFES

**1** ☐

A gang of fourteen robbers broke into a bank in Naples and entered the basement. They were hoping to steal millions of dollars from the 8,000 safety deposit boxes there. But the men had an unpleasant surprise.

**2** ☐

Ezedrick Jones, 18, tried to rob a fast-food restaurant in Tennessee. Although he was wearing a mask, Ezedrick was quickly recognised and arrested soon afterwards.

**3** ☐

A Detroit burglar arrived home after a 'successful' night. He was shocked when a few seconds later he opened the front door and saw his very happy dog … and the police.

**4** ☐

Neighbours in the city of Baku could hear music coming from an empty flat and decided to call the police. When the police arrived the thief didn't even try to escape.

**A**

The man **had left** his dog outside the house he **had burgled**. When the police arrived, they shouted 'Home boy!' and the dog happily led the police officer straight to the burglar's house.

**B**

The guard with the key to the boxes **had gone** for a coffee and they couldn't find him. They **hadn't prepared** an alternative plan so they left with almost nothing.

**C**

After he **had broken** into the flat, the thief decided to make himself at home. First, he had a bath, and then he had something to eat and drink. After he **had finished** his dinner, he saw a piano in the corner and started playing it. He was still singing songs when the police arrived.

**D**

Had Ezedrick **appeared** on TV and that's why staff recognised him? No, he hadn't. He **had** actually just **lost** his job at the restaurant. During the crime the manager kept on saying to him, 'Why are you doing this, Ezedrick?'

# GRAMMAR AND READING

**1** In pairs, check the meaning of the words, using a dictionary if you need to.

guard   robber   thief   steal   arrest
escape   break into   burglar

**2** Read stories 1–4 on page 96. In pairs, guess why the crimes were not successful.

A Perhaps there was nothing in the boxes.
B Maybe the guard saw the robbers and they ran away.

**3** Match explanations A–D with stories 1–4. Were your guesses in Exercise 2 correct?

## Work it out

**4** Read stories 1 and 2 again and tick the situations that happened first.

1 a The robbers **broke** into the bank. ☐
  b The guard **had gone** for a coffee. ☐

2 a Ezedrick **had lost** his job at the restaurant. ☐
  b He **tried** to rob the restaurant. ☐

**5** Study the sentences in Exercise 4 and choose the correct word in the rules below.

1 We use the Past Perfect to talk about an event that was completed *before / at the same time as* another event in the past.
2 With the Past Perfect we use *did + infinitive / had + Past Participle*.
3 The Past Perfect combines with the *Present Simple / Past Simple*.

## Check it out

### Past Perfect

We use the Past Perfect to talk about an action in the past that was completed before another action in the past. It combines with the Past Simple.

After he had finished his dinner, he started playing the piano.

| | |
|---|---|
| **Affirmative** | I/You/He/She/We/They had ('d) gone. |
| **Negative** | I/You/He/She/We/They had not (hadn't) gone. |
| **Questions** | Had I/you/he/she/we/they gone?<br>Yes, I/you/he/she/we/they had.<br>No, I/you/he/she/we/they hadn't. |

**6** **CD4.9** In pairs, use the Past Perfect of the verbs in brackets to complete the story. Can you guess what Pete had forgotten to do? Listen and check.

Pete [1]_____ (spend) a month observing the Parker family, so he knew they went away at weekends. He arrived at their house early on Sunday morning. The alarm didn't ring when he broke the window because he [2]_____ (already/cut) the cable. After he [3]_____ (climb) through the window he looked round the house. It was full of jewels and paintings. He [4]_____ (never/see) so many valuable things.

He smiled to himself as he drove away because he knew he [5]_____ (steal) a fortune. Suddenly he felt worried. [6]_____ (he/forget) something? Then he realised what it was. He hadn't …

**7** Look at the pictures of Kay's flat on page 122. Match verbs 1–5 with phrases a–e and say what the burglars had/hadn't done.

1 come in ☐     a some pizza
2 break ☐        b her clothes on the floor
3 eat ☐          c some money/the TV/
                    the DVD player
4 throw ☐        d the window
5 steal ☐        e through the window

When Kay came home, she saw that someone had broken into her flat. The burglars had come in through the window. They hadn't …

**8** Complete the sentences with *had* or *hadn't* where necessary. Remember the action which happened first takes the Past Perfect tense.

1 Kay _____ felt angry because she __hadn't__ closed the window.
2 After the police had examined the flat, they _____ found some fingerprints.
3 The police _____ found some fingerprints because the burglars _____ used gloves.
4 After the police _____ left, Kay _____ cleaned her flat.
5 The police _____ arrested the burglars two days later, after they _____ robbed another flat.
6 One of the burglars _____ explained that he had taken the hamster because he _____ always wanted to have a pet.
7 The burglars _____ left some of the pizza because they _____ already had dinner.

# LISTENING

**1** Check the meaning of the words. Use a dictionary if you need to.

dead  handgun  inherit  investigate
jealous  love affair  motive  murderer
personal assistant  silencer  suspect

**2** CD4.10 Read the newspaper extract and listen to Detective Marlowe. Then answer the questions.

1 Where and when was Tina murdered?
2 Who called the police?
3 How was she killed?

**3** CD4.11 Listen to Part 2 of the recording and match suspects 1–5 with motives a–e below.

**4** CD4.12 Listen to Part 3 and match suspects 1–5 with actions a–e.

1 Bobbie ☐   4 Billy ☐
2 Nicola ☐   5 Christine ☐
3 Delia ☐

a left the party early
b was the first guest to go onto the terrace
c heard a woman screaming
d had an argument with Tina
e was putting on her coat when Billy started shouting

**5** CD4.12 Match the beginnings and endings of the statements. Listen to Part 3 again and check.

Bobbie     When we got there, Tina was dead … ☐
Nicola     It was the most horrible thing … ☐
Delia      I was working when … ☐
Billy      When I got nearer, … ☐
Christine  I tried to help her, but … ☐

a she had already died.
b and Delia had already called the police.
c I had ever seen.
d I heard a shot.
e I saw she was dead.

**6** CD4.13 In groups, decide who killed Tina. Then listen to Part 4. What mistake had the murderer made?

## TINA MURDERED

Pop star Tina Squires has been murdered. It happened late last night during a dinner party. Tina, 23, was shot on the terrace of her luxury apartment near Central Park. The murderer had used a handgun with a silencer

**SUSPECT 1**

**Bobbie Davies**
Pop idol

**SUSPECT 2**

**Nicola Goodfellow**
Actress, going out with Bobbie Davies

Tina Squires

## MOTIVES

a  He will inherit Tina's money.

b  Tina had broken a promise to her.

c  She had stolen a lot of money from Tina.

d  He was angry with Tina because she kept calling him.

e  She was jealous of Tina and scared of losing her boyfriend.

**SUSPECT 3**

**Delia Adams**
Tina's personal assisstant

**SUSPECT 4**

**Billy Squires**
Tina's brother

**SUSPECT 5**

**Christine Cross**
Tina's manager

CONFIDENTI

# GRAMMAR

**1** CD4.14 In pairs, answer the questions below from memory. Then listen and check.

1 Where did Tina Squires die? How did it happen?
2 Who killed her? Why?
3 How did Detective Marlowe know who did it?

## Work it out

**2** Read the dialogue and Marlow's report. Then complete the table.

**Delia** I didn't murder Tina. I've never killed anyone.
**Marlowe** You're lying! You lied about hearing a gunshot. You forgot about the silencer on the gun.
**Delia** OK, I killed Tina. But I won't go to prison. You don't have any evidence.
**Marlowe** You will go to prison.

| Direct speech | Reported speech |
|---|---|
| **Present Simple** 'You don't have any evidence.' | **Past Simple** She said (that) I didn't have any evidence. |
| **Present Continuous** 'You're lying!' | **Past Continuous** I told her (that) she 1 _____ . |
| **Present Perfect** 'I've never killed anyone!' | **Past Perfect** She said (that) she 2 _____ . |
| **Past Simple** 'I didn't murder Tina. | **Past Perfect** She said (that) she 3 _____ . |
| **will** 'You will go to prison.' | **would** I told her (that) she 4 _____ . |

**3** Complete the sentences with Reported speech.

1 Billy: 'I **don't know** what I'll **do** with so much money!'
Billy told me that he **didn't know what** _____ .

2 Nicola: 'I'm trying to forget what **happened**, but it **won't be** easy.'
Nicola said that she _____ .

3 Bobbie: 'I've **never loved** anyone the way I **loved** Tina.'
Bobbie told Detective Marlowe that he _____ .

4 Christine: 'I've **found** a new job: I'm **working** in the prison and I **like** it a lot.'
Christine said that she _____ .
She also said that she _____ .

## Mind the trap!

In Reported speech we use *tell*, not *say* before a person's name or pronoun (*me*, *him*, *her*, etc.).

I told her/Delia (that) she was lying.

NOT I said her she was lying.   I told she was lying.

**4** Check you understand the crimes Ned was accused of. Then report what he said. Use *tell* if you know who he was talking to.

**Accused of …**
• **vandalism** 'I'm sorry I threw a brick through the window, Mrs Dibbs. I won't do it again!'
• **shoplifting** 'But Mum I bought the game! I'll show you the receipt … Oh no! I've lost it.'
• **mugging** 'I took Jane's iPod, but I didn't hurt her. I don't like violence and I've never hurt anyone.'
• **burglary** 'Honest, Officer, I'm not stealing these things, I'm just borrowing them.'

When Ned was accused of vandalism, he told Mrs Dibbs …

**5** In groups of four, follow the instructions on page 122.

## Tina Squires Case

Delia said she hadn't murdered Tina, that she had never killed anyone. I told her she was lying. I said she had lied about hearing a gunshot and that she had forgotten about the silencer on the gun. Then she changed her story. She said she had killed Tina. But she laughed and said that she wouldn't go to prison because I didn't have any evidence. I told her she would go to prison and then I played her the recording.

# WATCH OUT!

## There are con artists about!

We asked you to send in your letters about con tricks.

Here are the first three. More to come next week!

**A**

● I WAS in New York on holiday and I saw a crowd standing around a young man on a street. The man was holding up three playing cards, one of which was a Queen. He put the cards face down on a table and moved them around very quickly for a few seconds. Then he invited anyone in the crowd to 'find the lady' (the Queen). No one wanted to play, perhaps because they were scared of losing their money, but then a young woman <u>bet</u> $10 and won. It looked easy so I decided to try my luck. The first time I won and the second time too, but then I started losing. In the end I lost $90 before the young man <u>vanished</u> with my money. The young woman, who was clearly his <u>accomplice</u>, also disappeared. The truth is you can only beat a con artist when he wants you to win.

**Jon Wiggins, Blackpool**

**B**

● I WAS reading in the park when a man with a dog walked by. He asked me if I would look after his dog for an hour while he went to visit his sick mother in hospital. I said I would. After he left, another man walked by. 'Nice dog,' he said. He told me he was a vet and that the dog was very <u>valuable</u> and could cost as much as £1,000. When the first man returned from the hospital, he explained that he had just lost his job and was <u>hard up</u>. I offered to buy the dog and finally we agreed on a price of £200. I got the money from a <u>cashpoint</u> and paid the man. I really wanted to help him, but I also thought it was a fast way to make money. Later, I found out there was nothing special about the dog at all. I'd learnt an important lesson: there's no such thing as easy money.

**Marlene Rabanser, Swansea**

**C**

● A FEW months ago I received an email from a Mr Alika who said he worked for a bank in Nigeria. In the email he explained that three months before a foreigner had <u>deposited</u> $40 million in the bank. The next day the wealthy foreigner had died in a plane crash. The money was still in the bank. Mr Alika explained that he was writing to me because I had the same name and nationality as the dead man. He said that if I sent him $500, he would open an <u>account</u> in my name and transfer the $40 million to the new account. Then he promised we would <u>split</u> the money fifty-fifty. It was clearly a con, so I called the police straightaway.

**Nick Allenby, Montreal**

# READING AND VOCABULARY

**1** Look at the photo and use the phrases below to say what the man is doing.

cards   mix up   face down   cheat
choose a card   make money

**2** Read the newspaper letters page quickly and choose the correct definition for a con artist.

a a criminal who takes from the rich and gives to the poor (like Robin Hood).
b a prisoner who spends his time drawing, painting or making sculptures.
c someone who tricks or deceives people in order to get money from them.

**3** CD4.15 Read letters A–C, find the main idea of each one and match them with statements 1–5. There are two extra statements.

Con artists make you believe:
1 you are taking a risk. ☐
2 there's an easy way to win money. ☐
3 you have been specially chosen. ☐
4 something is worth more than it really is. ☐
5 you are punishing someone who deserves it. ☐

**4** Look at the underlined words in letters A and B. Decide what part of speech they are and put them in the table.

| Nouns | | |
|---|---|---|
| Verbs | | |
| Adjectives | | |

**5** Read the text before and after the underlined words in letters A and B, and use the context to work out their meanings. Complete these definitions.

1 A/An _____ is a machine you get money out of.
2 A/An _____ is a person who helps a criminal to commit a crime.
3 To _____ is to go away suddenly.
4 To _____ is to risk money on the result of a game, competition, or other future event.
5 If you don't have much money, you are _____ .
6 When something is worth a lot of money, we say it is _____ .

**6** Use Train Your Brain to work out the meaning of the underlined words in letter C. Check your answers in a dictionary.

> **TRAIN YOUR BRAIN | Reading skills**
>
> **Dealing with new words**
>
> When you come across new words in a text:
> 1 Don't panic – often you don't need them to understand the main ideas of the text.
> 2 Decide what part of speech they are.
> 3 Guess their meaning by looking carefully at the context.

**7** Read letters A–C again and choose the correct answers.

1 Jon Wiggins decided to play 'find the lady' because
a it was his turn.
b he thought he could win.
c the game looked like fun.
d he felt lucky.

2 When Marlene first met the man with the dog, she
a agreed to see his mother in hospital.
b told him she liked his dog.
c thought she could get some money from him.
d wanted to help him with a problem.

3 The man with the dog
a asked Marlene for £1,000.
b refused to sell his dog.
c accepted the first price Marlene offered him.
d wanted more money than Marlene first offered.

4 Mr Alika wrote to Nick Allenby to
a offer him a chance to steal some money.
b remind him he had $40 million in the bank.
c ask him if he knew who the rich foreigner was.
d tell him someone in his family had died.

5 Nick
a decided to send the money to Nigeria.
b knew immediately that Mr Alika was trying to cheat him.
c didn't want $40 million.
d wanted more than 50 percent of the money.

**8** Answer the questions in pairs.

1 Do you think the people who wrote letters A–C acted wisely? Why?/Why not?
2 Have you ever seen any films/watched any TV series/read any books about con artists? Which ones? What con tricks did they do?
3 Some people feel some admiration for the crimes that con artists commit. Why do you think that is? What do you feel?

**9** Form new pairs and report what your partners told you in Exercise 8. Use Reported speech.

# VOCABULARY | Crime

**1** CD4.16 Think Back! **Complete the table. Then listen and check.**

| Crime | Criminal | Action |
|---|---|---|
| 1 _____ | vandal | vandalise |
| 2 _____ | mugger | mug/rob/steal |
| 3 _____ | shoplifter | shoplift/rob/steal |
| theft | 4 _____ | rob/steal |
| robbery | 5 _____ | rob/steal |
| burglary | burglar | 6 _____ |
| murder | murderer | 7 _____ |

## Mind the trap!

We use the verbs *rob* and *steal* in a different way.

A criminal robs a person or a place.
The gang robbed three banks in one week.

A criminal steals something from a person or a place.
They stole more than $1 million.

**2** **Who does it? Match the people with the actions.**

a criminal ☐☐
a police officer ☐☐
a judge ☐☐

1 arrests somebody for a crime.
2 finds somebody guilty/innocent of a crime.
3 commits a crime.
4 accuses somebody of committing a crime.
5 breaks the law.
6 sentences somebody to twenty years in prison.

**3** **In groups, read the questionnaire. Then grade each idea/crime from 1 (not very serious) to 3 (very serious). Use the ideas below to discuss your answers.**

- It's/It's not (really) … annoying/common/ dangerous/serious/breaking the law/ committing a crime
- It's totally … dishonest/immoral/wrong/ unfair to other people
- Everybody does it.
- It can lead to more serious crimes.
- It causes a lot of damage.

**4** **In pairs, describe the photo and answer the questions.**

1 What is strange about this photo?
2 How big a problem is crime where you live?
3 Have you ever witnessed a crime? What happened?

### It's criminal

| | 1 | 2 | 3 |
|---|---|---|---|
| Cheating in an exam | ☐ | ☐ | ☐ |
| Computer-hacking (illegally entering a computer server) | ☐ | ☐ | ☐ |
| Fare dodging (travelling by public transport without a ticket) | ☐ | ☐ | ☐ |
| Shoplifting (stealing things from shops) | ☐ | ☐ | ☐ |
| Piracy (illegal copying of music, films, programs) | ☐ | ☐ | ☐ |
| Speeding (driving too fast) | ☐ | ☐ | ☐ |
| Vandalism (e.g. spraying graffiti on walls) | ☐ | ☐ | ☐ |

# LOST

6-MONTH / 3-YEAR OLD MALE /
FEMALE CHOW CHOW.

ANSWERS TO THE NAME OF MEESHOO / BENJI

PROBABLY LOST IN THE HAMILTON ROAD
AREA OF LONGTON ON MONDAY NOV 8TH.

PLEASE PHONE 05129777777 AND ASK
FOR FREYA / BECKY IF YOU HAVE ANY
INFORMATION.

## REWARD!

## SPEAKING AND WRITING

1 CD4.17 Listen to the conversation and choose the best options in the notice.

2 CD4.17 Study Speak Out. Then listen again and <u>underline</u> the expressions you hear.

---

**SPEAK OUT | Expressing feelings**

**Shock and surprise**
No way!
I don't believe it!
You're kidding!
Really? It can't be true!
I don't know what to say!
I'm (so) shocked!

**Fear**
I'm so worried!
I'm so scared!
I'm terrified!
I've never been so frightened in my life!

**Asking for explanations**
What's wrong?
What's the matter?
What's happened?

**Telling someone not to worry**
Don't be silly/scared!
Don't worry/panic!
Take it easy!

**Giving reassurance**
Cheer up!
It's not the end of the world.
Everything will be all right/OK.
(I'm sure) there's nothing to worry about!
There's probably a simple explanation.

---

3 CD4.18 Listen and repeat some of the phrases from Speak Out.

4 CD4.19 Listen to the dialogues and complete them with expressions from Speak Out. Then listen again and practise the dialogues in pairs.

1 **Boy** Oh no! Someone's stolen my motorbike!
**Girl** [shocked] _____

2 **Teacher** Congratulations! You got the highest mark in the exam.
**Student** [surprised] _____

3 **Little girl** Dad, I'm scared. I think there's a ghost. I heard a noise.
**Father** [telling her not to worry/ reassuring] _____

4 **Teacher** I'm afraid your son was cheating in the exam.
**Mother** [shocked] _____

5 **Man** Uh oh! One of them has got a gun!
**Woman** [fear] _____
**Man** [telling her not to worry] _____ They haven't seen us!

6 **Man** I think I've found your dog. It's Meeshoo, isn't it? He's fallen in love with my chow chow!
**Becky** [not believing] _____ !

5 In pairs, use alternative expressions from Speak Out to change the dialogues in Exercise 4. Then read your new dialogues to the rest of the class.

6 In pairs, use Speak Out to roleplay the conversation. Student A, look at page 123. Student B, look at page 124.

7 Write a notice about a lost mobile phone. Use the notice in Exercise 1 to help you.

• Mention the make/model/colour.
• Specify when and where you probably lost it.
• Give details so people can contact you.
• Say if there is a reward for finding it.

# Fit and well

**Read, listen and talk about** health and sport.
**Practise** modal verbs; the Second Conditional.
**Focus on** giving advice.
**Write** informal letters (openings).

**Harry** Uh! Darling! Could you come here, please?

**Carol** Do I have to? I'm watching television.

**Harry** Oh! Carol! Carol! Carol! I've got an awful pain in my chest. It says in my medical encyclopedia that the first signs of a heart attack are …

**Carol** You shouldn't read that book, Harry. It's probably just indigestion. You ate those sandwiches too quickly.

**Harry** But it's not just my chest. Feel my forehead. Maybe I've caught a dangerous virus too. And my throat is terribly red. Perhaps it's cancer of the …

**Carol** You've probably just got a cold and a sore throat. You should take an aspirin.

**Harry** An aspirin? What good is that going to do?

**Carol** My mother was right – Harry Hypochondriac she used to say. I'm going … I don't have to listen to this …

**Harry** Harry Hypochondriac indeed! I'm going to phone the doctor I am! Hello? Can I speak to Doctor Curtis, please? It's not possible?! But I must speak to him!
…
Hello? Oh, Dr Curtis. Hello, it's Harry Mac … Ah, you recognised me. I've got terrible pains in my … Oh?

**Carol** Well, what did he say?

**Harry** Dr Curtis says I have to stop reading my medical encyclopedia and …

**Carol** What else?

**Harry** He says that I mustn't phone him again!

# GRAMMAR AND VOCABULARY

**1** `CD4.20` In pairs, look at the photos. Is the man really ill? Listen and check.

**2** `CD4.20` Use a dictionary to check the meaning of the words. Then read and listen to the conversation in Exercise 1 again. Tick the problems which Harry thinks he has.

cancer ☐   indigestion ☐   a cold ☐
a sore throat ☐   a temperature ☐
a dangerous virus ☐   a heart attack ☐

## Work it out

**3** Find verbs 1–6 in the text in Exercise 2 and match them with their meanings a–e.

| | | |
|---|---|---|
| 1 shouldn't | ☐ | a It's a good idea to … |
| 2 should | ☐ | b It's not necessary to … |
| 3 don't have to | ☐ | c I'm not allowed to … |
| 4 must | ☐ | d It's not a good idea to … |
| 5 have to | ☐ | e It's necessary to … |
| 6 mustn't | ☐ | |

## Check it out

### Modal verbs

- *should* means something is a good idea
  You **should** take an aspirin.
  (It's a good idea to take an aspirin.)

- *shouldn't* means something isn't a good idea
  You **shouldn't** read that book.
  (It isn't a good idea to read that book.)

- *must* and *have to* mean something is necessary
  I **must** phone the doctor. (It is necessary to phone him.)
  He says I **have to** exercise more.
  (He says it is necessary for me to exercise more.)

- *don't have to* means something isn't necessary
  I **don't have to** listen to this.
  (It isn't necessary for me to listen to this.)

- *mustn't* means something is not allowed
  You **mustn't** phone me.
  (You're not allowed to phone me.)

**4** In pairs, read the advert and choose the correct answer.

---

### Mind the trap!

*Must* and *have to* both mean that it is necessary to do something but there is a difference between them.

*Must* means that the speaker personally feels that it is necessary to do something.
I **must** phone the doctor immediately! (I feel absolutely terrible!)

*Have to* means it is necessary to do something because it's a rule/the law or somebody else told the speaker to do something.
The doctor says I **have to** give up smoking.

**5** Complete the sentences with *must, mustn't, have to* or *don't have to*.

1 You _____ smoke in the hospital.
2 You _____ fill in all the form – your name and signature is enough.
3 I _____ remember to go to the pharmacy. I've got a sore throat.
4 I feel fine but my doctor tells me that I _____ take more exercise.
5 The sign says visitors _____ leave the hospital before 7 p.m.
6 Thanks but you really _____ help me – I can do it myself.
7 You _____ eat before your operation. It's dangerous!

**6** In pairs, write three sentences which give advice for each problem. Use the ideas below and *must/ mustn't/don't have to/should/shouldn't.*

- a broken leg
- a temperature/a fever
- a heart attack

---

call for an ambulance    lie down
take an aspirin    drink lots of water
see a doctor    take antibiotics
go to school/work    stay in bed
take some time off work    stop eating
ignore the problem    wear a bandage

---

If you have a fever, you must drink lots of water. You mustn't ignore the problem. You don't have to see a doctor.

## Bad Cold? Headache? Sore throat?

- You *shouldn't / have to* stop eating.
- You *should / mustn't* have a lot of hot drinks.
- You *must / shouldn't* stay in bed if you have a temperature.
- You *must / shouldn't* go to school or work.
- You *don't have to / must* see a doctor if you don't get better.

*And remember to take Citrocon, available without prescription from all good pharmacies!*

## VOCABULARY | Health problems

**1** [CD4.21] Look at pictures a–f and match them with the words below. Then listen and check.

hay fever ☐   backache ☐   toothache ☐
flu ☐   a headache ☐   stomachache ☐

**2** [CD4.21] In pairs, match problems 1–6 with the best advice a–f. Then listen and check.

1 a toothache ☐
2 hay fever ☐
3 stomachache ☐
4 flu ☐
5 a headache ☐
6 backache ☐

a Drink some peppermint tea.
b Take a painkiller and lie down.
c Stay indoors.
d Phone for a doctor.
e Take an aspirin.
f See a dentist.

**3** Read the questions and decide what the <u>underlined</u> words or phrases mean. Then answer the questions in pairs.

1 Which of the problems in Exercise 1 do you often <u>suffer from</u>? What do you usually do to help yourself?
2 When was the last time you <u>made an appointment</u> to see a doctor?
3 How often do you <u>go for a check-up</u> at the dentist's? Is this enough, in your opinion? Why?/Why not?
4 How do you usually feel before <u>having an injection</u>?
5 Have you ever <u>had an accident</u> while exercising/playing a sport? What happened?

## READING AND VOCABULARY

'**Can you tell me who won the last three World Cups?**'

**1** In pairs, look at the cartoon and answer the questions.

• What does the cartoon suggest the man is obsessed about?
• Do you know anyone with a similar obsession? What's your opinion of it?
• Is there a sport that you follow? Which local/national/international team do you support?

**2** [CD4.23] Read the article and choose the statement a–d which summarises it best.

a People who like football have incredible memories.
b Football fans behave in an unusual way, which can be very irritating.
c Some people are very passionate about football, but it can be dangerous for them.
d Being a football fan is bad for men's health but not for women's.

**106**

**Daily Sentinel**
Thursday 6th May | **OPINION**

# SPORTS MAD

by Sara Collins

They often have advice for some of the world's top referees and international football managers. They have opinions (usually negative) on most of the world's major football players. They can remember more scores than TV football commentators. And they probably haven't kicked a ball since primary school. Yes, it's that strange beast, the armchair football fan. In the same way that the back seat driver gives instructions to the driver in the front seat but may not even have a driving licence, the armchair football fan knows how to win every match but was probably the last person to be chosen for the school football team.

My brother is a very good example. Like all his friends, Ross never leaves the house without his football shirt, scarf, tracksuit trousers and trainers. Looking at him, you might think he was on his way to football training at the stadium. But no, the only exercise Ross does is when he occasionally has to run for the bus in the morning. He often complains that he has no head for remembering facts and isn't interested in History and yet he can remember that Aberdeen beat Lech Poznań 3–0 in the 1983 European Cup, twelve years before he was even born. He can remember who scored the second goal in the third match of last season but he finds it hard to memorise a few words for his French vocabulary tests.

Is it just a harmless obsession? In most cases, it probably is. I'm certainly not too worried about Ross at the moment. But we mustn't forget that there's also a more worrying side to being an armchair fan. Doctors say that you should exercise for at least half an hour, three times a week but statistics suggest that armchair sports fans are some of the unhealthiest people around and many are unwilling to exercise at all. What's more, watching sport can make you ill. Amazingly, doctors at Edinburgh Royal Infirmary, the city's major hospital, had to treat more than 150 patients who got ill while watching football at home during the 1998 World Cup. Problems included asthma, hyperventilation, heart attacks, temporary deafness and even mental problems. Similarly, researchers in the Netherlands found that the number of men who had heart attacks went up fifty percent on the day of an international football match. So it seems that although sport is good for us, being sports mad probably isn't.

**3** Read the article again and choose the correct answer.

**1** The author believes that typical armchair football fans
 **a** are probably friends with referees or football managers.
 **b** understand the game better than TV commentators.
 **c** are only interested in players from their own countries.
 **d** probably don't play football.

**2** An armchair football fan is similar to a back seat driver because they
 **a** spend a lot of time sitting down.
 **b** are both very talkative.
 **c** usually have more knowledge than skill.
 **d** are very big-headed.

**3** The author's brother
 **a** has a terrible memory.
 **b** wears sporty clothes.
 **c** hopes to become a professional football player.
 **d** is hopeless at French and History.

**4** It is true to say that
 **a** sports fans are as unhealthy as most other people.
 **b** you should exercise no more than an hour and a half a week.
 **c** many sports fans don't exercise even for short periods.
 **d** heart attacks are the most common problem for sports fans.

**4** Match the words 1–6 which collocate with phrases a–f.

**1** beat ☐    **a** a team
**2** football ☐    **b** a goal
**3** kick ☐    **c** a match
**4** score ☐    **d** a ball
**5** win/lose ☐    **e** Cup
**6** World ☐    **f** team/shirt/match/ manager/player

**5** In pairs, answer the questions.

**1** Do you consider yourself to be a 'sporty' person? Why?/Why not?
**2** Which sports do you particularly enjoy/not enjoy watching on TV?
**3** In your opinion, is it better to go to a football stadium to see a match or watch it live on TV? Why?
**4** Has your national team ever played in the World Cup? How did they do?

**107**

'You need to get some exercise, son.'

'Come to the pool with me, Kyle!'

'I haven't got enough time. If I had more time, I would do some _____ .'

'I don't know how to _____ . If I knew how to do it, I'd go with you, Kate.'

'Why don't you try this?'

'You spend too much time with that stupid machine!'

'It's really expensive. I'd play _____ if it wasn't so expensive.'

'It's always raining. I wouldn't play _____ so often if it didn't rain so much.'

## GRAMMAR AND SPEAKING

**1** Add the sports below to the correct category for you. Then compare your answers with a partner and use a dictionary to add more sports to each category.

aerobics   snowboarding   surfing   boxing
golf   horse-riding   baseball   scuba diving
bowling   hockey   basketball
skateboarding   mountain biking

Sports I've tried in real life

Sports I've tried in real life and on games consoles

Sports I've only tried on games consoles

Sports I've never tried

**2** Read what Kyle's friends and family tell him and complete his replies with the words below.

golf   sport   swim   video games

### Work it out

**3** Look at the sentences and answer the questions.

If I **had** more time, I **would do** some sport.
I **would play** golf if it **wasn't** so expensive.

1 Has Kyle got enough time for sport?
2 Is golf an expensive sport?
3 Do the underlined clauses describe real or unreal situations?
4 Which tense is used after *if* in these sentences?
5 Which verb is used before the infinitive in the other part of the sentence?

### Check it out

**The Second Conditional**

We use the Second Conditional to talk about:

- unreal situations in the present
  I wouldn't play video games so often if it didn't rain so much. (but it rains a lot so I often play video games)

- things that are unlikely or impossible to happen in the future (fantasies, unreal plans)
  If Kyle knew how to swim, he'd go with Kate. (but he doesn't know how to swim so he won't go with her)
  What would you do if you were Kyle? (you're not Kyle)

| The condition | The result |
|---|---|
| *If* + Past Simple, | *would* + infinitive |

**Mind the trap!**

With the Second Conditional we often use *were* – instead of *was* – after *I*, *he*, *she* and *it*, especially in written English or formal situations.

I would go for a run if I weren't so tired.

If it were nearer my house, I'd go to that gym.

**4** Complete these Second Conditional sentences with the correct form of the verbs in brackets.

1 If I _____ (be) taller, I _____ (play) basketball.
2 If she _____ (have) more money, she _____ (join) a gym.
3 I _____ (try) to get more exercise if I _____ (be) you.
4 We _____ (go) hiking this weekend if we _____ (not have) an exam on Monday.
5 You _____ (not feel) so stressed out if you _____ (play) sport more often.
6 If there _____ (be) a swimming pool near here, _____ (you go) swimming more often?

**5** Which sports from Exercise 1 would you like to try? In pairs, make sentences using the ideas to help you.

- live nearer the mountains/the sea
- have enough money
- have someone to go with
- be braver/fitter/better at/not so clumsy …
- have more free time

If I were better at swimming, I'd love to try scuba diving.

**6** In pairs, think of excuses for not doing these things using the Second Conditional.

1 Let's go bungee jumping!
  I'm scared of heights. If I wasn't scared of heights, I'd go bungee jumping.
2 Do you want to go sailing with me?
3 Why don't you train for a marathon!
4 How about going windsurfing this weekend?
5 Would you like to try kick boxing?
6 I'm going skiing. Do you want to come?
7 Let's play sports on the games console!

**7** In groups, answer the questions below.

- If you had to choose between playing your favourite sport in real life, playing it on a games console or watching it on TV, what would you do?
- If you could be any famous sports star, who would you choose to be? Why?
- If you had the opportunity to take part in any extreme sport, which would you choose?
- If a doctor told you that you had to lose weight and get fit, what would you do?

**109**

## SPEAKING

**1** In pairs, look at the picture and answer the questions.

- How does the girl feel? Why does she feel like that?
- What would you do if you were in her situation?
- How do you usually feel on Monday mornings? What is your routine like?

**2** *CD4.24* Listen to the radio programme and choose the correct answers.

1 Dr Moody is
  a a TV and radio presenter.
  b a university professor.
  c a doctor and psychologist.

2 He says
  a Chris's problem is unusual.
  b people get depressed because they have to get up early on Mondays.
  c listening to music can make Monday mornings better.

3 He suggests getting up early in order to
  a do some work.
  b get some exercise.
  c study.

4 In his opinion, on Monday evenings you should
  a relax at home.
  b do something special.
  c find something pleasant to do at work.

**110**

**3** *CD4.24* Study Speak Out. Then listen again and fill in the expressions Dr Moody uses in the gaps below. In pairs, say what you think of his advice.

To make Monday mornings more pleasant …
1 _____ get up an hour earlier than usual.
2 _____ listen to your favourite CD.
3 _____ go for a walk or a run.
4 _____ do something nice on Monday evenings.
5 _____ make a list of things to do for the next week on Friday.

---

### SPEAK OUT | Advice

**Asking for advice**
What should I do?
Could you give me some advice?
Have you any ideas about how to [+ infinitive] …?
Have you any tips on how to …?

**Giving advice**
If I were you, I'd …
I (don't) think you should …
You should/shouldn't …
(I think) it's/it isn't a good idea to …
It's better (not) to …
Why don't you [+ infinitive]?

---

**4** *CD4.25* Listen and repeat some of the phrases from Speak Out.

**5** *CD4.26* In pairs, complete the sentences with phrases from Speak Out. Then listen and check.

Amy      I want to live to be a hundred. Could ¹_____ ?
Dr Moody  Well, I think you ²_____ get some exercise. It isn't ³_____ go everywhere by car. It ⁴_____ cycle or walk. You ⁵_____ also eat more fruit and vegetables. And if ⁶_____ stop smoking.
Amy      That's easy to say, but have ⁷_____ on ⁸_____ do that?
Dr Moody  Why ⁹_____ go and see a hypnotist?

**6** In groups, use phrases from Speak Out and the prompts below to think of advice to help people live to be a hundred. Then look at page 122 to check.

take vitamins   drink alcohol   sleep a lot
smoke   watch TV   stay thin   get exercise
eat fast food   go out at night   stay single
play professional sport   get married
drink a lot of water   have a lot of friends

**7** Would you like to live to be a hundred? Why?/ Why not?

# WRITING | Opening paragraph

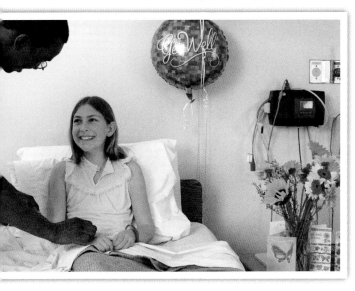

**1** Look at the picture and answer the questions.

1 Where is the girl? Why do you think she is there?
2 How would you feel if you were in her situation?
3 What would you do to help the time pass faster?

**2** Read the email to Becky from her classmates. What's the situation and what advice do you think she asked for? Choose the correct phrases.

```
NEW MESSAGE                                    =✉

To:       becky_davids@mailbox.con
From:     sam25@mailbox.con
Subject:  Get well soon!
```

Hi Becky,

We're all so glad you're feeling better. In less than a month you'll be out of hospital and back with us in the classroom! You'll catch up in no time, but here are a few suggestions.

First of all, ¹*why don't you / you shouldn't* contact our form tutor and explain the problem? I'm sure she'll be sympathetic. Also, ²*I think you should / it isn't a good idea to* read Hamlet. Mrs Dewar said the final exam is going to be on Shakespeare. Finally, ³*it's better not to / I think you should* relax. At the end of the day, your health is the most important thing.

Good luck!
Sam

PS. Ali, Karen, Gwen, Mark and Chris send their love. We all miss you!

**SEND**

**3** In pairs, look at the first paragraph in the email and answer the questions. Then look at Train Your Brain to check.

1 How many sentences are there? Are they short or long?
2 Why has Sam written the email? Is it clear from the first paragraph?
3 What is the connection between the third sentence and the second paragraph?

---

**TRAIN YOUR BRAIN | Writing skills**

**The opening paragraph in informal letters and emails**

**1** It's often a good idea to show interest in the person you're writing to, e.g. by referring to the last time you were in contact or to some recent news. Use these expressions:
I'm so glad that …    Thanks for …
Congratulations on …    Have you heard …?
I hope you're well.    I'm sorry for …
It was great to hear from you again.
**2** Explain why you're writing. (*This is just a quick note to … / I wonder if you …*)
**3** Don't write too much, it's better to be concise.
**4** Connect the last sentence with the subject of the second paragraph.

**4** Form three opening paragraphs by matching sentences a–f below with first sentences 1–3.

**First sentences**
1 Thanks for the postcard. ☐ ☐
2 It was great to hear from you again after so long. ☐ ☐
3 This is just a quick note to thank you for the present. ☐ ☐

**Second sentences**
a It was nice of you to remember my birthday.
b I'm glad you're enjoying your holiday in France.
c I'm really pleased you want to come back here to work.

**Third sentences**
d I'm going to have a party when the exams are over and I hope you can come.
e I've got a few tips for you on how to find a job.
f Give me a call when you get back home.

**5** Which of the sentences d–f lead into a second paragraph which offers advice?

**6** Read texts a and b and think of some good advice for each case.

**a**
**Message:**
I'm sorry for not writing back sooner, but I've been really busy. I've got an exam next week and I'm really worried about it. Could you give me some advice on what to do the evening before a big exam?

**SEND**

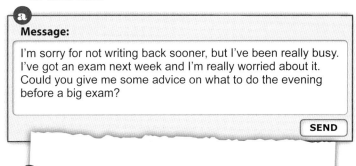

**b** I wonder if you can help me. I need to lose weight and get fit but I don't have much time or money. What should I do?

**7** Write replies to a and b above. Use Train Your Brain and Speak Out on page 110 to help you. Give advice in the second paragraph of each reply.

## VOCABULARY AND GRAMMAR

**1** Complete the sentences. For each gap write one word. The first letter of each word is given. (9 points)

1 If you've got toothache, make an **a**_____ to see the **d**_____ .
2 I've got a **t**_____ , a terrible **h**_____ and a **s**_____ throat. Maybe I've got the flu.
3 The football **c**_____ criticised the **r**_____ for his controversial decision.
4 He's mad about **s**_____ and usually spends the weekends on his boat in the Lake District.
5 She's really keen on water sports, especially **w**_____ .

**2** Match 1–6 with a–f to make collocations and compound nouns. (6 points)

1 accuse sb ☐    a a crime
2 break ☐    b of a crime
3 cheat ☐    c hacking
4 commit ☐    d in an exam
5 go to ☐    e the law
6 computer ☐    f prison

**3** Read the email. For each gap choose the correct answer. (6 points)

✕ NEW MESSAGE                                    ≡ ✉

To:       ann@town.ox.uk
From:     julie@village.ox.uk
Subject:  We're back home

Hi Ann,

At last we're back from our holidays! We got home early on Saturday morning, tired but happy. But when we opened the front door, I couldn't believe my eyes. I ¹___ anything like it before! Our house had been burgled! I immediately phoned our neighbours, the Simpsons. They told me that the police ²___ a young man in our street. Later on, in the afternoon we ³___ by a young policewoman. She ⁴___ us that we had forgotten to lock the back door! We ⁵___ really be more careful in the future.

I ⁶___ finish now, there's somebody at the door.

Take care
Julie

[SEND]

1 a never saw       b was never seen
  c had never seen
2 a have already caught    b caught already
  c had already caught
3 a interviewed     b were interviewed
  c had interviewed
4 a told      b was told      c was telling
5 a shouldn't      b should      c mustn't
6 a had to      b don't have to      c have to

**4** Complete the sentences so that they have the same meaning as the original sentences. (5 points)

1 'But Jane … Tom doesn't like extreme sports.'
  I told Jane that _____
  _____ .
2 'The thieves have robbed four banks in one week!'
  The police reported that the thieves _____
  _____ .
3 'Mr Cross, you murdered Ben Box!'
  The lawyer said _____
  _____ .
4 'You will never catch me!'
  The man said that the police _____
  _____ .
5 'Watson, the women aren't guilty!'
  Sherlock Holmes told Dr Watson _____
  _____ .

**5** Complete the sentences so that they have the same meaning as the original sentences. (4 points)

1 He's a hypochondriac. He feels ill all the time.
  If he _____
  _____ .
2 He has asthma and has to take a lot of medicines.
  If he _____
  _____ .
3 She often breaks promises so people don't trust her.
  If she _____
  _____ .
4 She doesn't go to the gym very often. She's not very fit.
  If she _____
  _____ .

## PRONUNCIATION

**6** CD4.27 Listen and put the words in the box in the correct column. Then listen, repeat and check.

| voiced /ð/ | voiceless /θ/ |
|---|---|
| brother | anthem |
|  |  |

both   north   other   than   thank   there
thing   birthday   together   tooth
weather   without

## a CAMP NOU

The Camp Nou is a football stadium in Barcelona, Spain. It is the largest stadium in Europe and the tenth largest in the world. Many international matches are played there. The FC Barcelona museum is considered the best football museum in the world. There are multi-media displays about the club and its history as well as a fantastic panoramic view of the stadium. The Camp Nou is also a place where you can enjoy major concerts and other non-football events.

## b Beijing National Stadium

Beijing National Stadium, also called the Bird's Nest, is a stadium in China. It was designed for use during the 2008 Summer Olympics and Paralympics. It is the world's largest steel structure. It has a four-star hotel with eighty rooms, an elegant restaurant with views of the athletics track, and an underground shopping centre. The stadium has recently been transformed into a centre for winter sports.

## c Wembley Stadium

Wembley Stadium is located in Wembley Park in London, England. The England national football team play most of their home matches here. The stadium is also used for other sporting events. It is the second largest stadium in Europe (after Camp Nou) and one of the largest and tallest in the world, with every seat under a roof. It was very expensive to build.

## d Maracanã Stadium

Maracanã Stadium is an open-air stadium in Rio de Janeiro, Brazil. It was opened in 1950 for the FIFA World Cup. Since then, it has mainly been used for football matches between the major football clubs in Rio de Janeiro. It is the largest stadium in South America.

## READING SKILLS

**7** Read the descriptions of four famous stadiums and the statements below. Match statements 1–10 with descriptions a–d.  (10 points)

1 This stadium is the biggest steel structure in the world. ☐
2 Sporting events for disabled athletes took place there. ☐
3 You can learn a lot about a famous football team if you visit this stadium. ☐
4 Local football teams usually play here. ☐
5 Sports fans can eat an expensive meal at this stadium. ☐
6 It is the biggest stadium on the European continent. ☐
7 Fans are protected from bad weather at this stadium. ☐
8 You can visit various shops here. ☐
9 If you're keen on skating, visit this stadium. ☐
10 People sometimes come here to watch events that are not connected with sport. ☐

## SPEAKING SKILLS

**8** Roleplay the conversation.

Your two English-speaking friends are staying with you for the weekend. Decide what you should do together. Choose from the list below and give reasons for your choice.
• Go skateboarding
• Go bowling
• Watch a football match on TV
• Play basketball
• Go to a swimming pool
• Go hiking
• Go horse-riding

## WRITING SKILLS

**9** Follow the instructions and write a notice.

During your summer language course in Bath, you lose a bag with your personal belongings and medicine which you need to take every day. Write a notice in which you:
• describe the bag and say why it is important for you to find it.
• write where you think you lost it.
• give contact details.

# CULTURE SHOCK 1

## EDUCATION IN BRITAIN

**Glossary**   attend school   Bachelor's degree
compulsory   corporal punishment   gap year
nursery school/playgroup   optional   P.E.
pre-school education   school uniform
specialise

**1** In pairs, look at the table and answer the questions.

1 How old are children in England when they start their education?

2 At what age can they legally finish their education?

3 How many years of compulsory education do students have before they take their school-leaving exams (A-levels)?

4 How old are most students when they finish university?

**2** CD4.28 **Listen to five school-leavers talking about secondary-school life. Match the speakers with the topics. There are two answers that you don't need.**

1 Frank   ☐
2 Kirsty   ☐
3 Jo   ☐
4 Rob   ☐
5 Naomi   ☐

a The school day
b Physical Education (P.E.)
c Different types of school
d School uniform
e School clubs and societies
f Punishments
g Subjects

## THE ENGLISH SCHOOL SYSTEM

| Typical Age | Type of Education | Type of School | School Years and Exams |
|---|---|---|---|
| 3–4 | **Pre-School Education** This is not compulsory but 47% of children attend. | Nursery School/Playgroup | |
| 4/5–10 | **Primary Education** | Primary School | Year 1–Year 6 |
| 11–18 | **Secondary Education** At present students can leave school after Year 11 (16 years old) but more than 50% continue education for two years (Years 12 and 13). The school-leaving age will go up to 17 in 2013 and 18 in 2015. | **Secondary School** (Usually Comprehensive schools which are for students of all abilities.) Some students choose to study for their A-levels at Colleges of Further Education. | Year 7– Year 11 *GCSEs   Year 12–Year 13 *A-levels |
| 19–22 | **Higher Education** About 40% of 19-year-olds enter higher education. | **University** Three or four years which finish with a Bachelor's degree – many students take a break (a gap year) before they start university. | |

**Exams**

*GCSEs   General Certificate of Secondary Education – Students usually take GCSEs in five to ten subjects at the age of 16.

*A-levels   Advanced Level – Students usually take two or three subjects at the age of 18. You usually need A-levels to go to university.

# School life

S ome aspects of school life date back to the nineteenth century. One example is the school assembly, a meeting of the whole school every morning before classes. Another is school uniform, which is still very common – about [1] *fifteen percent / fifty percent* of pupils in England wear school uniform.

The school day in both primary and secondary schools is fixed – the first lesson begins at 9.15 a.m. and classes end at [2] *2.30 p.m. / 3.30 p.m.* every day. Classes on Saturdays are very unusual.

Compared with many countries, pupils in England specialise quite early. Pupils study many subjects until the age of fourteen, but then they usually study only three subjects during the last [3] *two / three* years of school. Sport is an important part of school life. P.E. is compulsory. Typically boys play football or rugby in winter and cricket in spring; and girls usually do aerobics or play [4] *basketball / netball*.

England was one of the last countries to stop using corporal punishment in schools (it only became illegal in 1985). Nowadays teachers can punish their students with lines or detention, which means that students have to [5] *stay after school / do extra homework.*

A university graduation day

Students at a secondary school

An English primary school

**3** CD4.28 Read the text and choose the correct words. Then listen again and check your answers.

**4** In pairs, look at your answers to Exercise 3. How is life in English schools different from schools in your country?

**5** Crossing Cultures. In groups, answer the question. Use your answers to Exercises 1 and 4 and the ideas below to help you.

'Is there anything in the English education system that you think is a particularly good or bad idea compared with your country? Why?'

too old/young    liberal    long/short childhood    a big/small percentage
strict    fair/unfair    a large/small choice of subjects    optional/compulsory
more exams    start your first job    specialise early/late    mature/immature

A I think school uniform is a good idea. You don't have to worry about wearing really fashionable clothes every day.

B I think children in England are too young when they start school. Their childhood is really short!

**115**

# CULTURE SHOCK 2

## Fascinating places and events across the country

### Where in the UK can you …

1 see from one side of the country to the other?
2 enjoy one of the world's finest surfing beaches?
3 travel back in time to watch a Shakespeare play?
4 meet rich and famous people (and some horses too)?
5 attend a huge cultural festival and not hear a word of English?

When most people go to the theatre, they sit down to enjoy the play. However, 400 years ago it was very different. Only rich people could pay for a seat in William Shakespeare's **Globe Theatre**. Poorer people paid a penny to stand in front of the stage. They were called 'groundlings'. A replica of the Globe opened in 1997 and now shows Shakespeare plays from May to September. Seats cost £12–£33, but groundlings only pay £5. And they get the best view too!

**Ben Lawers** is not a very high mountain; it is only 1,214 metres above sea level. However, on a clear day from the top you can see both the Atlantic Ocean to the west and the North Sea to the east. The UK is a long narrow country and the distance from coast to coast in this part of Scotland is just over 150 km.

When you think of surfing, you think of Hawaii or Australia, not the UK. But **Fistral Beach** in Newquay, Cornwall is one of the best surfing beaches in the world. The beach is long (750 m), straight and offers the high waves that surfers love. International surfing competitions take place there and you can hire surfboards and wetsuits if you want to try it yourself.

Horse racing is popular in the UK and every June over 300,000 people go to the races at **Royal Ascot**. The meeting, which dates from 1711, is an important event for the British social elite and the Queen and other members of the royal family always attend. Many spectators seem more interested in their clothes, particularly their hats, than they are in the horses.

An **eisteddfod** is a Welsh arts festival in which singers, poets, dancers, actors and musicians participate in competitions. It is an ancient tradition that dates from the 12th century or earlier. The International Eisteddfod is in Llangollen in July, but the most important eisteddfod is the eight-day-long National Eisteddfod of Wales in August. It is Europe's largest competitive festival of music and poetry. The participants speak only in Welsh.

**E** The Globe

4 **CD4.29** Listen again and decide which place from Exercise 1 the people are visiting in each situation.

1 _____
2 _____
3 _____
4 _____

5 **Crossing Cultures.** Work in groups and follow the instructions using the phrases below to help you.

- Individually, think of a fascinating place or event in your country and write a question about it: *Where in _____ can you …?*
- Ask your group your question and see if they can guess the place or event you're thinking of.
- Give them a clue every time they guess wrong.
- Discuss which place or event in your questions you would prefer to visit. Say why.

**Questions**

dress up… mix with… listen to…
take part in … see historic buildings/narrow
streets … attend … travel back in time to…
enjoy the nightlife/shopping/countryside/
wonderful views

**Clues**

it's in the north-west/south-east/centre …
It's open from … to … theatre …
It's famous for its cathedral/museums/
You can hire … The university/castle/palace
dates from the … th century
A street market/music festival/sports
competition takes place there every year

**D** Royal Ascot

# WHERE IN THE UK CAN YOU …?

Glossary coast competitive date from
replica sea level spectators stage
take place waves

1 Match questions 1–5 above with photos A–E. Then read the texts to check your answers.

2 Read the texts again and answer the questions below. Sometimes there is more than one answer. Then say which of the places or events you would like to go to and why.

Which place or event:
1 has winners and losers?
2 is an exact copy of an older place?
3 do you need to be fit to enjoy?
4 offers an artistic performance?
5 first took place about 300 years ago?
6 can you enjoy at any time in the year?

3 **CD4.29** Listen and match each extract with the situation. There is one extra situation.

☐ ☐ ☐ ☐ ☐

Asking for directions
In a taxi
On a guided tour
In a hotel reception
Asking for travel information

**A** Fistral Beach

**B** The Eisteddfod

**C** Ben Lawers

# CULTURE SHOCK3

## THE LONDON UNDERGROUND

The London Underground or the Tube is the world's oldest underground railway: the first line, the Metropolitan, opened in 1863. It is also the longest metro system in the world with about 400 km of track and 270 stations. It carries more than a billion passengers every year, making it the third busiest underground system in Europe after Moscow and Paris.

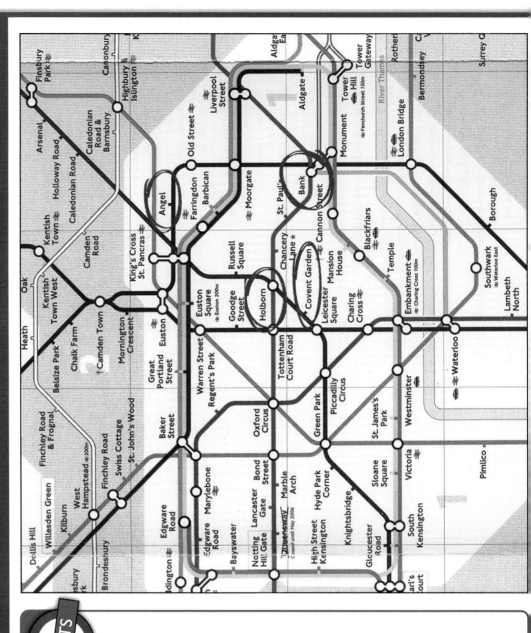

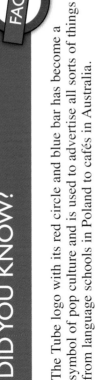

## DID YOU KNOW?

**FACTS**

The Tube logo with its red circle and blue bar has become a symbol of pop culture and is used to advertise all sorts of things from language schools in Poland to cafés in Australia.

The Tube map was designed by Harry Beck in 1933. He believed that passengers were only interested in how to get from one station to another and where to change lines, and didn't care if the map was realistic or not. So he drew a map that did not show real distances but was simple to read. His idea has inspired many similar maps around the world.

During the Second World War Tube stations were used as shelters to protect Londoners from German bombs.

The longest line is the Central line. It is 74 km long and it takes 1 hour 28 minutes to go from one end to the other.

The longest escalator in Western Europe (318 steps) is at Angel station. It takes 80 seconds to carry passengers up or down.

On average the air in the London Underground is 10°C hotter than the air outside. Temperatures as high as 47°C were reported in the summer of 2006.

There are perhaps half a million mice living in the London Underground. You can often see them running around the tracks.

There are also stories of ghosts living in the Underground. On the platforms of Bank station the 'Black Nun' looks for her brother, a bank worker who was executed in 1811. And an Ancient Egyptian walks a secret tunnel from the Egyptian room of the British Museum to Holborn station.

# GOING UNDERGROUND

Glossary    escalator    line    logo    Mind the gap!    passenger
platform    railway    rucksack    rush hour    shelter    single ticket
standard fare    track    tunnel

1    **Look at the map and read the text. Then answer questions 1–8.**

1  How old is the London Underground?

2  Are there any other metro systems in the world which are busier, longer or
   older than the London Tube? If so, which ones?

3  Why did Harry Beck not draw the real distances between stations on his
   Tube map?

4  What other function for Tube stations is mentioned in the text?

5  How many lines do you have to take to go from Covent Garden to the
   station with Europe's longest escalator?

6  Which type of animal can you find on the Tube? How many of them are there?

7  There are two ghosts living in the longest line in the Tube. What's the name of
   the line and what colour is it on the map?

2    **Work in pairs. Which things in the text do you find most surprising? Why?**

3    CD4.30 **In pairs, read the Dos and Don'ts and say why you think they're good advice.
     Then listen and check.**

4    **Crossing Cultures. In groups, write a list of Dos and Don'ts for travelling on public
     transport where you live.**

*Don't buy standard fare single tickets because they're more expensive
than other tickets.*

* Avoid the rush hour.
* Stand on the right on the
  escalators.
* Look before you sit down.
* Keep away from the doors.
* Mind the gap!

* Don't buy standard fare single
  tickets.
* Don't always believe the map.
* Don't read other people's
  books or newspapers.
* Don't travel with a big rucksack
  on your back.
* Don't put your bags on a seat.

# Student activities

Unit 1, Vocabulary, Exercise 6, page 10.

**CD1.8** Listen to the song and complete gaps a–i with phrases 1–9.

1 I'm someone filled with self-belief
2 Sometimes I'm not sure who I am
3 Sometimes I make no sense
4 Sometimes I'm miserable
5 I've got all the answers
6 Sometimes I'm perfect
7 I like to be by myself
8 I hate to be alone
9 I am special

Then, in pairs, discuss if the girl in the song is happy. Say why.

## I Am

I'm an angel, I'm a devil
I am sometimes in between
I'm as bad as it can get and good as it can be
Sometimes I'm a million colours
Sometimes I'm black and white, I am all extremes
Try to figure me out, you never can
There's so many things I am

*Chorus*
a _____ , I am beautiful, I am wonderful
*And powerful, unstoppable*
b _____ , sometimes I'm pitiful
*But that's so typical of all the things I am*

c _____ , I'm haunted by self-doubt
d _____ , I've got nothing figured out
e _____ , f _____

I'm up and I am down but that's part of the thrill
Part of the plan, part of all of the things I am

*Chorus*

I'm a million contradictions, g _____
h _____ , sometimes I'm a mess
i _____

*Chorus (×2)*

Of all the things I am
Sometimes I'm miserable, sometimes I'm pitiful
But that's so typical of all the things I am
Of all the things I am

Unit 1, Grammar and Writing, Exercise 3, page 11.

Quiz results

| |
|---|
| **8–10 ticks**<br>You are a very outgoing, extrovert person – you love being spontaneous and enjoy being the centre of attention. Some people find you too dominating – but you don't care. |
| **4–7 ticks**<br>You are fairly outgoing and enjoy spending time with other people. |
| **0–3 ticks**<br>You are an introvert – you are a rather shy person and enjoy peace and quiet |

Unit 2, Reading and Listening, Exercise 8, page 16.

**Work in groups of three or four and follow the instructions.**

• You have two weeks to travel around Europe with an InterRail Pass. You can travel as much as you want in any of the countries on the map on page 17. You are planning to sleep on the train or stay in youth hostels.
• Choose a city you want to start your trip in and the places you want to visit. Stay for two or three days in the places that interest you more. Also decide which things from Exercise 2 on page 16 to take with you.
• Tell the class about your plans for your InterRail holiday.

We're starting our trip in … We're going to stay there for … nights. Then we're travelling to … We're going to take …

Unit 4, Reading, Exercise 7, page 35.

**Look at the photo. In pairs, answer the questions. Use these ideas to help you.**

revising before an exam    tired    stay up late
sleepy    stressed    drink coffee    memorise

1 What is the person doing? Why?
2 How do you think he is feeling?
3 Before an important exam, do you prefer to study all night or go to bed early? Why?

Unit 4, Writing, Exercise 5, page 39.

Check your answers to the email on page 39.

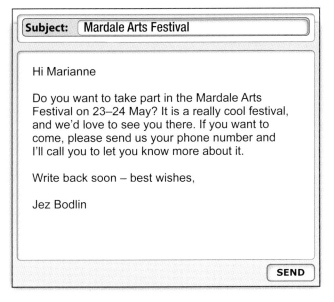

| Subject: | Mardale Arts Festival |

Hi Marianne

Do you want to take part in the Mardale Arts Festival on 23–24 May? It is a really cool festival, and we'd love to see you there. If you want to come, please send us your phone number and I'll call you to let you know more about it.

Write back soon – best wishes,

Jez Bodlin

SEND

Unit 5, Vocabulary, Exercises 4 and 5, page 47.

CD2.15 Read the text and choose the correct words. Then listen and check. What kind of room is the person describing?

I really love this room – it's very bright and [1] *cosy / uncomfortable*. It's [2] *downstairs / upstairs* on the first floor. You get a wonderful view of the trees in the back garden from the window. There's a big [3] *skylight / attic* too, so you get a lot of sunshine in here in the mornings, which I love. It's not very [4] *roomy / tiny* but I think it's big enough for one person. It can be rather cold in winter, so I have to turn on the [5] *freezer / heater* sometimes.

I like the decoration; it's quite tasteful. There are a lot of colourful posters on the [6] *floor / door* and an [7] *ugly / attractive* old Indian rug. There's a lamp in the corner, a large desk where I keep my computer and printer and a [8] *chest of drawers / bookshelf* for my books. There's a comfortable old [9] *armchair / stool* too.

Sometimes I sit and listen to music in the evenings, especially when my girlfriend goes to bed early. But most of the time I work in here. I'm finishing my studies so I've got a lot of work to do. I used to just work in the bedroom but we decided it was better to have another room where I could work in peace.

Unit 5, Speaking, Exercise 3, page 48.

Read the description and answer the questions on page 48.

The photo shows a housing estate in a city. I don't know where it is exactly but it might be somewhere in Europe. Perhaps it's in Germany or it might be Sweden. There are some blocks of flats – one on the left and some more in the background. The blocks of flats look really colourful and there is a lot of grass and trees. Some of the balconies have flowers on them. There might be a school with a playground on the right but I'm not sure. In the foreground there's a woman with a big rucksack. She's wearing shorts and a sun hat and she's walking through the estate. She looks like a typical tourist. It's surprising because the housing estate doesn't look like a typical place for tourists to visit. Perhaps she's lost! The estate seems quiet and pleasant – it's probably quite a nice place to live.

Unit 8, Grammar and Reading, Exercise 3, page 68.

Check your scores. Then compare your results with a partner.

Points

| 1 | A 50 | B 5  |   | 5 | A 5  | B 40 |
|---|------|------|---|---|------|------|
| 2 | A 10 | B 25 |   | 6 | A 10 | B 25 |
| 3 | A 20 | B 10 |   | 7 | A 5  | B 50 |
| 4 | A 20 | B 10 |   | 8 | A 30 | B 5  |

Results

| Points | Ideal jobs |
|--------|-----------|
| 60–90 | librarian, therapist, priest, accountant, scientist, nurse |
| 91–150 | engineer, computer programmer, pilot, police officer, doctor, architect |
| 151–220 | psychologist, writer, translator, fashion designer, teacher, musician |
| 221–250 | businessman/woman, lawyer, judge, salesperson, insurance agent, marketing manager |
| 251+ | company director, banker, politician, TV presenter, reporter, actor |

Unit 10, Writing, Exercise 8, page 93.

Check your answers to Vicky's reply to Pete on page 93.

Pete

Meeting my cousin on Saturday evening so can't go. Want to meet for a coffee on Sunday at 3? Will be upstairs in Toni's. Let me know if you can't come.

Vicky xxx

Unit 11, Grammar and Reading, Exercise 7, page 97.

Look at the pictures of Kay's flat and answer the questions on page 97.

Before the burglary

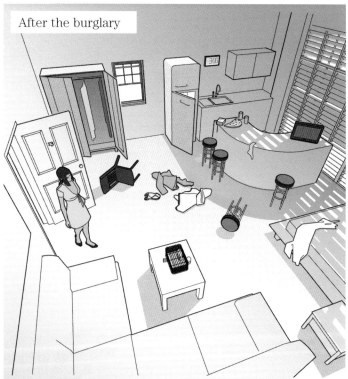

After the burglary

Unit 11, Grammar, Exercise 5, page 99.

In groups of four, follow the instructions.

- Form two pairs and answer questions 1–4.
- Form two new pairs and do it again, but this time *change one or more of your answers*.
- Talk to the last person in your group and compare what your first two partners told you. Are there any differences?

1 Have you ever seen a crime? How did you feel? What happened?
2 Do you like TV detectives? If so, which ones?
3 Do you think people will always commit crimes?
4 Are you thinking of joining the police when you leave school? Why?/Why not?

A Anna said that she had never seen a crime.
B Yes, she told me that too ... She said that she loved watching CSI.
A Really? She told me she hated TV detectives.

Unit 12, Speaking, Exercise 6, page 110.

Check your answers to think of advice to help people live to be a hundred.

# *health*
## Ten tips to live to be a hundred

**1** To live a long and healthy life it is important to keep your weight down. In general, people in developed countries eat too much and should try to eat less.

**2** You should eat less meat and processed foods and more fresh fruit and vegetables.

**3** It is not necessary to take a lot of vitamin supplements.

**4** Fish oil, which contains a lot of Omega 3, is very good for you.

**5** It is not a good idea to smoke or to drink alcohol.

**6** You should try to drink a lot of water, at least a litre a day.

**7** You should take regular exercise, but you shouldn't push your body too far.

**8** People with a lot of friends and close family contacts tend to live longer, but going out to party every night is not a good idea.

**9** Men who are married live longer, but for women it's better to stay single.

**10** It's good for you to sleep well, but it isn't necessary to sleep more than eight hours a night. Many older people survive perfectly well with only four or five hours' sleep a night.

# Student A activities

Unit 2, Speaking and Listening, Exercise 8, page 18.

**Student A**
Follow the instructions. Use Speak Out on page 18 to help you. Start the conversation.

You are spending a long weekend at a youth hostel in the mountains. You are discussing your plans for the next day.

- Make a suggestion: go fishing tomorrow.
- Politely reject your friend's suggestion.
- Suggest an alternative: go for a long walk.

Unit 6, Grammar and Vocabulary, Exercise 7, page 51.

## FACT BOX

### THE MELANDER FAMILY OF BARGTEHEIDE, GERMANY

| | |
|---|---|
| They buy a lot of … | oranges, cabbage, beef, milk, yoghurt, cream, ham, mineral water, fruit juice, bread, muesli, cocoa. |
| They buy too much/many … | beer, frozen pizzas. |
| They buy some … | apples, bananas, tomatoes, onions, potatoes, pork, cheese, ice cream, wine, coffee, tea, pasta, flour. |
| They don't buy much/many … | eggs, grapes, bacon, fish, olives, tinned food. |
| They buy a few/a little … | mushrooms, croissants, chocolate, cake, butter. |
| They don't buy any … | chicken, prawns, jam, sweets, chewing gum. |

**Student A**

1 Study the fact box about the weekly food shopping of this family.
2 Answer your partner's questions and tell him/her about what they eat and drink. Use the phrases from Check it out on page 51 to help you.
3 Then ask questions about meat, fruit, drinks, etc. to find out about the food shopping of the family your partner has information on.
4 Guess what country they are from (*China, Greenland* or *Poland*) and say if their diet is healthy or not.

Unit 8, Listening and Speaking, Exercise 7, page 73.

**Student A**
Follow the instructions. Use Speak Out on page 73 to help you.

Your name is Martin/Martha McKenzie. You are looking for a summer job. Your friend Lily told you that a friend of hers, Jacob, has some information about a job in a hotel in England. Call Jacob to find out about the job. If he's not there, leave a message for him.

- say who you are
- say why you are calling
- ask him to get in touch with you
- spell your name and leave your phone number

Unit 11, Speaking and Writing, Exercise 6, page 103.

**Student A**
Follow the instructions. Use Speak Out from page 103 to help you.

You're shocked. You have just got to school and you want to call your mother, but you can't find your mobile phone.

- Tell a friend that you're afraid that someone has stolen it.
- Tell your friend that you're sure you didn't leave your phone at home because you phoned your boyfriend/girlfriend on the way to school.
- You think your friend has made a good suggestion. Thank him/her.

# Student B activities

Unit 2, Speaking and Listening, Exercise 8, page 18.

**Student B**
Follow the instructions. Use Speak Out on page 18 to help you.

You are spending a long weekend at a youth hostel in the mountains. You are discussing your plans for the next day.

- Politely reject your friend's suggestion.
- Suggest an alternative: go climbing.
- Agree to your friend's new suggestion.

Unit 5, Speaking, Exercise 8, page 49.

**Look at the photo and follow the instructions on page 49.**

Unit 6, Grammar and Vocabulary, Exercise 7, page 51.

## FACT BOX

### THE MADSEN FAMILY OF CAP HOPE, GREENLAND

| | |
|---|---|
| They buy a lot of … | tinned fruit, dried soup, fruit juice, powdered milk. |
| They buy too much/many … | meat (polar bear, beef, walrus), sweets, chocolate, fizzy drinks, crisps. |
| They buy some … | fish, coffee, tea, butter, rice, pasta, breakfast cereals. |
| They don't buy much/many … | bread, bacon, eggs, biscuits, tomato sauce, mayonnaise. |
| They buy a few/a little … | onions, sausages, ham, mashed potato mix. |
| They don't buy any … | fresh milk, fresh fruit, olive oil, green vegetables, tomatoes, pizzas. |

### Student B

1 Ask questions about meat, fruit, drinks, etc. to find out about the food shopping of the family your partner has information on.
2 Guess what country they are from (*Germany*, *Italy* or *the USA*) and say if their diet is healthy or not.
3 Then study the fact box about the weekly food shopping of this family.
4 Answer your partner's questions and tell him/her about what they eat and drink. Use the phrases from Check it out on page 51 to help you.

Unit 8, Listening and Speaking, Exercise 7, page 73.

### Student B
Follow the instructions. Use Speak Out on page 73 to help you.

You are Tim, Lily and Jacob's flatmate. Someone wants to speak to Jacob but he's not in at the moment.

• Say that Jacob's not in at the moment.
• Ask him/her if he/she wants to leave a message.
• Ask him/her to spell his/her name and note down his/her phone number.
• Say you will pass on the message.

Unit 11, Speaking and Writing, Exercise 6, page 103.

### Student B
Follow the instructions. Use Speak Out on page 103 to help you. Start the conversation.

Your friend is looking very unhappy.

• Ask him/her what has happened.
• Tell your friend not to worry. Perhaps he/she has left it at home.
• Reassure your friend. Suggest that he/she writes a notice and puts it up in the school entrance.

# Word list

## UNIT 1

| | |
|---|---|
| always | ˈɔːlwəz |
| apply for a passport/visa | əˌplaɪ fər ə ˈpɑːspɔːt, ˈviːzə |
| association | əˌsəʊsiˈeɪʃən |
| at the moment | ət ðə ˈməʊmənt |
| belong to | bɪˈlɒŋ tə |
| big-headed | ˌbɪɡˈhedɪd |
| bilingual | baɪˈlɪŋgwəl |
| border (n) | ˈbɔːdə |
| boring | ˈbɔːrɪŋ |
| boss | bɒs |
| bossy | ˈbɒsi |
| Brazil | brəˈzɪl |
| brilliant | ˈbrɪljənt |
| bring together | ˌbrɪŋ təˈgeðə |
| caring | ˈkeərɪŋ |
| chat online | ˌtʃæt ɒnˈlaɪn |
| cheer (v) | tʃɪə |
| cheerful | ˈtʃɪəfəl |
| chef | ʃef |
| classic novels | ˌklæsɪk ˈnɒvəlz |
| classical | ˈklæsɪkəl |
| clever | ˈklevə |
| club | klʌb |
| community | kəˈmjuːnəti |
| compete | kəmˈpiːt |
| competition | ˌkɒmpəˈtɪʃən |
| confident | ˈkɒnfədənt |
| count | kaʊnt |
| crime novel | ˈkraɪm ˌnɒvəl |
| dance (v) | dɑːns |
| delighted | dɪˈlaɪtɪd |
| difference | ˈdɪfərəns |
| division | dɪˈvɪʒən |
| do puzzles | duː ˈpʌzəlz |
| do well at school | duː ˌwel ət ˈskuːl |
| dominating | ˈdɒməneɪtɪŋ |
| dozen | ˈdʌzən |
| draw (v) | drɔː |
| emigrate to | ˈeməgreɪt tə |
| enemy | ˈenəmi |
| English | ˈɪŋglɪʃ |
| enjoy | ɪnˈdʒɔɪ |
| explanation | ˌekspləˈneɪʃən |
| extrovert | ˈekstrəvɜːt |
| flag | flæg |
| folk | fəʊk |
| foreign | ˈfɒrɪn |
| friendly | ˈfrendli |
| funny | ˈfʌni |
| generous | ˈdʒenərəs |
| get on with | ˌget ˈɒn wɪð, wɪθ |
| get to know | ˌget tə ˈnəʊ |
| global | ˈgləʊbəl |
| go to the gym | ˌgəʊ tə ðə ˈdʒɪm |
| hard-working | ˌhɑːd ˈwɜːkɪŋ |
| helpful | ˈhelpfəl |
| hip-hop | ˈhɪp hɒp |
| hold hands | ˌhəʊld ˈhændz |
| home town | ˈhəʊmtaʊn |

| | |
|---|---|
| horror | ˈhɒrə |
| identity | aɪˈdentəti |
| indie | ˈɪndi |
| indoors | ˌɪnˈdɔːz |
| international | ˌɪntəˈnæʃənəl |
| introvert | ˈɪntrəvɜːt |
| jazz | dʒæz |
| joke (n) | dʒəʊk |
| keep fit | ˌkiːp ˈfɪt |
| laid-back | ˌleɪd ˈbæk |
| lazy | ˈleɪzi |
| lively | ˈlaɪvli |
| loud | laʊd |
| make clothes | ˌmeɪk ˈkləʊðz, ˈkləʊz |
| marry | ˈmæri |
| mean (adj) | miːn |
| metal | ˈmetl |
| mind (v) | maɪnd |
| miserable | ˈmɪzərəbəl |
| mixed nationality | ˌmɪkst ˌnæʃəˈnæləti |
| mixture | ˈmɪkstʃə |
| mock exam | ˌmɒk ɪgˈzæm |
| modest | ˈmɒdɪst |
| multilingual | ˌmʌltiˈlɪŋgwəl |
| nation | ˈneɪʃən |
| national anthem | ˌnæʃənəl ˈænθəm |
| nationality | ˌnæʃəˈnæləti |
| neighbourhood | ˈneɪbəhʊd |
| never | ˈnevə |
| now | naʊ |
| nowadays | ˈnaʊədeɪz |
| often | ˈɒfən |
| optimistic | ˌɒptəˈmɪstɪk |
| outgoing | ˌaʊtˈgəʊɪŋ |
| paint (v) | peɪnt |
| passionate | ˈpæʃənət |
| passport | ˈpɑːspɔːt |
| personality | ˌpɜːsəˈnæləti |
| pessimistic | ˌpesəˈmɪstɪk |
| play board/computer/role/sports games | ˌpleɪ ˈbɔːd, kəmˈpjuːtə, ˈrəʊl, ˈspɔːts geɪmz |
| play/listen to music | ˌpleɪ ˈmjuːzɪk, ˌlɪsən tə |
| polite | pəˈlaɪt |
| pop | pɒp |
| popular | ˈpɒpjələ |
| Portuguese | ˌpɔːtʃəˈgiːz |
| pride | praɪd |
| proud | praʊd |
| punctual | ˈpʌŋktʃuəl |
| quiet | ˈkwaɪət |
| rarely | ˈreəli |
| read | riːd |
| reggae | ˈregeɪ |
| regularly | ˈregjələli |
| reserved | rɪˈzɜːvd |
| respect (v) | rɪˈspekt |
| rock | rɒk |
| romantic | rəʊˈmæntɪk |
| rude | ruːd |

**125**

| | |
|---|---|
| science fiction | ˌsaɪəns ˈfɪkʃən |
| novel | ˈnɒvəl |
| Scotland | ˈskɒtlənd |
| Scottish | ˈskɒtɪʃ |
| security check | sɪˈkjʊərəti tʃek |
| self-belief | ˌself bəˈliːf |
| selfish | ˈselfɪʃ |
| sense of | ˌsens əv ˈhjuːmə |
| humour | |
| serious | ˈsɪəriəs |
| share | ʃeə |
| short story | ˌʃɔːt ˈstɔːri |
| shy | ʃaɪ |
| sing | sɪŋ |
| society | səˈsaɪəti |
| sometimes | ˈsʌmtaɪmz |
| sophisticated | səˈfɪstəkeɪtɪd |
| soul | səʊl |
| spontaneous | spɒnˈteɪniəs |
| stupid | ˈstjuːpɪd |
| subject | ˈsʌbdʒɪkt |
| surname | ˈsɜːneɪm |
| Sweden | ˈswiːdən |
| Swedish | ˈswiːdɪʃ |
| take part in | ˌteɪk ˈpɑːt ɪn |
| talkative | ˈtɔːkətɪv |
| techno | ˈteknəʊ |
| term | tɜːm |
| these days | ðiːz ˈdeɪz |
| tolerant | ˈtɒlərənt |
| tradition | trəˈdɪʃən |
| uncomfortable | ʌnˈkʌmftəbəl |
| unusual | ʌnˈjuːʒʊəl |
| usually | ˈjuːʒʊəli |
| visa | ˈviːzə |
| wave (v) | weɪv |

## UNIT 2

| | |
|---|---|
| accommodation | əˌkɒməˈdeɪʃən |
| adult | ˈædʌlt, əˈdʌlt |
| adaptor plug | əˈdæptə ˌplʌg |
| advantage | ədˈvɑːntɪdʒ |
| advert | ˈædvɜːt |
| airport | ˈeəpɔːt |
| anti-sickness | ˌænti ˈsɪknəs |
| tablets | ˌtæbləts |
| arrive | əˈraɪv |
| art gallery | ˈɑːt ˌgæləri |
| arts centre | ˈɑːts ˌsentə |
| at the last | ˌət ðə ˌlɑːst ˈmɪnɪt |
| minute | |
| available | əˈveɪləbəl |
| babysit | ˈbeɪbisɪt |
| battery | ˈbætəri ˌtʃɑːdʒə |
| charger | |
| beach | biːtʃ |
| bored | bɔːd |
| breakfast | ˌbrekfəst ɪnˈkluːdəd, |
| included | ɪnˈkluːdɪd |
| by plane/train/ | baɪ ˈpleɪn, ˈtreɪn, |
| coach | ˈkəʊtʃ |
| camera | ˈkæmərə |
| camping | ˈkæmpɪŋ |
| campsite | ˈkæmpsaɪt |

| | |
|---|---|
| cancel | ˈkænsəl |
| capital | ˈkæpətl |
| catch a train/ | ˌkætʃ ə ˈtreɪn, |
| plane | ˈpleɪn |
| cathedral | kəˈθiːdrəl |
| celebrate | ˌseləbreɪt ə |
| a birthday | ˈbɜːθdeɪ |
| cinema | ˈsɪnəmə |
| city centre | ˌsɪti ˈsentə |
| climbing | ˈklaɪmɪŋ |
| cloud | klaʊd |
| club | klʌb |
| clubbing | ˈklʌbɪŋ |
| coast | kəʊst |
| come home | ˌkʌm ˈhəʊm |
| concert hall | ˈkɒnsət hɔːl |
| convenient | kənˈviːniənt |
| cost (v) | kɒst |
| country | ˈkʌntri |
| crowded | ˈkraʊdɪd |
| cycle (v) | ˈsaɪkəl |
| cycling | ˈsaɪklɪŋ |
| daily | ˈdeɪli |
| delayed (for | dɪˈleɪd fər ən ˌaʊə |
| an hour) | |
| destination | ˌdestəˈneɪʃən |
| disabled | dɪsˈeɪbəld |
| disadvantage | ˌdɪsədˈvɑːntɪdʒ |
| distance | ˈdɪstəns |
| district | ˈdɪstrɪkt |
| double room | ˌdʌbəl ˈruːm, ˈrʊm |
| earn | ɜːn |
| enter | ˈentə |
| exhibition | ˌeksəˈbɪʃən |
| experience (v) | ɪkˈspɪəriəns |
| explore | ɪkˈsplɔː |
| factory | ˈfæktəri |
| fancy (v) | ˈfænsi |
| ferry | ˈferi |
| find sth easy/ | ˌfaɪnd sʌmθɪŋ |
| difficult | ˈiːzi, ˈdɪfɪkəlt |
| fishing | ˈfɪʃɪŋ |
| flight | flaɪt |
| floor | flɔː |
| fly | flaɪ |
| fortnight | ˈfɔːtnaɪt |
| frustrating | frʌˈstreɪtɪŋ |
| guest house | ˈgesthaʊs |
| guidebook | ˈgaɪdbʊk |
| hiking | ˈhaɪkɪŋ |
| hill | hɪl |
| holiday | ˈhɒlədi ˌbrəʊʃə |
| brochure | |
| hotel | həʊˈtel |
| huge | hjuːdʒ |
| inconvenient | ˌɪnkənˈviːniənt |
| industrial | ɪnˈdʌstriəl |
| industry | ˈɪndəstri |
| jewellery | ˈdʒuːəlri |
| lake | leɪk |
| land (v) | lænd |
| leave for the | ˌliːv fər ðə |
| station/airport | ˈsteɪʃən, ˈeəpɔːt |
| leisure | ˈleʒə |
| length | leŋθ |
| letter of | ˌletər əv |
| complaint | kəmˈpleɪnt |

| | |
|---|---|
| lively | ˈlaɪvli |
| look forward to sth | ˌlʊk ˈfɔːwəd tə ˌsʌmθɪŋ |
| lost property office | ˌlɒst ˈprɒpəti ˌɒfɪs |
| medicine | ˈmedsən |
| money belt | ˈmʌni belt |
| motorbike | ˈməʊtəbaɪk |
| mountain | ˈmaʊntən |
| museum | mjuːˈziːəm |
| on foot | ɒn ˈfʊt |
| outdoor | ˈaʊtdɔː |
| pack (v) | pæk |
| pass the time | ˌpɑːs ðə ˈtaɪm |
| peace and quiet | ˌpiːs ən ˈkwaɪət |
| penknife | ˈpen-naɪf |
| photography | fəˈtɒɡrəfi |
| platform | ˈplætfɔːm |
| playing card | ˈpleɪ-ɪŋ kɑːd |
| pop in | ˌpɒp ˈɪn |
| poster | ˈpəʊstə |
| practise sb's French/ English | ˌpræktɪs ˌsʌmbədiz ˈfrentʃ, ˈɪŋglɪʃ |
| queue (n, v) | kjuː |
| rail pass | ˈreɪl ˌpɑːs |
| rail timetable | ˌreɪl ˈtaɪmteɪbəl |
| relax | rɪˈlæks |
| relaxing | rɪˈlæksɪŋ |
| reservation | ˌrezəˈveɪʃən |
| rucksack | ˈrʌksæk |
| rush (v) | rʌʃ |
| sailing | ˈseɪlɪŋ |
| satisfied | ˈsætɪsfaɪd |
| science | ˈsaɪəns |
| shampoo | ʃæmˈpuː |
| shopping centre | ˈʃɒpɪŋ ˌsentə |
| sightseeing | ˈsaɪtˌsiːɪŋ |
| skiing | ˈskiː-ɪŋ |
| skill | skɪl |
| sleeping bag | ˈsliːpɪŋ bæg |
| snorkelling | ˈsnɔːkəlɪŋ |
| stadium | ˈsteɪdiəm |
| stay at a youth hostel/ with a friend | ˌsteɪ ət ə ˈjuːθ ˌhɒstl, wɪð ə ˈfrend |
| stimulating | ˈstɪmjəleɪtɪŋ |
| stressful | ˈstresfəl |
| suitcase | ˈsuːtkeɪs |
| sunbathing | ˈsʌnbeɪðɪŋ |
| suntan lotion | ˈsʌntæn ˌləʊʃən |
| take photos | ˌteɪk ˈfəʊtəʊz |
| tent | tent |
| theatre | ˈθɪətə |
| ticket | ˈtɪkɪt |
| tip | tɪp |
| tiring | ˈtaɪərɪŋ |
| toothbrush | ˈtuːθbrʌʃ |
| tourist attraction | ˈtʊərəst əˌtrækʃən |
| tourist information office | ˌtʊərəst ɪnfəˈmeɪʃən ˌɒfɪs |
| towel | ˈtaʊəl |
| travel agent's | ˈtrævəl ˌeɪdʒənts |

| | |
|---|---|
| travel to | ˈtrævəl tə |
| trip | trɪp |
| under (+ age) | ˈʌndə |
| unlimited | ʌnˈlɪmətɪd |
| visit (v) | ˈvɪzɪt |
| waterproof jacket | ˌwɔːtəpruːf ˈdʒækət |
| youth hostel | ˈjuːθ ˌhɒstl |

## UNIT 3

| | |
|---|---|
| amazed | əˈmeɪzd |
| amazing | əˈmeɪzɪŋ |
| annoyed | əˈnɔɪd |
| annoying | əˈnɔɪ-ɪŋ |
| anxious | ˈæŋkʃəs |
| appearance | əˈpɪərəns |
| aquarium | əˈkweəriəm |
| be bad at sth | ˌbi ˈbæd ət ˌsʌmθɪŋ |
| be good at sth | bi ˈɡʊd ət ˌsʌmθɪŋ |
| be in the same year as | ˌbi ɪn ðə ˌseɪm ˈjɪər əz |
| bell | bel |
| billion | ˈbɪljən |
| bored | bɔːd |
| boring | ˈbɔːrɪŋ |
| born | bɔːn |
| borrow | ˈbɒrəʊ |
| brain | breɪn |
| brand new | ˌbrænd ˈnjuː |
| break (v) | breɪk |
| calculator | ˈkælkjəleɪtə |
| calm | kɑːm |
| cause (n) | kɔːz |
| check your email | ˌtʃek jər ˈiːmeɪl |
| Chemistry | ˈkeməstri |
| clap | klæp |
| class | klɑːs |
| classmate | ˈklɑːsmeɪt |
| classroom | ˈklɑːsruːm |
| creative | kriˈeɪtɪv |
| dictionary | ˈdɪkʃənəri |
| disability | ˌdɪsəˈbɪləti |
| disappointed | ˌdɪsəˈpɔɪntɪd |
| disappointing | ˌdɪsəˈpɔɪntɪŋ |
| drop out of school | ˌdrɒp ˈaʊt əv ˈskuːl |
| dyslexia | dɪsˈleksiə |
| dyslexic | dɪsˈleksɪk |
| education | ˌedjʊˈkeɪʃən |
| embarrassed | ɪmˈbærəst |
| embarrassing | ɪmˈbærəsɪŋ |
| essay | ˈeseɪ |
| excited | ɪkˈsaɪtɪd |
| exciting | ɪkˈsaɪtɪŋ |
| fail an exam | ˌfeɪl ən ɪɡˈzæm |
| fascinated | ˈfæsəneɪtəd, ˈfæsɪneɪtəd |
| fascinating | ˈfæsəneɪtɪŋ |
| fish | fɪʃ |
| form tutor | ˈfɔːm ˌtjuːtə |
| frightened | ˈfraɪtnd |
| frightening | ˈfraɪtn-ɪŋ |

| | |
|---|---|
| funny | ˈfʌni |
| genetic | dʒəˈnetɪk |
| genius | ˈdʒiːniəs |
| grow up | ˌɡrəʊ ˈʌp |
| grown-up (adj) | ˌɡrəʊn ˈʌp |
| hate | heɪt |
| have sth in common | ˌhæv sʌmθɪŋ ɪn ˈkɒmən |
| hidden | ˈhɪdn |
| imagination | ɪˌmædʒəˈneɪʃən |
| in | ɪn |
| inside | ɪnˈsaɪd |
| intelligent | ɪnˈtelədʒənt |
| interested | ˈɪntrəstɪd |
| interesting | ˈɪntrəstɪŋ |
| inventor | ɪnˈventə |
| invite | ɪnˈvaɪt |
| last night/ week/year/ Saturday | ˌlɑːst ˈnaɪt, ˈwiːk, ˈjɪə, ˈsætədi |
| laugh out loud | ˌlɑːf aʊt ˈlaʊd |
| learn by heart | ˌlɜːn baɪ ˈhɑːt |
| look (v) | lʊk |
| make a mistake | ˌmeɪk ə mɪˈsteɪk |
| make friends | meɪk ˈfrendz |
| make yourself at home | ˌmeɪk jəself ət ˈhəʊm |
| make-up | ˈmeɪk ʌp |
| mark (n) | mɑːk |
| Maths | mæθs |
| mean (v) | miːn |
| memorise | ˈmeməraɪz |
| musical instrument | ˌmjuːzɪkəl ˈɪnstrəmənt |
| noisy | ˈnɔɪzi |
| one day/ morning | ˌwʌn ˈdeɪ, ˈmɔːnɪŋ |
| pass an exam | ˌpɑːs ən ɪɡˈzæm |
| pen | pen |
| pencil case | ˈpensəl keɪs |
| piercing | ˈpɪəsɪŋ |
| pirate | ˈpaɪərət |
| playground | ˈpleɪɡraʊnd |
| primary school | ˈpraɪməri ˌskuːl |
| pupil | ˈpjuːpəl |
| ring (v) | rɪŋ |
| ruler | ˈruːlə |
| satisfied | ˈsætɪsfaɪd |
| satisfying | ˈsætɪsfaɪ-ɪŋ |
| say goodbye to sb | ˌseɪ ɡʊdˈbai tə ˌsʌmbədi |
| scared | skeəd |
| school gate | ˌskuːl ˈɡeɪt |
| school holiday | ˌskuːl ˈhɒlədi |
| school uniform | ˌskuːl ˈjuːnəfɔːm |
| score (n) | skɔː |
| secondary school | ˈsekəndəri ˌskuːl |
| shocked | ʃɒkt |
| shocking | ˈʃɒkɪŋ |
| similar | ˈsɪmələ |
| sit cross-legged | ˌsɪt krɒs ˈleɡɪd |
| slim | slɪm |
| smelly | ˈsmeli |
| smoke (v) | sməʊk |

| | |
|---|---|
| soap | səʊp |
| spell (v) | spel |
| spot (n) | spɒt |
| start/leave school | ˌstɑːt ˈskuːl, ˈliːv |
| strange | streɪndʒ |
| strict | strɪkt |
| surprised | səˈpraɪzd |
| surprising | səˈpraɪzɪŋ |
| Take a seat. | ˌteɪk ə ˈsiːt |
| ten years ago | ˌten ˈjɪəz əˌɡəʊ |
| terrified | ˈterəfaɪd |
| terrifying | ˈterəfaɪ-ɪŋ, ˈterɪfaɪ-ɪŋ |
| test (n) | test |
| textbook | ˈtekstbʊk |
| tired | taɪəd |
| tiring | ˈtaɪərɪŋ |
| university | ˌjuːnəˈvɜːsəti |
| unpleasant | ʌnˈplezənt |
| voice | vɔɪs |
| wear | weə |
| What a surprise! | ˌwɒt ə səˈpraɪz |
| yesterday | ˈjestədi |

## UNIT 4

| | |
|---|---|
| according to | əˈkɔːdɪŋ tə |
| after a while | ˌɑːftər ə ˈwaɪl |
| after that | ˌɑːftə ˈðæt |
| afterwards | ˈɑːftəwədz |
| ago | əˈɡəʊ |
| all sorts of | ˌɔːl ˈsɔːts əv |
| annual | ˈænjuəl |
| apartment | əˈpɑːtmənt |
| arts festival | ɑːts ˈfestəvəl |
| audience | ˈɔːdiəns |
| author | ˈɔːθə |
| band | bænd |
| battle | ˈbætl |
| be asleep | ˌbi əˈsliːp |
| be fed up | bi ˌfed ˈʌp |
| be lucky | bi ˈlʌki |
| be unlucky | bi ʌnˈlʌki |
| bestseller | ˌbestˈselə |
| blank | blæŋk |
| blind | blaɪnd |
| boyfriend | ˈbɔɪfrend |
| break into | ˌbreɪk ˈɪntə |
| candle | ˈkændl |
| catchy | ˈkætʃi |
| chill out | ˌtʃɪl ˈaʊt |
| choice | tʃɔɪs |
| Christmas | ˈkrɪsməs |
| cigar | sɪˈɡɑː |
| cinema | ˈsɪnəmə |
| Colombian | kəˈlʌmbiən |
| come up | ˌkʌm ˈʌp |
| come up with | ˌkʌm ˈʌp wɪð, wɪθ |
| compose | kəmˈpəʊz |
| composer | kəmˈpəʊzə |
| composition | ˌkɒmpəˈzɪʃən |
| concentrate | ˈkɒnsəntreɪt |
| concert | ˈkɒnsət |
| condition | kənˈdɪʃən |

| | |
|---|---|
| couple | ˈkʌpəl |
| creative | kriˈeɪtɪv |
| dance (n) | dɑːns |
| dawn | dɔːn |
| depressed | dɪˈprest |
| desk | desk |
| diary | ˈdaɪəri |
| disaster | dɪˈzɑːstə |
| disorganised | dɪsˈɔːɡənaɪzd |
| distraction | dɪˈstrækʃən |
| dramatic | drəˈmætɪk |
| dream (n) | driːm |
| drop (v) | drɒp |
| drum solo | ˈdrʌm ˌsəʊləʊ |
| eventually | ɪˈventʃuəli |
| exhibition | ˌeksəˈbɪʃən |
| fall (v) | fɔːl |
| fall asleep | ˌfɔːl əˈsliːp |
| farmhouse | ˈfɑːmhaʊs |
| feel ill | ˌfiːl ˈɪl |
| feel inspired | ˌfiːl ɪnˈspaɪəd |
| finally | ˈfaɪnl-i |
| find out | ˌfaɪnd ˈaʊt |
| first | fɜːst |
| get down to | ˌget ˈdaʊn tə |
| guitar | ɡɪˈtɑː |
| have a bath | hæv ə ˈbɑːθ |
| have a good idea | hæv ə ˌɡʊd aɪˈdɪə |
| have a picnic | hæv ə ˈpɪknɪk |
| idea | aɪˈdɪə |
| imaginative | ɪˈmædʒənətɪv |
| inspiration | ˌɪnspəˈreɪʃən |
| inspiring | ɪnˈspaɪərɪŋ |
| interruption | ˌɪntəˈrʌpʃən |
| intrigued | ɪnˈtriːɡd |
| irritated | ˈɪrəteɪtəd, ˈɪrɪteɪtəd |
| irritating | ˈɪrəteɪtɪŋ, ˈɪrɪteɪtɪŋ |
| jamming | ˈdʒæmɪŋ |
| join in | ˌdʒɔɪn ˈɪn |
| keep on | ˌkiːp ˈɒn |
| key | kiː |
| knock at the door | ˌnɒk ət ðə ˈdɔː |
| last summer | ˌlɑːst ˈsʌmə |
| late | leɪt |
| later | ˈleɪtə |
| library | ˈlaɪbrəri |
| lie (v) | laɪ |
| light (v) | laɪt |
| literature | ˈlɪtərətʃə |
| lose | luːz |
| matter (v) | ˈmætə |
| melodic | məˈlɒdɪk, mɪˈlɒdɪk |
| melody | ˈmelədi |
| middle | ˈmɪdl |
| mind (n) | maɪnd |
| moon | muːn |
| multi-tasking | ˈmʌlti ˌtɑːskɪŋ |
| mysterious | mɪˈstɪəriəs |
| next | nekst |
| Nobel prize | nəʊˈbel ˌpraɪz |
| noise | nɔɪz |
| novelist | ˈnɒvəlɪst |
| open to | ˈəʊpən tə |
| organised | ˈɔːɡənaɪzd |

| | |
|---|---|
| painting | ˈpeɪntɪŋ |
| palace | ˈpælɪs |
| perform | pəˈfɔːm |
| piano | piˈænəʊ |
| pin (v) | pɪn |
| play the guitar/ piano/violin | ˌpleɪ ðə ɡɪˈtɑː, piˈænəʊ, ˌvaɪəˈlɪn |
| play live | ˌpleɪ ˈlaɪv |
| pleasant | ˈplezənt |
| pleased | pliːzd |
| plug in | ˌplʌɡ ˈɪn |
| poem | ˈpəʊəm |
| poet | ˈpəʊɪt |
| poetry | ˈpəʊətri |
| prestigious | preˈstɪdʒəs |
| prize | praɪz |
| publish | ˈpʌblɪʃ |
| recording studio | rɪˈkɔːdɪŋ ˌstjuːdiəʊ |
| reply (v) | rɪˈplaɪ |
| request (n) | rɪˈkwest |
| revise | rɪˈvaɪz |
| robber | ˈrɒbə |
| Romantic poets | rəʊˌmæntɪk ˈpəʊəts |
| scientist | ˈsaɪəntɪst |
| second | ˈsekənd |
| sentimental | ˌsentəˈmentl |
| shine | ʃaɪn |
| short story | ˌʃɔːt ˈstɔːri |
| silly | ˈsɪli |
| sleepy | ˈsliːpi |
| solve | sɒlv |
| something else | ˌsʌmθɪŋ ˈels |
| stay up | ˌsteɪ ˈʌp |
| stranger | ˈstreɪndʒə |
| stressed | strest |
| table tennis | ˈteɪbəl ˌtenɪs |
| take a break | ˌteɪk ə ˈbreɪk |
| text (v) | tekst |
| theatre | ˈθɪətə |
| then | ðen |
| truth | truːθ |
| Vienna | viˈenə |
| violin | ˌvaɪəˈlɪn |
| vision | ˈvɪʒən |
| wheel | wiːl |
| wheelchair | ˈwiːltʃeə |
| whistle (n) | ˈwɪsəl |
| work (n) | wɜːk |
| write back | ˌraɪt ˈbæk |
| write down | ˌraɪt ˈdaʊn |
| writer | ˈraɪtə |

## UNIT 5

| | |
|---|---|
| admit | ədˈmɪt |
| alien | ˈeɪliən |
| apartment | əˈpɑːtmənt |
| appliance | əˈplaɪəns |
| architect | ˈɑːkətekt |
| armchair | ˈɑːmtʃeə |
| attic | ˈætɪk |
| attract | əˈtrækt |

| | |
|---|---|
| attractive | əˈtræktɪv |
| back door | ˌbæk ˈdɔː |
| balcony | ˈbælkəni |
| basement | ˈbeɪsmənt |
| bathroom | ˈbɑːθruːm |
| bed | bed |
| bedroom | ˈbedruːm |
| blind | blaɪnd |
| block of flats | ˌblɒk əv ˈflæts |
| bookshelf | ˈbʊkʃelf |
| bright | braɪt |
| bubble | ˈbʌbəl |
| build | bɪld |
| carpet | ˈkɑːpɪt |
| ceiling | ˈsiːlɪŋ |
| centre | ˈsentə |
| chat (v) | tʃæt |
| cheap | tʃiːp |
| cheerful | ˈtʃɪəfəl |
| chest of drawers | ˌtʃest əv ˈdrɔːz |
| chimney | ˈtʃɪmni |
| church | tʃɜːtʃ |
| close to | ˈkləʊs tə |
| colourful | ˈkʌləfəl |
| column | ˈkɒləm |
| comfortable | ˈkʌmftəbəl |
| common | ˈkɒmən |
| communicate | kəˈmjuːnəkeɪt |
| competition | ˌkɒmpəˈtɪʃən |
| corner | ˈkɔːnə |
| cosy | ˈkəʊzi |
| cottage | ˈkɒtɪdʒ |
| country | ˈkʌntri |
| cupboard | ˈkʌbəd |
| curtain | ˈkɜːtn |
| curved | kɜːvd |
| decoration | ˌdekəˈreɪʃən |
| design (v) | dɪˈzaɪn |
| detached house | dɪˌtætʃt ˈhaʊs |
| dining room | ˈdaɪnɪŋ ruːm |
| dishwasher | ˈdɪʃˌwɒʃə |
| district | ˈdɪstrɪkt |
| doorbell | ˈdɔːbel |
| downstairs | ˌdaʊnˈsteəz |
| drive | draɪv |
| DVD player | ˌdiː viː ˈdiː ˌpleɪə |
| elegant | ˈeləgənt |
| enormous | ɪˈnɔːməs |
| escape (v) | ɪˈskeɪp |
| estate agent | ɪˈsteɪt ˌeɪdʒənt |
| expensive | ɪkˈspensɪv |
| far (adj, adv) | fɑː |
| fashion designer | ˈfæʃən dɪˌzaɪnə |
| feel sick | ˌfiːl ˈsɪk |
| fence | fens |
| fit | fɪt |
| fitted kitchen | ˌfɪtəd ˈkɪtʃən, ˈfɪtɪd |
| flat | flæt |
| flatmate | ˈflætmeɪt |
| floor | flɔː |
| for sale | fə ˈseɪl |
| forest | ˈfɒrɪst |
| freezer | ˈfriːzə |
| friendly | ˈfrendli |
| front door | ˌfrʌnt ˈdɔː |
| fun (adj) | fʌn |
| furniture | ˈfɜːnɪtʃə |
| games console | ˈgeɪmz ˌkɒnsəʊl |
| garage | ˈgærɑːʒ |
| garden | ˈgɑːdn |
| giant (adj) | ˈdʒaɪənt |
| grass | grɑːs |
| guy | gaɪ |
| hall | hɔːl |
| hang out (with) | ˌhæŋ ˈaʊt wɪð, wɪθ |
| healthy | ˈhelθi |
| heater | ˈhiːtə |
| hedge | hedʒ |
| horrible | ˈhɒrəbəl |
| housing estate | ˈhaʊzɪŋ ɪˌsteɪt |
| however | haʊˈevə |
| in the foreground | ɪn ðə ˈfɔːgraʊnd |
| in the background | ɪn ðə ˈbækgraʊnd |
| indoor | ˈɪndɔː |
| inexpensive | ˌɪnɪkˈspensɪv |
| island | ˈaɪlənd |
| kettle | ˈketl |
| key (n) | kiː |
| kind | kaɪnd |
| lavatory | ˈlævətəri |
| lawn | lɔːn |
| letterbox | ˈletəbɒks |
| light (n) | laɪt |
| living room | ˈlɪvɪŋ ruːm |
| location | ləʊˈkeɪʃən |
| loft | lɒft |
| lonely | ˈləʊnli |
| lovely | ˈlʌvli |
| market | ˈmɑːkɪt |
| message | ˈmesɪdʒ |
| microwave | ˈmaɪkrəweɪv |
| modern | ˈmɒdn |
| monastery | ˈmɒnəstri |
| move (n) | muːv |
| near | nɪə |
| neighbour | ˈneɪbə |
| nice | naɪs |
| noisy | ˈnɔɪzi |
| obviously | ˈɒbviəsli |
| odd | ɒd |
| original | əˈrɪdʒɪnəl |
| outside (adj, adv) | ˈaʊtsaɪd |
| oval | ˈəʊvəl |
| owner | ˈəʊnə |
| peaceful | ˈpiːsfəl |
| picture | ˈpɪktʃə |
| pleasant | ˈplezənt |
| porch | pɔːtʃ |
| poster | ˈpəʊstə |
| practical | ˈpræktɪkəl |
| protest (v) | prəˈtest |
| reason | ˈriːzən |
| remote control | rɪˌməʊt kənˈtrəʊl |
| rent (v) | rent |
| represent | ˌreprɪˈzent |
| resident | ˈrezədənt |
| rock (n) | rɒk |

| | |
|---|---|
| rocky | ˈrɒki |
| room | ruːm |
| roomy | ˈruːmi |
| round | raʊnd |
| row of | ˈrəʊ əv |
| rug | rʌg |
| sell | sel |
| semi-detached house | ˌsemi dɪˈtætʃt ˈhaʊs |
| shape (n) | ʃeɪp |
| share a flat | ʃeər ə ˈflæt |
| shower | ˈʃaʊə |
| sink | sɪŋk |
| skylight | ˈskaɪlaɪt |
| sofa | ˈsəʊfə |
| south | saʊθ |
| spacious | ˈspeɪʃəs |
| spectacular | spekˈtækjələ |
| stairs | steəz |
| state (n) | steɪt |
| station | ˈsteɪʃən |
| stool | stuːl |
| study (n) | ˈstʌdi |
| suburb | ˈsʌbɜːb |
| sunshine | ˈsʌnʃaɪn |
| tasteful | ˈteɪstfəl |
| tasteless | ˈteɪstləs |
| terraced house | ˌterəst ˈhaʊs |
| tiny | ˈtaɪni |
| trust (v) | trʌst |
| turn (n) | tɜːn |
| typical | ˈtɪpɪkəl |
| ugly | ˈʌgli |
| uncomfortable | ʌnˈkʌmftəbəl |
| upside down | ˌʌpsaɪd ˈdaʊn |
| upstairs | ˌʌpˈsteəz |
| vacuum cleaner | ˈvækjuəm ˌkliːnə |
| view (n) | vjuː |
| violence | ˈvaɪələns |
| wall | wɔːl |
| wardrobe | ˈwɔːdrəʊb |
| washbasin | ˈwɒʃˌbeɪsən |
| washing machine | ˈwɒʃɪŋ məˌʃiːn |
| win | wɪn |
| window | ˈwɪndəʊ |
| wrong | rɒŋ |

## UNIT 6

| | |
|---|---|
| Aborigine | ˌæbəˈrɪdʒəni, ˌæbəˈrɪdʒini |
| accident | ˈæksədənt |
| although | ɔːlˈðəʊ |
| analyse | ˈænl-aɪz |
| ancestor | ˈænsəstə |
| anthropologist | ˌænθrəˈpɒlədʒɪst |
| apology | əˈpɒlədʒi |
| apple | ˈæpəl |
| apple pie | ˌæpəl ˈpaɪ |
| avocado | ˌævəˈkɑːdəʊ |
| bacon | ˈbeɪkən |
| bad for you | ˈbæd fə jʊ |
| bag | bæg |

| | |
|---|---|
| banana | bəˈnɑːnə |
| be to blame | bi tə ˈbleɪm |
| bean | biːn |
| beef | biːf |
| beer | bɪə |
| bill | bɪl |
| biscuit | ˈbɪskɪt |
| bitter | ˈbɪtə |
| branch | brɑːntʃ |
| bread | bred |
| break down | ˌbreɪk ˈdaʊn |
| breakfast cereal | ˈbrekfəst ˌsɪəriəl |
| broccoli | ˈbrɒkəli |
| brussels sprout | ˌbrʌsəlz ˈspraʊt |
| burger | ˈbɜːgə |
| butter | ˈbʌtə |
| cabbage | ˈkæbɪdʒ |
| café | ˈkæfeɪ |
| cake | keɪk |
| canteen | kænˈtiːn |
| cappuccino | ˌkæpəˈtʃiːnəʊ, ˌkæpʊˈtʃiːnəʊ |
| careless | ˈkeələs |
| carrot | ˈkærət |
| carton | ˈkɑːtn |
| cereal | ˈsɪəriəl |
| cheese | tʃiːz |
| chewing gum | ˈtʃuːɪŋ gʌm |
| chicken curry | ˌtʃɪkən ˈkʌri |
| chip | tʃɪp |
| chocolate | ˈtʃɒklət |
| chocolate bar | ˈtʃɒklət bɑː |
| clue | kluː |
| cocoa | ˈkəʊkəʊ |
| coffee | ˈkɒfi |
| compensation | ˌkɒmpənˈseɪʃən |
| complaint | kəmˈpleɪnt |
| control | kənˈtrəʊl |
| convenience food | kənˈviːniəns fuːd |
| cream | kriːm |
| crisp (n) | krɪsp |
| Croatia | krəʊˈeɪʃə |
| croissant | ˈkwɑːsɒŋ |
| cruel | ˈkruːəl |
| customer | ˈkʌstəmə |
| cut down on | ˌkʌt ˈdaʊn ɒn |
| dairy products | ˈdeəri ˌprɒdʌkts |
| date | deɪt |
| delicious | dɪˈlɪʃəs |
| dessert | dɪˈzɜːt |
| diet | ˈdaɪət |
| dried (soup) | draɪd |
| drink (v, n) | drɪŋk |
| eat out | ˌiːt ˈaʊt |
| economical | ˌekəˈnɒmɪkəl |
| egg | eg |
| fall (v) | fɔːl |
| fashionable | ˈfæʃənəbəl |
| fast food | ˌfɑːst ˈfuːd |
| fast food restaurant | ˌfɑːst ˈfuːd restərɒnt |
| fat (n) | fæt |
| fault | fɔːlt |
| filling | ˈfɪlɪŋ |

| | |
|---|---|
| fish | fɪʃ |
| fizzy drink | ˌfɪzi ˈdrɪŋk |
| flour | flaʊə |
| food | fuːd |
| fresh | freʃ |
| freshness | ˈfreʃnəs |
| fridge | frɪdʒ |
| from abroad | frəm əˈbrɔːd |
| frozen | ˈfrəʊzən |
| fruit | fruːt |
| fruit juice | ˈfruːt dʒuːs |
| garlic bread | ˌgɑːlɪk ˈbred |
| generation | ˌdʒenəˈreɪʃən |
| give up | ˌgɪv ˈʌp |
| good for you | ˈgʊd fə jʊ |
| goulash | ˈguːlæʃ |
| grape | greɪp |
| greasy | ˈgriːsi |
| green bean | ˌgriːn ˈbiːn |
| grow | grəʊ |
| gut | gʌt |
| ham | hæm |
| have a sweet tooth | hæv ə ˌswiːt ˈtuːθ |
| health | helθ |
| healthy | ˈhelθi |
| hot dog | ˌhɒt ˈdɒg |
| ice cream | ˌaɪs ˈkriːm |
| ignore | ɪgˈnɔː |
| improve | ɪmˈpruːv |
| inedible | ɪnˈedəbəl, ɪnˈedɪbəl |
| ingredient | ɪnˈgriːdiənt |
| insect | ˈɪnsekt |
| invention | ɪnˈvenʃən |
| jam | dʒæm |
| kebab | kəˈbæb, kɪˈbæb |
| ketchup | ˈketʃəp |
| kill | kɪl |
| lamb | læm |
| lasagne | ləˈsænjə, -ˈzæn- |
| lemonade | ˌleməˈneɪd |
| lend | lend |
| lifestyle | ˈlaɪfstaɪl |
| loathe | ləʊð |
| low fat | ˌləʊ ˈfæt |
| main course | ˌmeɪn ˈkɔːs |
| margarine | ˌmɑːdʒəˈriːn |
| mashed potato mix | ˌmæʃt pəˈteɪtəʊ mɪks |
| mayonnaise | ˌmeɪəˈneɪz |
| meal | miːl |
| meat | miːt |
| melon | ˈmelən |
| menu | ˈmenjuː |
| mild | maɪld |
| milk | mɪlk |
| milkshake | ˈmɪlkʃeɪk |
| mineral water | ˈmɪnərəl ˌwɔːtə |
| molar | ˈməʊlə |
| movement | ˈmuːvmənt |
| muesli | ˈmjuːzli |
| mug (n) | mʌg |
| munch | mʌntʃ |
| mushroom | ˈmʌʃruːm |
| natural | ˈnætʃərəl |

| | |
|---|---|
| noodle | ˈnuːdl |
| nut | nʌt |
| nutritious | njuːˈtrɪʃəs |
| oil | ɔɪl |
| olive | ˈɒlɪv |
| olive oil | ˈɒlɪv ɔɪl |
| onion | ˈʌnjən |
| orange | ˈɒrɪndʒ |
| order (n, v) | ˈɔːdə |
| out-of-date | ˌaʊt əv ˈdeɪt |
| packaged | ˈpækɪdʒd |
| packed lunch | ˌpækt ˈlʌntʃ |
| packet | ˈpækɪt |
| pain | peɪn |
| pasta | ˈpæstə |
| peckish | ˈpekɪʃ |
| percentage | pəˈsentɪdʒ |
| pineapple | ˈpaɪnæpəl |
| pizza | ˈpiːtsə |
| pizzeria | ˌpiːtsəˈriːə |
| planet | ˈplænət |
| population | ˌpɒpjəˈleɪʃən |
| pork | pɔːk |
| potato | pəˈteɪtəʊ |
| powdered milk | ˌpaʊdəd ˈmɪlk |
| prawn | prɔːn |
| prehistoric | ˌpriːhɪˈstɒrɪk |
| product | ˈprɒdʌkt |
| promise (v) | ˈprɒmɪs |
| quality | ˈkwɒləti |
| realise | ˈrɪəlaɪz |
| receipt | rɪˈsiːt |
| recipe | ˈresəpi |
| red pepper | ˌred ˈpepə |
| refund (n) | ˈriːfʌnd |
| refuse (v) | rɪˈfjuːz |
| religion | rɪˈlɪdʒən |
| reputation | ˌrepjəˈteɪʃən |
| review (n) | rɪˈvjuː |
| rice | raɪs |
| root | ruːt |
| salad | ˈsæləd |
| sandwich | ˈsænwɪdʒ |
| satisfactory | ˌsætɪsˈfæktəri |
| sausage | ˈsɒsɪdʒ |
| save | seɪv |
| seafood | ˈsiːfuːd |
| seed | siːd |
| sell-by date | ˈsel baɪ ˌdeɪt |
| serve | sɜːv |
| service | ˈsɜːvɪs |
| several | ˈsevərəl |
| slave | sleɪv |
| snack | snæk |
| spaghetti Bolognese | spəˌgeti bɒləˈneɪz |
| spicy | ˈspaɪsi |
| stale | steɪl |
| starter | ˈstɑːtə |
| steak | steɪk |
| stomach | ˈstʌmək |
| store (n) | stɔː |
| strawberry | ˈstrɔːbəri |
| substantial | səbˈstænʃəl |
| sugar | ˈʃʊgə |

**132**

| | |
|---|---|
| suitable for | ˈsuːtəbəl fə |
| supermarket | ˈsuːpəˌmɑːkɪt |
| sweet (n, adj) | swiːt |
| tasty | ˈteɪsti |
| tea | tiː |
| tin | tɪn |
| tinned | tɪnd |
| to make matters worse | tə ˌmeɪk mætəz ˈwɜːs |
| tomato | təˈmɑːtəʊ |
| tomato sauce | təˌmɑːtəʊ ˈsɔːs |
| tomato soup | təˌmɑːtəʊ ˈsuːp |
| tortilla chip | tɔːˈtiːjə tʃɪp |
| tub | tʌb |
| tube | tjuːb |
| tuna | ˈtjuːnə |
| turkey | ˈtɜːki |
| unacceptable | ˌʌnəkˈseptəbəl |
| unchanged | ʌnˈtʃeɪndʒd |
| unhealthy | ʌnˈhelθi |
| vegetable | ˈvedʒtəbəl |
| vegetarian (n, adj) | ˌvedʒəˈteəriən |
| vegetarianism | ˌvedʒəˈteəriənɪzəm, ˌvedʒɪˈteəriənɪzəm |
| vitamin | ˈvɪtəmən |
| waitress | ˈweɪtrəs |
| waiter | ˈweɪtə |
| watermelon | ˈwɔːtəˌmelən |
| wine | waɪn |
| yoghurt | ˈjɒɡət |

## UNIT 7

| | |
|---|---|
| 3-D | ˌθriː ˈdiː |
| acid rain | ˌæsɪd ˈreɪn |
| act (v) | ækt |
| aeroplane | ˈeərəpleɪn |
| air | eə |
| alive | əˈlaɪv |
| army | ˈɑːmi |
| artificial | ˌɑːtəˈfɪʃəl |
| astrology | əˈstrɒlədʒi |
| atomic | əˈtɒmɪk |
| balanced | ˈbælənst |
| banknote | ˈbæŋknəʊt |
| believe | bəˈliːv |
| bottle bank | ˈbɒtl bæŋk |
| brave | breɪv |
| cancer | ˈkænsə |
| carry | ˈkæri |
| century | ˈsentʃəri |
| certainly | ˈsɜːtnli |
| circle (v) | ˈsɜːkəl |
| climate | ˈklaɪmət |
| climate change | ˈklaɪmət tʃeɪndʒ |
| cloakroom | ˈkləʊkruːm |
| cloudy | ˈklaʊdi |
| coin | kɔɪn |
| cold (n) | kəʊld |
| company | ˈkʌmpəni |
| computer | kəmˈpjuːtə |
| create | kriˈeɪt |
| cure (n) | kjʊə |
| dawn | dɔːn |

| | |
|---|---|
| decorate | ˈdekəreɪt |
| defence | dɪˈfens |
| definitely | ˈdefɪnətli |
| deliver | dɪˈlɪvə |
| democrat | ˈdeməkræt |
| destroy | dɪˈstrɔɪ |
| domestic waste | dəˌmestɪk ˈweɪst |
| dry | draɪ |
| DVD player | ˌdiː viː ˈdiː ˌpleɪə |
| Earth | ɜːθ |
| ecology | ɪˈkɒlədʒi |
| economy | ɪˈkɒnəmi |
| electricity | ɪˌlekˈtrɪsəti |
| electricity cut | ˌelɪkˈtrɪsəti ˌkʌt |
| encourage | ɪnˈkʌrɪdʒ |
| energy | ˈenədʒi |
| engine | ˈendʒɪn |
| environment | ɪnˈvaɪərənmənt |
| equality | ɪˈkwɒləti |
| exist | ɪgˈzɪst |
| facility | fəˈsɪləti, fəˈsɪlɪti |
| faint | feɪnt |
| fast (adj) | fɑːst |
| finance | ˈfaɪnæns |
| flu | fluː |
| foot | fʊt |
| forest | ˈfɒrɪst |
| future | ˈfjuːtʃə |
| gadget | ˈgædʒɪt |
| get married | ˌget ˈmærid |
| get rid of | ˌget ˈrɪd əv, ɒv |
| get wet | get ˈwet |
| government | ˈgʌvəmənt |
| horoscope | ˈhɒrəskəʊp |
| hybrid (n) | ˈhaɪbrəd, ˈhaɪbrɪd |
| in danger | ɪn ˈdeɪndʒə |
| increase (v) | ɪnˈkriːs |
| independent | ˌɪndəˈpendənt |
| Internet café | ˌɪntənet ˈkæfeɪ |
| introduce | ˌɪntrəˈdjuːs |
| invest in | ɪnˈvest ɪn |
| journey | ˈdʒɜːni |
| key (adj) | kiː |
| laser | ˈleɪzə |
| Latin | ˈlætɪn |
| leisure | ˈleʒə |
| life expectancy | ˈlaɪf ɪkˌspektənsi |
| likely | ˈlaɪkli |
| lower (v) | ˈləʊə |
| luxury | ˈlʌkʃəri |
| major (adj) | ˈmeɪdʒə |
| man-made | ˌmæn ˈmeɪd |
| masculine | ˈmæskjələn |
| maximum | ˈmæksəməm |
| mess | mes |
| mile | maɪl |
| military (n) | ˈmɪlətəri |
| mineral | ˈmɪnərəl |
| missile | ˈmɪsaɪl |
| mobile phone | ˌməʊbaɪl ˈfəʊn |
| motor | ˈməʊtə |
| muscle | ˈmʌsəl |
| musical (n) | ˈmjuːzɪkəl |
| necessary | ˈnesəsəri |
| nuclear | ˈnjuːkliə |
| on average | ɒn ˈævərɪdʒ |

**133**

| | |
|---|---|
| one day | ˌwʌn ˈdeɪ |
| opportunity | ˌɒpəˈtjuːnəti |
| opposition | ˌɒpəˈzɪʃən |
| own (v) | əʊn |
| pale | peɪl |
| panel | ˈpænl |
| parcel | ˈpɑːsəl |
| party | ˈpɑːti |
| pedestrian | pəˈdestriən |
| perhaps | pəˈhæps |
| petrol | ˈpetrəl |
| pollution | pəˈluːʃən |
| possible | ˈpɒsəbəl |
| power | ˈpaʊə |
| power station | ˈpaʊə ˌsteɪʃən |
| prediction | prɪˈdɪkʃən |
| president | ˈprezədənt |
| probably | ˈprɒbəbli |
| produce (v) | prəˈdjuːs |
| progress | ˈprəʊgres |
| promise (n) | ˈprɒmɪs |
| proportions | prəˈpɔːʃənz |
| protect | prəˈtekt |
| protein | ˈprəʊtiːn |
| public transport | ˌpʌblɪk ˈtrænspɔːt |
| punishment for | ˈpʌnɪʃmənt fə |
| radar | ˈreɪdɑː |
| radio station | ˈreɪdiəʊ ˌsteɪʃən |
| realistic | ˌrɪəˈlɪstɪk |
| recycle | ˌriːˈsaɪkəl |
| reduce | rɪˈdjuːs |
| reflect | rɪˈflekt |
| renewable | rɪˌnjuːəbəl |
|     energy | ˈenədʒi |
| replace | rɪˈpleɪs |
| replant | ˌriːˈplɑːnt |
| rescue | ˈreskjuː |
| retired | rɪˈtaɪəd |
| revolution | ˌrevəˈluːʃən |
| rise (v) | raɪz |
| rubbish | ˈrʌbɪʃ |
| rule (n) | ruːl |
| satellite | ˈsætəlaɪt |
| school report | ˌskuːl rɪˈpɔːt |
| seaside | ˈsiːsaɪd |
| second-hand | ˌsekəndˈhænd ʃɒp |
|     shop | |
| shoelace | ˈʃuːleɪs |
| signal (n) | ˈsɪgnəl |
| slow down | ˌsləʊ ˈdaʊn |
| solar panel | ˌsəʊlə ˈpænl |
| solar power | ˌsəʊlə ˈpaʊə |
| solution | səˈluːʃən |
| sort (v) | sɔːt |
| speed (n) | spiːd |
| spending | ˈspendɪŋ |
| suffer from | ˈsʌfə frəm |
| supersonic | ˌsuːpəˈsɒnɪk |
| survive | səˈvaɪv |
| swimming pool | ˈswɪmɪŋ puːl |
| switch to | ˈswɪtʃ tə |
| tax | tæks |
| technological | ˌteknəˈlɒdʒɪkəl |
| technology | tekˈnɒlədʒi |
| television set | ˌteləˈvɪʒən set |
| temperature | ˈtemprətʃə |

| | |
|---|---|
| throw out | ˌθrəʊ ˈaʊt |
| timetable | ˈtaɪmˌteɪbəl |
| top (adj) | tɒp |
| transport (v) | trænˈspɔːt |
| truck | trʌk |
| undone | ˌʌnˈdʌn |
| unemployment | ˌʌnɪmˈplɔɪmənt |
| unlikely | ʌnˈlaɪkli |
| video recorder | ˈvɪdiəʊ rɪˌkɔːdə |
| vote (v) | vəʊt |
| war | wɔː |
| waste (n) | weɪst |
| wave power | ˈweɪv ˌpaʊə |
| weather | ˈweðə ˌfɔːkɑːst |
|     forecast | |
| western | ˈwestən |
| wet | wet |
| wildlife | ˈwaɪldlaɪf |
| wind farm | ˈwɪnd fɑːm |
| wind power | ˈwɪnd ˌpaʊə |
| work from home | ˌwɜːk frəm ˈhəʊm |

## UNIT 8

| | |
|---|---|
| ability | əˈbɪləti |
| accountant | əˈkaʊntənt |
| act (v) | ækt |
| actor | ˈæktə |
| additionally | əˈdɪʃənəli |
| adventure | ədˈventʃə |
| advice | ədˈvaɪs |
| appear | əˈpɪə |
| applicant | ˈæplɪkənt |
| application | ˌæplɪˈkeɪʃən |
| apply for a job | əˌplaɪ fər ə ˈdʒɒb |
| architect | ˈɑːkətekt |
| artist | ˈɑːtɪst |
| avoid | əˈvɔɪd |
| badly-paid | ˌbædli ˈpeɪd |
| banker | ˈbæŋkə |
| barbecue (n) | ˈbɑːbɪkjuː |
| be comfortable | ˌbi ˈkʌmftəbəl wɪð, |
|     with | wɪθ |
| be fluent in | bi ˈfluːənt ɪn |
| be fond of | bi ˈfɒnd əv |
|     sb/sth | ˌsʌmbədi, |
| | ˌsʌmθɪŋ |
| be the centre of | bi ðə ˌsentər əv |
|     attention | əˈtenʃən |
| benefit | ˈbenəfɪt |
| biologist | baɪˈɒlədʒɪst |
| break (n) | breɪk |
| bungee jump (v) | ˈbʌndʒi ˌdʒʌmp |
| businesswoman | ˈbɪznəsˌwʊmən |
| businessman | ˈbɪznəsmən |
| busy | ˈbɪzi |
| call/phone back | ˌkɔːl ˈbæk, ˌfəʊn |
| candidate | ˈkændədət |
| career | kəˈrɪə |
| caretaker | ˈkeəˌteɪkə |
| cause (v) | kɔːz |
| certain | ˈsɜːtn |
| certificate | səˈtɪfɪkət |
| change one's | ˌtʃeɪndʒ wʌnz |
|     mind | ˈmaɪnd |

**134**

| | |
|---|---|
| charity worker | ˈtʃærəti ˌwɜːkə |
| commute to | kəˈmjuːt tə |
| company director | ˌkʌmpəni dəˈrektə, daɪ- |
| computer programmer | kəmˌpjuːtə ˈprəʊgræmə |
| contract | ˈkɒntrækt |
| covering letter | ˌkʌvərɪŋ ˈletə |
| current (adj) | ˈkʌrənt |
| currently | ˈkʌrəntli |
| CV | ˌsiː ˈviː |
| deal with | ˈdiːl wɪð, wɪθ |
| delivery driver | dɪˈlɪvəri ˌdraɪvə |
| direct (v) | dəˈrekt |
| director | dəˈrektə |
| doctor | ˈdɒktə |
| dream job | ˌdriːm ˈdʒɒb |
| driving licence | ˈdraɪvɪŋ ˌlaɪsəns |
| earn | ɜːn |
| employer | ɪmˈplɔɪə |
| enclose | ɪnˈkləʊz |
| engineer | ˌendʒəˈnɪə |
| entertaining | ˌentəˈteɪnɪŋ |
| essential | ɪˈsenʃəl |
| except | ɪkˈsept |
| experience (n) | ɪkˈspɪəriəns |
| fascinate | ˈfæsəneɪt |
| fashion designer | ˈfæʃən dɪˌzaɪnə |
| finalist | ˈfaɪnl-ɪst |
| fire-fighter | ˈfaɪə ˌfaɪtə |
| First Aid | ˌfɜːst ˈeɪd |
| Formula 1 driver | ˌfɔːmjələ ˈwʌn ˌdraɪvə |
| frequent | ˈfriːkwənt |
| full-time job | ˌfʊl taɪm ˈdʒɒb |
| games tester | ˈgeɪmz ˌtestə |
| gardener | ˈgɑːdnə |
| get bored | get ˈbɔːd |
| get in touch with | ˌget ɪn ˈtʌtʃ wɪð, wɪθ |
| giraffe | dʒɪˈrɑːf |
| golf buggy | ˈgɒlf ˌbʌgi |
| groceries | ˈgrəʊsəriz |
| hard (adj) | hɑːd |
| impress | ɪmˈpres |
| in addition | ɪn əˈdɪʃən |
| in front of | ɪn ˈfrʌnt əv |
| include | ɪnˈkluːd |
| insurance agent | ɪnˈʃʊərəns ˌeɪdʒənt |
| involve | ɪnˈvɒlv |
| job (n) | dʒɒb |
| job interview | ˈdʒɒb ˌɪntəvjuː |
| judge | dʒʌdʒ |
| keen on | ˈkiːn ɒn |
| knowledge of sth | ˈnɒlɪdʒ əv ˌsʌmθɪŋ |
| last (v) | lɑːst |
| lawyer | ˈlɔːjə |
| leader | ˈliːdə |
| librarian | laɪˈbreəriən |
| mad about | ˈmæd əˌbaʊt |
| mainland | ˈmeɪnlənd |
| manage | ˈmænɪdʒ |
| marketing | ˈmɑːkətɪŋ |
| manager | ˌmænɪdʒə |
| mature (adj) | məˈtʃʊə |
| minimum (adj) | ˈmɪnəməm |
| model | ˈmɒdl |
| motivated | ˈməʊtəveɪtəd, ˈməʊtɪveɪtəd |
| musician | mjuːˈzɪʃən |
| nanny | ˈnæni |
| note down | ˌnəʊt ˈdaʊn |
| nurse | nɜːs |
| organiser | ˈɔːgənaɪzə |
| ostrich | ˈɒstrɪtʃ |
| part-time | ˌpɑːt ˈtaɪm |
| peel (v) | piːl |
| permanent | ˈpɜːmənənt |
| physical | ˈfɪzɪkəl |
| pilot | ˈpaɪlət |
| police officer | pəˈliːs ˌɒfəsə |
| politician | ˌpɒləˈtɪʃən |
| politics | ˈpɒlətɪks |
| priest | priːst |
| proficient in | prəˈfɪʃənt ɪn |
| programme (v) | ˈprəʊgræm |
| psychologist | saɪˈkɒlədʒɪst |
| psychology | saɪˈkɒlədʒi |
| publicity | pʌˈblɪsəti |
| qualification | ˌkwɒləfəˈkeɪʃən |
| recent | ˈriːsənt |
| receptionist | rɪˈsepʃənɪst |
| report (v) | rɪˈpɔːt |
| reporter | rɪˈpɔːtə |
| require | rɪˈkwaɪə |
| responsible | rɪˈspɒnsəbəl |
| ride (v) | raɪd |
| routine | ˌruːˈtiːn |
| salary | ˈsæləri |
| salesperson | ˈseɪlzˌpɜːsən |
| scientist | ˈsaɪəntɪst |
| show sb around | ˌʃəʊ ˌsʌmbədi əˈraʊnd |
| snorkel (v) | ˈsnɔːkəl |
| sociable | ˈsəʊʃəbəl |
| stand (v) | stænd |
| straightaway | ˌstreɪtəˈweɪ |
| stressful | ˈstresfəl |
| take a message | ˌteɪk ə ˈmesɪdʒ |
| take place | ˌteɪk ˈpleɪs |
| take risks | ˌteɪk ˈrɪsks |
| taster | ˈteɪstə |
| teacher | ˈtiːtʃə |
| temporary | ˈtempərəri |
| therapist | ˈθerəpəst, ˈθerəpɪst |
| therapy | ˈθerəpi |
| tour guide | ˈtʊə gaɪd |
| tourism | ˈtʊərɪzəm |
| translator | trænsˈleɪtə |
| tropical | ˈtrɒpɪkəl |
| turn up | ˌtɜːn ˈʌp |
| TV presenter | ˌtiː ˈviː prɪˌzentə |
| uniform | ˈjuːnəfɔːm |
| used to doing sth | ˈjuːst tə ˈduːɪŋ ˌsʌmθɪŋ |
| vet | vet |
| wage | weɪdʒ |
| well-paid | ˌwel ˈpeɪd |

| | |
|---|---|
| what's more | ˌwɒts ˈmɔː |
| winner | ˈwɪnə |
| wonder (n) | ˈwʌndə |
| working conditions | ˈwɜːkɪŋ kənˌdɪʃənz |
| worth | wɜːθ |
| writer | ˈraɪtə |

## UNIT 9

| | |
|---|---|
| accept | əkˈsept |
| alone | əˈləʊn |
| argue | ˈɑːɡjuː |
| argument | ˈɑːɡjəmənt |
| back (n) | bæk |
| bark (v) | bɑːk |
| bass | beɪs |
| be homesick | bi ˈhəʊmˌsɪk |
| be in sb's teens/ twenties/ forties | ˌbi: ɪn ˌsʌmbədiz ˈtiːnz, ˈtwentiz, ˈfɔːtiz |
| be the best of friends | bi ðə ˌbest əv ˈfrendz |
| be wrong | bi ˈrɒŋ |
| beg | beg |
| blind date | ˌblaɪnd ˈdeɪt |
| boyfriend | ˈbɔɪfrend |
| celebrate | ˈseləbreɪt |
| clear the table | ˌklɪər ðə ˈteɪbəl |
| colleague | ˈkɒliːg |
| come true | ˌkʌm ˈtruː |
| contact (v) | ˈkɒntækt |
| control (v) | kənˈtrəʊl |
| darkness | ˈdɑːknəs |
| depend | dɪˈpend |
| disagree | ˌdɪsəˈgriː |
| do the vacuuming | ˌduː ðə ˈvækjʊmɪŋ |
| do the washing-up | ˌduː ðə ˌwɒʃɪŋ ˈʌp |
| dream (v) | driːm |
| drummer | ˈdrʌmə |
| drums | drʌmz |
| even (adv) | ˈiːvən |
| ever | ˈevə |
| fall in love with | ˌfɔːl ɪn ˈlʌv wɪð, wɪθ |
| fall out | ˌfɔːl ˈaʊt |
| feed | fiːd |
| fight (v) | faɪt |
| fill | fɪl |
| footstep | ˈfʊtstep |
| freedom | ˈfriːdəm |
| gang | gæŋ |
| get angry with | ˌget ˈæŋgri wɪð, wɪθ |
| get married | ˌget ˈmærid |
| girlfriend | ˈgɜːlfrend |
| glad | glæd |
| go out with | ˌgəʊ ˈaʊt wɪð, wɪθ |
| hall of residence | ˌhɔːl əv ˈrezədəns |
| have a good talk (with sb) | hæv ə ˌgʊd ˈtɔːk wɪð ˌsʌmbədi |
| have sth in | hæv ˌsʌmθɪŋ ɪn |

| | |
|---|---|
| common | ˈkɒmən |
| hit (n) | hɪt |
| Hold on a minute. | ˌhəʊld ˈɒn ə ˌmɪnət |
| housework | ˈhaʊswɜːk |
| How come? | ˌhaʊ ˈkʌm |
| hugs and kisses | ˌhʌgz ən ˈkɪsəz |
| imagine | ɪˈmædʒɪn |
| independent | ˌɪndəˈpendənt |
| interrupt | ˌɪntəˈrʌpt |
| irritate | ˈɪrəteɪt |
| jealous of | ˈdʒeləs əv |
| joke (v) | dʒəʊk |
| just (adv) | dʒəst |
| light up | ˌlaɪt ˈʌp |
| look after | ˌlʊk ˈɑːftə |
| love at first sight | ˌlʌv ət fɜːst ˈsaɪt |
| loyal | ˈlɔɪəl |
| make your bed | ˌmeɪk jə ˈbed |
| mate | meɪt |
| miss (v) | mɪs |
| poor | pʊə |
| prison | ˈprɪzən |
| ray | reɪ |
| recently | ˈriːsəntli |
| record (n) | ˈrekɔːd |
| record (v) | rɪˈkɔːd |
| relationship | rɪˈleɪʃənʃɪp |
| rent (n) | rent |
| responsibility | rɪˌspɒnsəˈbɪləti |
| ridiculous | rɪˈdɪkjələs |
| ring (n) | rɪŋ |
| romantic | rəʊˈmæntɪk |
| roof | ruːf |
| rub (v) | rʌb |
| sadness | ˈsædnəs, ˈsædnɪs |
| set the table | ˌset ðə ˈteɪbəl |
| shopping centre | ˈʃɒpɪŋ ˌsentə |
| sigh (v) | saɪ |
| single (n) | ˈsɪŋgəl |
| split up with | ˌsplɪt ˈʌp wɪð, wɪθ |
| stand by | ˌstænd ˈbaɪ |
| step out of | ˌstep ˈaʊt əv |
| still (adv) | stɪl |
| take care of sb/sth | teɪk ˈkeər əv ˌsʌmbədi, ˌsʌmθɪŋ |
| tattoo | təˈtuː |
| text message | ˈtekst ˌmesɪdʒ |
| tidy one's room | ˌtaɪdi wʌnz ˈruːm, ˈrʊm |
| tour (n) | tʊə |
| trust (v) | trʌst |
| turn round | ˌtɜːn ˈraʊnd |
| unfair | ˌʌnˈfeə |
| upset | ʌpˈset |
| wig | wɪg |
| wonder (v) | ˈwʌndə |
| yawn (v) | jɔːn |
| yet | jet |

## UNIT 10

| | |
|---|---|
| access the Internet | ˌækses ði ˈɪntənet |

**136**

| | |
|---|---|
| action film | ˈækʃən fɪlm |
| adaptation | ˌædæpˈteɪʃən |
| advert | ˈædvɜːt |
| amusing | əˈmjuːzɪŋ |
| arrest (v) | əˈrest |
| award (n) | əˈwɔːd |
| ballet dancer | ˈbæleɪ ˌdɑːnsə |
| blog | blɒg |
| board game | ˈbɔːd geɪm |
| bone | bəʊn |
| box office hit | ˌbɒks ɒfɪs ˈhɪt |
| break (n) | breɪk |
| broadcast (v) | ˈbrɔːdkɑːst |
| caller | ˈkɔːlə |
| car crash | ˈkɑː kræʃ |
| cartoon | kɑːˈtuːn |
| cartoon strip | kɑːˈtuːn strɪp |
| cash (n) | kæʃ |
| celebrity | səˈlebrəti |
| character | ˈkærɪktə |
| cinema | ˈsɪnəmə |
| column | ˈkɒləm |
| comedy series | ˈkɒmədi ˌsɪəriːz |
| commercial success | kəˌmɜːʃəl səkˈses |
| connect to | kəˈnekt tə |
| contest | ˈkɒntest |
| contestant | kənˈtestənt |
| critic | ˈkrɪtɪk |
| crossword | ˈkrɒswɜːd |
| daily/weekly publication | ˌdeɪli pʌbləˈkeɪʃən, ˌwiːkli |
| debate | dɪˈbeɪt |
| dialogue | ˈdaɪəlɒg |
| direct (v) | dəˈrekt |
| disappear | ˌdɪsəˈpɪə |
| disorienting | dɪsˈɔːrientɪŋ |
| documentary | ˌdɒkjəˈmentri |
| download | ˌdaʊnˈləʊd |
| drama school | ˈdrɑːmə ˌskuːl |
| eccentric (adj) | ɪkˈsentrɪk |
| entertainment guide | ˌentəˈteɪnmənt ˌgaɪd |
| enthusiastic | ɪnˌθjuːziˈæstɪk |
| fancy | ˈfænsi |
| fantasy film | ˈfæntəsi fɪlm |
| fashion tips | ˈfæʃən tɪps |
| friendship | ˈfrendʃɪp |
| game/quiz show | ˈgeɪm ʃəʊ, ˈkwɪz |
| get a divorce | ˌget ə dɪˈvɔːs |
| glamorous | ˈglæmərəs |
| gossip (n) | ˈgɒsɪp |
| graduate (v) | ˈgrædʒueɪt |
| happy ending | ˌhæpi ˈendɪŋ |
| historical drama | hɪˌstɒrɪkəl ˈdrɑːmə |
| horror film | ˈhɒrə fɪlm |
| informative | ɪnˈfɔːmətɪv |
| introduce | ˌɪntrəˈdjuːs |
| journalist | ˈdʒɜːnəlɪst |
| lead role | ˌliːd ˈrəʊl |
| local news | ˌləʊkəl ˈnjuːz |
| major (adj) | ˈmeɪdʒə |
| memorable | ˈmemərəbəl |
| memory | ˈmeməri |
| modest | ˈmɒdɪst |
| music video | ˈmjuːzɪk ˌvɪdiəʊ |

| | |
|---|---|
| news channel | ˈnjuːz ˌtʃænl |
| news programme | ˈnjuːz ˌprəʊgræm |
| newspaper | ˈnjuːsˌpeɪpə |
| online (adj) | ˈɒnlaɪn |
| online (adv) | ˌɒnˈlaɪn |
| ordinary | ˈɔːdənəri |
| paper version | ˈpeɪpə ˌvɜːʃən |
| part (n) | pɑːt |
| performance | pəˈfɔːməns |
| phone-in | ˈfəʊn ɪn |
| photographer | fəˈtɒgrəfə |
| plot | plɒt |
| praise (v) | preɪz |
| presenter | prɪˈzentə |
| psychological thriller | ˌsaɪkəˈlɒdʒɪkəl ˈθrɪlə |
| radio drama | ˈreɪdiəʊ ˌdrɑːmə |
| radio station | ˈreɪdiəʊ ˌsteɪʃən |
| readers' letter | ˌriːdəz ˈletə |
| reality show | riˈæləti ʃəʊ |
| remake (v) | ˌriːˈmeɪk |
| review (n) | rɪˈvjuː |
| role | rəʊl |
| romantic comedy | rəʊˌmæntɪk ˈkɒmədi |
| scary | ˈskeəri |
| scene | siːn |
| science fiction film | ˌsaɪəns ˈfɪkʃən fɪlm |
| scissors | ˈsɪzəz |
| search engine | ˈsɜːtʃ ˌendʒɪn |
| section | ˈsekʃən |
| send out | ˌsend ˈaʊt |
| soap opera | ˈsəʊp ˌɒpərə |
| social networking site | ˌsəʊʃəl ˈnetwɜːkɪŋ ˌsaɪt |
| soundtrack | ˈsaʊndtræk |
| special effects | ˌspeʃəl əˈfekts |
| sports news | ˈspɔːts njuːz |
| sports page | ˈspɔːts peɪdʒ |
| sports programme | ˈspɔːts ˌprəʊgræm |
| star (n, v) | stɑː |
| status | ˈsteɪtəs |
| stunt | stʌnt |
| suburban | səˈbɜːbən |
| superstar | ˈsuːpəstɑː |
| take sb seriously | ˌteɪk ˌsʌmbədi ˈsɪəriəsli |
| talent show | ˈtælənt ʃəʊ |
| talk show | ˈtɔːk ʃəʊ |
| teen idol | ˈtiːn ˌaɪdl |
| the media | ðə ˈmiːdiə |
| travel report | ˈtrævəl rɪˌpɔːt |
| TV channel | ˌtiː ˈviː ˌtʃænl |
| TV guide | ˌtiː ˈviː gaɪd |
| unknown | ˌʌnˈnəʊn |
| upload | ˌʌpˈləʊd |
| virus | ˈvaɪərəs |
| website | ˈwebsaɪt |
| well-known | ˌwel ˈnəʊn |
| world news | ˌwɜːld ˈnjuːz nuz |

| | |
|---|---|
| accomplice | əˈkʌmpləs, əˈkʌmplɪs |
| account | əˈkaʊnt |
| accuse of | əˈkjuːz əv |
| admiration | ˌædməˈreɪʃən |
| alarm (n) | əˈlɑːm |
| arrrest (v) | əˈrest |
| bet (v) | bet |
| boredom | ˈbɔːdəm |
| break into | ˌbreɪk ˈɪntə |
| break the law | ˌbreɪk ðə ˈlɔː |
| brick | brɪk |
| burglar | ˈbɜːglə |
| burglary | ˈbɜːgləri |
| burgle | ˈbɜːgəl |
| cable | ˈkeɪbəl |
| call the police | kɔːl ðə pəˈliːs |
| cashpoint | ˈkæʃpɔɪnt |
| cheat | tʃiːt |
| cheer up | ˌtʃɪər ˈʌp |
| climb through | ˌklaɪm ˈθruː |
| commit a crime | kəˌmɪt ə ˈkraɪm |
| computer hacking | kəmˌpjuːtə ˈhækɪŋ |
| con trick | ˈkɒn trɪk |
| con artist | ˈkɒn ˌɑːtɪst |
| Congratulations! | kənˌgrætʃəˈleɪʃənz, kənˌgrætʃʊˈleɪʃənz |
| copy (v) | ˈkɒpi |
| crime | kraɪm |
| criminal (n, adj) | ˈkrɪmənəl |
| crowd | kraʊd |
| dead | ded |
| deceive | dɪˈsiːv |
| deposit (v) | dɪˈpɒzɪt |
| deserve | dɪˈzɜːv |
| detective | dɪˈtektɪv |
| die | daɪ |
| dishonest | dɪsˈɒnəst |
| drug (n) | drʌg |
| entrance | ˈentrəns |
| escape (v) | ɪˈskeɪp |
| evidence | ˈevədəns |
| face down | ˌfeɪs ˈdaʊn |
| fare dodging | ˈfeə ˌdɒdʒɪŋ |
| fingerprint | ˈfɪŋgəˌprɪnt |
| foreigner | ˈfɒrənə |
| frustration | frʌˈstreɪʃən |
| gang | gæŋ |
| ghost | gəʊst |
| glove | glʌv |
| graffiti | grəˈfiːti |
| guard (n) | gɑːd |
| guilty | ˈgɪlti |
| gun | gʌn |
| gunshot | ˈgʌnʃɒt |
| hamster | ˈhæmstə |
| handgun | ˈhændgʌn |
| hard up | ˌhɑːd ˈʌp |
| hurt | hɜːt |
| illegal | ɪˈliːgəl |
| immediately | ɪˈmiːdiətli |
| immoral | ɪˈmɒrəl |
| inherit | ɪnˈherɪt |
| innocent | ˈɪnəsənt |
| investigate | ɪnˈvestəgeɪt |
| jewel | ˈdʒuːəl |
| judge (n) | dʒʌdʒ |
| kill | kɪl |
| lead to | ˈliːd tə |
| lie (v) | laɪ |
| love affair | ˈlʌv əˌfeə |
| make (n) | meɪk |
| mask | mɑːsk |
| mix up | ˌmɪks ˈʌp |
| model (n) | ˈmɒdl |
| motive | ˈməʊtɪv |
| mug | mʌg |
| mugger | ˈmʌgə |
| mugging | ˈmʌgɪŋ |
| murder (n, v) | ˈmɜːdə |
| murderer | ˈmɜːdərə |
| No way! | ˌnəʊ ˈweɪ |
| observe | əbˈzɜːv |
| panic (v) | ˈpænɪk |
| personal assistant | ˌpɜːsənəl əˈsɪstənt |
| piracy | ˈpaɪərəsi |
| playing card | ˈpleɪ-ɪŋ kɑːd |
| police | pəˈliːs |
| police officer | pəˈliːs ˌɒfəsə |
| prison | ˈprɪzən |
| prisoner | ˈprɪzənə |
| punish | ˈpʌnɪʃ |
| Queen | kwiːn |
| recognise | ˈrekəgnaɪz |
| recording | rɪˈkɔːdɪŋ |
| reward (n) | rɪˈwɔːd |
| risk (v) | rɪsk |
| rob | rɒb |
| robber | ˈrɒbə |
| robbery | ˈrɒbəri |
| run away | ˌrʌn əˈweɪ |
| safety deposit box | ˌseɪfti dɪˈpɒzɪt bɒks |
| scream (v) | skriːm |
| sculpture | ˈskʌlptʃə |
| sentence to | ˈsentəns tə |
| shoot | ʃuːt |
| shoplift | ˈʃɒpˌlɪft |
| shoplifter | ˈʃɒpˌlɪftə |
| shoplifting | ˈʃɒpˌlɪftɪŋ |
| silencer | ˈsaɪlənsə |
| speeding | ˈspiːdɪŋ |
| split | splɪt |
| staff | stɑːf |
| steal | stiːl |
| suspect (n) | ˈsʌspekt |
| Take it easy! | ˌteɪk ɪt ˈiːzi |
| the poor | ðə ˈpʊə |
| the rich | ðə ˈrɪtʃ |
| theft | θeft |
| thief | θiːf |
| throw | θrəʊ |
| transfer (v) | trænsˈfɜː |
| trick (v) | trɪk |
| valuable | ˈvæljəbəl |
| vandal | ˈvændl |
| vandalise | ˈvændəlaɪz |
| vandalism | ˈvændəlɪzəm |
| vanish | ˈvænɪʃ |
| violence | ˈvaɪələns |

| | |
|---|---|
| wealthy | ˈwelθi |
| What's the matter? | ˌwɒts ðə ˈmætə |
| What's wrong? | ˌwɒts ˈrɒŋ |
| wisely | ˈwaɪzli |
| You're kidding! | jɔː ˈkɪdɪŋ |

## UNIT 12

| | |
|---|---|
| aerobics | eəˈrəʊbɪks |
| alcohol | ˈælkəhɒl |
| ambulance | ˈæmbjələns |
| antibiotic | ˌæntɪbaɪˈɒtɪk |
| aspirin | ˈæsprɪn |
| asthma | ˈæsmə |
| awful | ˈɔːfəl |
| back seat driver | ˌbæk siːt ˈdraɪvə |
| backache | ˈbækeɪk |
| bandage | ˈbændɪdʒ |
| baseball | ˈbeɪsbɔːl |
| basketball | ˈbɑːskɪtbɔːl |
| be obsessed about | bi əbˈsest əˌbaʊt |
| beast | biːst |
| beat (v) | biːt |
| bowling | ˈbəʊlɪŋ |
| boxing | ˈbɒksɪŋ |
| brave | breɪv |
| broken | ˈbrəʊkən |
| bungee jumping | ˈbʌndʒi ˌdʒʌmpɪŋ |
| cancer | ˈkænsə |
| catch (v) | kætʃ |
| catch up | ˌkætʃ ˈʌp |
| check-up | ˈtʃek ʌp |
| chemist's | ˈkeməsts, ˈkemɪsts |
| chest | tʃest |
| clumsy | ˈklʌmzi |
| cold (n) | kəʊld |
| commentator | ˈkɒmənteɪtə |
| cycle (v) | ˈsaɪkəl |
| deafness | ˈdefnəs |
| dentist | ˈdentɪst |
| exercise (n, v) | ˈeksəsaɪz |
| extreme sport | ɪkˌstriːm ˈspɔːt |
| fever | ˈfiːvə |
| fill in | ˌfɪl ˈɪn |
| fish oil | ˈfɪʃ ɔɪl |
| fit | fɪt |
| flu | fluː |
| football fan | ˈfʊtbɔːl fæn |
| football manager | ˈfʊtbɔːl ˌmænɪdʒə |
| football player | ˈfʊtbɔːl ˌpleɪə |
| football shirt | ˈfʊtbɔːl ʃɜːt |
| football team | ˈfʊtbɔːl tiːm |
| forehead | ˈfɒrəd |
| form (n) | fɔːm |
| get better | get ˈbetə |
| get ill | get ˈɪl |
| get some exercise | ˌget səm ˈeksəsaɪz |
| give up smoking | ˌgɪv ʌp ˈsməʊkɪŋ |
| go for a run | ˌgəʊ fər ə ˈrʌn |
| go up | ˌgəʊ ˈʌp |

| | |
|---|---|
| goal | gəʊl |
| golf | gɒlf |
| gym | dʒɪm |
| have no head for | hæv ˌnəʊ ˈhed fə |
| hay fever | ˌheɪ ˈfiːvə |
| headache | ˈhedeɪk |
| heart attack | ˈhɑːt əˌtæk |
| height | haɪt |
| hiking | ˈhaɪkɪŋ |
| hockey | ˈhɒki |
| hopeless | ˈhəʊpləs |
| horse-riding | ˈhɔːs ˌraɪdɪŋ |
| hospital | ˈhɒspɪtl |
| hyperventilation | ˌhaɪpəventəˈleɪʃən, ˌhaɪpəventɪˈleɪʃən |
| hypochondriac | ˌhaɪpəˈkɒndriæk |
| ignore the problem | ɪgˌnɔː ðə ˈprɒbləm |
| ill | ɪl |
| indigestion | ˌɪndɪˈdʒestʃən |
| injection | ɪnˈdʒekʃən |
| kick (v) | kɪk |
| kick boxing | ˈkɪk ˌbɒksɪŋ |
| knowledgeable | ˈnɒlɪdʒəbəl |
| leg | leg |
| lie down | ˌlaɪ ˈdaʊn |
| lose weight | ˌluːz ˈweɪt |
| make an appointment | ˌmeɪk ən əˈpɔɪntmənt |
| marathon | ˈmærəθən |
| match (n) | mætʃ |
| medical encyclopedia | ˌmedɪkəl ɪnˌsaɪkləˈpiːdiə |
| mental problems | ˈmentl ˌprɒbləmz |
| mountain biking | ˈmaʊntən ˌbaɪkɪŋ |
| obsession | əbˈseʃən |
| operation | ˌɒpəˈreɪʃən |
| pain | peɪn |
| painkiller | ˈpeɪnˌkɪlə |
| pass (v) | pɑːs |
| patient (n) | ˈpeɪʃənt |
| peppermint tea | ˌpepəmɪnt ˈtiː |
| phone for a doctor/an ambulance | ˌfəʊn fər ə ˈdɒktə, ən ˈæmbjələns |
| player | ˈpleɪə |
| prescription | prɪˈskrɪpʃən |
| processed | ˈprəʊsest |
| professional (adj) | prəˈfeʃənəl |
| referee | ˌrefəˈriː |
| sailing | ˈseɪlɪŋ |
| sb is allowed to do something | ˌsʌmbədi ɪz əˌlaʊd tə ˈduː ˌsʌmθɪŋ |
| scarf | skɑːf |
| score (n, v) | skɔː |
| scuba diving | ˈskuːbə ˌdaɪvɪŋ |
| season | ˈsiːzən |
| see a doctor | ˌsiː ə ˈdɒktə |
| sign | saɪn |
| signature | ˈsɪgnətʃə |
| skateboarding | ˈskeɪtˌbɔːdɪŋ |
| skiing | ˈskiː-ɪŋ |
| snowboarding | ˈsnəʊˌbɔːdɪŋ |
| sore | sɔː |
| sporty | ˈspɔːti |

| | | | |
|---|---|---|---|
| stadium | ˈsteɪdɪəm | throat | θrəʊt |
| statistics | stəˈtɪstɪks | toothache | ˈtuːθ-eɪk |
| stay in bed | ˌsteɪ ɪn ˈbed | tracksuit | ˈtræksuːt |
| stomachache | ˈstʌmək-eɪk | train for | ˈtreɪn fə |
| stressed out | ˌstrest ˈaʊt | trainer | ˈtreɪnə |
| suffer from | ˈsʌfə frəm | training | ˈtreɪnɪŋ |
| supplement (n) | ˈsʌpləmənt | treat (v) | triːt |
| surfing | ˈsɜːfɪŋ | unhealthy | ʌnˈhelθi |
| swim (v) | swɪm | unwilling | ʌnˈwɪlɪŋ |
| swimming pool | ˈswɪmɪŋ puːl | virus | ˈvaɪərəs |
| sympathetic | ˌsɪmpəˈθetɪk | visitor | ˈvɪzətə |
| take | teɪk | vitamin | ˈvɪtəmən |
| temperature | ˈtemprətʃə | weight | weɪt |
| tend to live longer | ˌtend tə ˈlɪv ˌlɒŋgə | windsurfing | ˈwɪndˌsɜːfɪŋ |
| thin | θɪn | World Cup | ˌwɜːld ˈkʌp |

# Irregular verbs

| Verb | Past Simple | Past Participle |
|------|-------------|-----------------|
| babysit | babysat | babysat |
| be | was/were | been |
| beat | beat | beaten |
| become | became | become |
| begin | began | begun |
| bet | bet | bet |
| break | broke | broken |
| bring | brought | brought |
| broadcast | broadcast | broadcast |
| build | built | built |
| buy | bought | bought |
| can | could | been able |
| catch | caught | caught |
| choose | chose | chosen |
| come | came | come |
| cost | cost | cost |
| cut | cut | cut |
| deal | dealt | dealt |
| do | did | done |
| draw | drew | drawn |
| dream | dreamed/ dreamt | dreamed/ dreamt |
| drink | drank | drunk |
| drive | drove | driven |
| eat | ate | eaten |
| fall | fell | fallen |
| feed | fed | fed |
| feel | felt | felt |
| fight | fought | fought |
| find | found | found |
| fly | flew | flown |
| forget | forgot | forgotten |
| get | got | got |
| give | gave | given |
| go | went | gone/been |
| grow | grew | grown |
| hang | hung | hung |
| have | had | had |
| hear | heard | heard |
| hide | hid | hidden |
| hit | hit | hit |
| hold | held | held |
| hurt | hurt | hurt |
| keep | kept | kept |
| know | knew | known |
| lead | led | led |

| Verb | Past Simple | Past Participle |
|------|-------------|-----------------|
| learn | learned/learnt | learned/learnt |
| leave | left | left |
| lend | lent | lent |
| let | let | let |
| lie | lay | lain |
| light | lit | lit |
| lose | lost | lost |
| make | made | made |
| mean | meant | meant |
| meet | met | met |
| pay | paid | paid |
| put | put | put |
| read /riːd/ | read /red/ | read /red/ |
| remake | remade | remade |
| ride | rode | ridden |
| ring | rang | rung |
| rise | rose | risen |
| run | ran | run |
| say | said | said |
| see | saw | seen |
| sell | sold | sold |
| send | sent | sent |
| set | set | set |
| shine | shone | shone |
| shoot | shot | shot |
| show | showed | shown |
| sing | sang | sung |
| sit | sat | sat |
| sleep | slept | slept |
| speak | spoke | spoken |
| spell | spelled/spelt | spelled/spelt |
| spend | spent | spent |
| split | split | split |
| stand | stood | stood |
| steal | stole | stolen |
| swim | swam | swum |
| take | took | taken |
| teach | taught | taught |
| tell | told | told |
| think | thought | thought |
| throw | threw | thrown |
| understand | understood | understood |
| wake | woke | woken |
| wear | wore | worn |
| win | won | won |
| write | wrote | written |

# Pronunciation table

## CONSONANTS

| Symbol | Key word | Other common spellings |
|--------|----------|------------------------|
| /p/ | **p**ark | ha**pp**y |
| /b/ | **b**ath | ru**bb**ish |
| /t/ | **t**ie | bu**tt**er walk**ed** |
| /d/ | **d**ie | te**dd**y bear |
| /k/ | **c**at | **k**ey s**ch**ool che**ck** |
| /g/ | **g**ive | **gh**ost bi**gg**er |
| /tʃ/ | **ch**air | ma**tch** na**t**ural |
| /dʒ/ | **j**eans | a**g**e ga**dg**et sol**di**er |
| /f/ | **f**ace | co**ff**ee **ph**one lau**gh** |
| /v/ | **v**isit | o**f** |
| /θ/ | **th**row | |
| /ð/ | **th**ey | |
| /s/ | **s**ell | **c**inema li**s**ten **ps**ychology **sc**enery me**ss**age |
| /z/ | **z**oo | no**s**e bu**zz** |
| /ʃ/ | **sh**op | **s**ure ambi**ti**on |
| /ʒ/ | mea**s**ure | revi**si**on |
| /h/ | **h**ot | **wh**o |
| /m/ | **m**ap | su**mm**er |
| /n/ | **n**ot | **kn**ow sun**n**y |
| /ŋ/ | si**ng** | thi**n**k |
| /l/ | **l**ot | ba**ll** |
| /r/ | **r**oad | so**rr**y **wr**ite |
| /j/ | **y**ellow | **u**sually **Eu**rope b**eau**tiful n**ew** |
| /w/ | **w**arm | **o**ne **wh**ale q**u**ick |

## VOWELS

| Symbol | Key word | Other common spellings |
|--------|----------|------------------------|
| **Long and short vowels** | | |
| /iː/ | f**ee**t | n**ie**ce r**ea**d th**e**se k**ey** rec**ei**pt p**o**lice |
| /ɪ/ | f**i**t | g**y**m g**u**itar pr**e**tty |
| /i/ | happ**y** | spaghett**i** marr**ie**d |
| /e/ | b**e**d | **a**ny br**ea**d fr**ie**nd |
| /æ/ | b**a**d | |
| /ɑː/ | b**a**th | **a**rt h**a**lf **au**nt h**ea**rt |
| /ɒ/ | b**o**ttle | w**a**tch |
| /ɔː/ | b**ough**t | sp**or**t y**our** d**augh**ter sm**a**ll dr**aw** w**ar** fl**oor** |
| /ʊ/ | p**u**t | b**oo**k c**oul**d |
| /uː/ | b**oo**t | r**u**de bl**ue** fr**ui**t m**o**ve sh**oe** gr**ou**p fl**ew** |
| /ʌ/ | b**u**t | s**o**me c**ou**sin |
| /ɜː/ | b**ir**d | s**er**ve **ear**ly t**ur**n |
| /ə/ | broth**er** | th**e** **a**bout act**or** col**our** |
| **Diphthongs (two vowel sounds pronounced as one)** | | |
| /eɪ/ | gr**ey** | l**a**ke w**ai**t pl**ay** **eigh**t br**ea**k |
| /əʊ/ | g**o**ld | sh**ow** c**oa**t |
| /aɪ/ | b**y** | l**i**ke d**ie** h**igh** h**eigh**t **eye**s b**uy** |
| /aʊ/ | br**ow**n | ab**ou**t |
| /ɔɪ/ | b**oy** | n**oi**sy |
| /ɪə/ | h**ear** | h**ere** b**eer** |
| /eə/ | h**air** | th**ere** th**eir** squ**are** b**ear** |
| /ʊə/ | s**ure** | p**oor** t**our** |
| **Triphthongs (three vowel sounds pronounced as one)** | | |
| /eɪə/ | pl**aye**r | |
| /əʊə/ | l**owe**r | |
| /aɪə/ | t**ire**d | |
| /aʊə/ | fl**owe**r | |

Pearson Education Limited,
Edinburgh Gate, Harlow
Essex, CM20 2JE, England
and Associated Companies throughout the world

www.pearsonelt.com

First published 2012
Set in 10.5/11.5pt ITC Century Light
Printed in China   (GCC/01)
ISBN 978-1-4082-7151-3

Location photography by Gareth Boden

**Illustrated by:** Rowan Barnes-Murphy (Nick Diggory Illustration) page 32;
Fred Blunt pages 106 (right), 110; Ollie Cuthbertson pages 82–83;
Kath Walker pages 10, 13, 14, 55, 72, 106 (left); Peter Richardson
pages 62–63, 98–99; Kate Rochester pages 17, 71; David Semple page 105;
Jamie Sneddon page 122; Victor Tavares (Beehive Illustration) page 37;
Anthony Trimmer (Beehive Illustration) page 96; Ken Turner (Beehive
Illustration) page 61.

#### Authors' acknowledgements

Stuart McKinlay would like to thank his friends and family for all the
support he has received. Bob Hastings would like to thank his colleagues,
students, friends and family for all the inspiration and support they have
given him.

The authors and publishers would like to thank the following people for
their help in the development of this course:

Abdullah Arslan, Monika Adamowicz, Nurşen Cin Akçay, Hatice Akgün,
Magdalena Augustynek, Ayşe Zeren, Engin Aytekin, Jiřina Babáková, Eva
Baierová, Edyta Bajda-Kowalczyk, Lidia Bajerska, Małgorzata Barczyńska,
Agnieszka Batko, Dilek Bayazıt, Sevin Bayraktar, Mariusz Bęcławski,
Sebastian Bednarz, Gülay Bilgan, Nuran Bilginer, Agnieszka Biskup,
Elżbieta Bobrowska, Kamila Borkowska, Ebru Bozca, Beata Brzostek, Jitka
Buchlová, Raisa Butjugina, Gözde Çalışkan, Fatih Canpolat, Justyna
Cholewa, Jadwiga Chrząstek, Dagmara Chudy, Dorota Ciężkowska-Gajda,
Ewa Ciok, Elżbieta Ciurzyńska, Barbara Cybuch, Monika Cynar, Elżbieta
Czarnogórska, Maria Czechowicz, Ewa Dąbrowska, Jolanta Dąbrowska,
Selma Dalbastı, Sylwia Dańczak, Lucyna Daniec-Zych, Monika Dargas-
Miszczak, Monika Dębska, Agata Demidowicz, Bahar Burcu Demirtola,
Urszula Deszcz, Jolanta Dola-Niewiadomska, Joanna Domańska, Konrad
Dutkowski, Bożena Dypa, Halina Działecka, Jolanta Dziewulska, Marzena
Dziurzyńska, Sebestyén Emese, Seda Erdein, Fulya Erdemet, Bircan
Ergün, Csontos Erzsébet, Hüseyin Evcim, E. Didem Evrensel, Elżbieta
Fabisiak, Ömer Faruk İpek, Renata Fijałkowska, Agnieszka Fijałkowska-
Grabowiecka, Tamara Filatova, Jagoda Filipecka, Agnieszka Filipowicz-
Wesołowska, Agata Fronczak, Małgorzata Gajcy-Czapigo, Hanna Gajewska-
Wolna, Dominika Gala, Joanna Galant, Grażyna Garus, Agnieszka Gatz,
Katarzyna Gierałtowska, Anna Gil-Kisiecka, Joanna Gładyszewska, Anna
Głowacka, Bogusława Godlewska, Michał Gołda, Ewa Goldnik-Ciok, Monika
Grabowska-Królik, Jadwiga Greszta, Beata Gromek, Rafał Grynienko,
Urszula Guszczyn, Ondřej Hašlar, Andrea Hejduková, Marta Hilgier, Anita
Horbat, Naďa Hrušková, Joanna Idem, Müsteyde İrikoğlu, Barbara Iwanicz,
Agnieszka Jakubiec, Elżbieta Jaśków, Agnieszka Jastak, Robert Jastrzębski,
Anna Jaźwińska, Małgorzata Jedlińska, Małgorzata Jojdziałło-Odrobińska,
Magdalena Junkieles, Mirosław Kaczorek, Veronika Kadeřábková, Gülin
Kale, Oğuzhan Kalkan, Ewa Kamińska, Ewa Kamka, Feray Karayel,
Agnieszka Karolak, Maciej Karwowski, Vladimíra Kasalová, Magadalena
Kica, Anna Kielan, Kazimierz Klekotko, Katarzyna Kłobukowska, Beata
Kochanowska, Mehmet Koçyiğit, Ewa Komorowska, Magdalena Konczak,
Katarzyna Korejwo, H. Şule Korkmaz, Małgorzata Kowal, Anna
Kowalewska, Ewa Kubisz, Agnieszka Kucharska-Widera, Anna Kuklik-
Petrykowska, Barbara Kurianiuk, Fulya Kurtuluş, Galina Kuznetsova,
Magdalena Kwasiborska, Anna Kwaśniewska, Janina Lachowska, Jadwiga
Łakomek, Urszula Langer, Maria Lasek, Celina Łazowska, Julianna
Leczkowska, Agata Lesińska-Domagała, Mirosława Letachowicz, Katarzyna
Licińska, Agata Lisicka, Magdalena Loska, Bogusław Lubański, Katarzyna
Łukasiewicz, Vendula Macková, Barbara Madej, Agnieszka Michna, Andrzej
Mikołajczak, Waldemar Mileszczyk, Anna Milewska, Paweł Mirecki, Selim
Mucharski, Denisa Muller, Marzena Muszyńska, Irene Nekrasova,
Małgorzata Nibor-Grabowska, Joanna Niedbała, Kinga Niemczuk, Věra
Novotná, Anna Nowotka, Sylwia Obłudek, Katarzyna Ochnio, Bożena
Ogrodniczek, Przemysław Ogrodowczyk, Ewa Okrasa, Irene Olhovskaya,
Anita Omelańczuk, Özer Öner, Marina Osipova, Barbara Owczarek, Hatice
Özbasmacı, Mehmet Özcan, Ekrem Özkoçak, Mariola Palcewicz, Ali
Parmaksız, Łukasz Pielasa, Joanna Pieróg, Joanna Pilecka, Marta Piróg-
Riley, Magdalena Płaneta, Mirosława Podgórska, Yelena Povolotskaya, Marie
Prokešová, Ewa Prokopowicz, Anna Rabiega, Elżbieta Radulska, Maria
Rakowska, Pınar Reisoğlu, Agnieszka Rodak, Grażyna Rusiecka, İsmail
Şahin, Sylwia Sawczuk, İlyas Saykılı, Ewa Schubert, Gülban Keyran
Şenyuva, Mariola Serowy-Ziółkowska, Renata Sitarz, Ewa Skoczeń, Dorota
Sobakiewicz, Roksana Sobieralska, Katarzyna Sobkowicz, Marzanna
Stasiak, Kateřina Šteklová, Vladimíra Šulcová, Barbara Superson, Monika
Świerczyńska, Monika Szałwińska, Anna Szuchalska, Wiktor Szwaja, Irina
Tarayan, Nida Tatar, Yasemin Tezgiden, Katarzyna Tobolska, Katarzyna
Tokaj, Ayşe Tolunay, Ewa Toporek Niemczyk, Beata Trapnell, Ewa
Trochimczyk, Maria Tsangaras, Dorota Tyburska, Małgorzata Tygielska,
Halina Tykocińska, Urbaniak Karolina, Jitka Vaňková, Ida Vohryzková,
Lenka Volfová, Jolanta Walterska, Anna Waluch, Sławomir Wandycz, Joanna
Wap, Hanna Wasilewska, Elżbieta Więcław, Grażyna Wilczyńska, Ewa
Wiśniewska-Matraszek, Adam Wójcicki, Michał Wójcik, Małgorzata Wolak,
Leszek Wolski, Andrzej Woyda, Anna Wroniecka, Burcu Yaşar, Sevinç Yerli,
Hana Zadražílová, Katarzyna Zadrożna-Attia, Ewa Zalewska, Joanna
Zalewska, Sławomir Zasuński, Sonia Zbraniborska, Eugeniusz Żebrowski,
Andrzej Zejdler, Piotr Żemła, Iwona Ziębicka, Barbara Ziębowicz, Maria
Zielińska, Anna Ziemińska, Justyna Zubowicz

#### Acknowledgements

We are grateful to the following for permission to reproduce copyright material:

Lyrics on page 82 from *Ain't No Sunshine*, Words & Music by Bill Withers
© Copyright 1971 Interior Music Corporation, USA, Universal/MCA Music
Limited. All Rights Reserved. International Copyright Secured. Used by
permission of Music Sales Limited; Extracts (1B, 4C) on page 96 adapted
from *The Book of Criminal Blunders*, by P. Mason and J. Burns,
published by Corgi. Reprinted by permission of The Random House
Group Ltd. and excerpts (1B, 4C) from *The Book of Criminal Blunders*
(© Peter Mason and John Burns, 1985) are reproduced by permission of
PFD (www.pfd.co.uk) on behalf of Peter Mason and John Burns; Extract
(3A) on page 96 adapted from *The Book of Heroic Failures*, first
published by Penguin Books Ltd. (Pile, S. 1979) p. 96, Copyright ©
Stephen Pile, 1989. Reproduced by permission of the author c/o Rogers,
Coleridge & White Ltd., 20 Powis Mews, London W11 1JN; Lyrics on page
120 from *I Am*. Words and Music by Diane Warren © 2004 Realsongs
(ASCAP). All Rights Reserved. Used by Permission of Alfred Publishing
Co., Inc.; Graph on page 52 based on information from the European
Vegetarian Union: http://www.euroveg.eu/lang/en/info/howmany.php.

In some instances we have been unable to trace the owners of copyright
material, and we would appreciate any information that would enable us to
do so.

The publisher would like to thank the following for their kind permission to
reproduce their photographs:

(Key: b-bottom; c-centre; l-left; r-right; t-top)

**Alamy Images**: Alistair Laming 43, avatra images 34l, Barry Mason 19,
Bubbles Photolibrary 95, Chris Howes / Wild Places Photography 49r,
Chuck Pefley 54tl, CountrySideCollection – Homer Sykes 117bc, daniel grill
65l, David Coleman 119l, Hola Images 84, james andrew 69c, Jeff Morgan
education 115t, Juice Images 111, keith morris 66, Kim Karpeles 38bl,
Kuttig – Travel 46tr, LOETSCHER CHLAUS 117br, mylife photos 12tr,
Photofusion Picture Library 48–49c, PhotoStock-Israel 100, Radius Images
59b, Red Cover 44, STOCKFOLIO® 54tr, StudioSource 86, Ted Foxx 38t,
The Photolibrary Wales 48l, 121, Trevor Smith 119r, vario images GmbH &
Co.KG 54bl, VIEW Pictures Ltd 42r, VStock 104bc; Corbis: Bill Varie 120,
Eric Robert / Sygma 46bl, Hulton-Deutsch Collection 27br, Image Source
20, Stefan Kraszewski / epa 46tl, The Art Archive 27t, The Gallery
Collection The Gallery Collection / © DACS, © Succession Picasso/DACS
2010 27bc, TONY BARTLETT / epa 71t, William Perlman / Star Ledger 34r;
**Getty Images**: Comstock Images 12tl, Comstock Images 12tl, Hulton
Archive 37, Johan Elbers / Time & Life Pictures 36, Oli Scarff 59t, Suzanne
Plunkett / Bloomberg 117bl; **Ronald Grant Archive**: Artisan
Entertainment 89tr; **iStockphoto**: Andresr 107, billnoll 21 (background),
claudiaveja 68r, daniel sainthorant 103, kelvin wakefield 42l, Oleg
Prikhodko 38br, Sean Locke 90; **James Kirkikis/Photographers Direct**:
46br; **Kobal Collection Ltd**: 20TH CENTURY FOX 89tl, BEND IT FILMS /
FILM COUNCIL / PARRY, CHRISTINE 89br, NEW LINE / SAUL ZAENTZ /
WING NUT FILMS / VINET, PIERRE 89bl; **Pearson Education Ltd**: Ian
Wedgewood 115c, Jules Selmes 17t, 115b, MindStudio Collection 17b,
Photodisc. Andy Sotiriou 69t, Photodisc. C Squared Studios. Tony Gable
68l, Photodisc. Hisham F. Ibrahim 69b; **Peter Menzel/menzelphoto.com**:
50t, 50b; **Photofusion Picture Library**: Janine Wiedel 65r;
**Photolibrary.com**: Kablonk! 21; **Rex Features**: Everett Collection 27bl,
James D. Morgan 71b, Jeremy Young 117tl, Robert Hallam 117cl, Sipa Press
67; **TfL from the London Transport Museum collection**: 118;
**Thinkstock**: iStockphoto 18, 85l, 85r, Jupiterimages 12bl; **TopFoto**: Kent
Meireis / The Image Works 74

All other images © Pearson Education Limited

Every effort has been made to trace the copyright holders and we
apologise in advance for any unintentional omissions. We would be pleased
to insert the appropriate acknowledgement in any subsequent edition of
this publication.

Special thanks to the following for their help during location photography:

Brays Grove Community College; Fanhams Hall Hotel, Ware; Fitzwilliam
Museum, Cambridge; The Dynamou family; The Evans family; Sheering
C of E Primary School

Front cover images supplied by: Corbis/Ken Kaminesky (orange);
Punchstock/Photodisk (purple); Punchstock/Digital Vision (blue, red and
green); Stockbyte (blue-green).